TUDOR

SURVIVOR

King Henry the eyght.

TUDOR
SURVIVOR

THE LIFE &
TIMES OF
WILLIAM PAULET

MARGARET
SCARD

Frontispiece: Henry VIII and the Privy Council, by an unknown artist.(©National Portrait Gallery, London)

Front of jacket: William Paulet, 1st Marquess of Winchester, unknown artist, detail NPG 65. (©National Portrait Gallery, London)

Back of jacket: 'The Family of Henry VIII: An Allegory of the Tudor Succession', detail, c.1572, attributed to Flemish artist Lucas de Heere (1534–1584). The panel is now at Sudeley Castle. To the left are Philip II of Spain and Mary. Edward kneels at Henry's feet. Elizabeth on his right holds the hand of Peace. According to the inscription the painting was a gift from Elizabeth to Francis Walsingham. (Bridgeman Art Library)

First published 2011

The History Press
The Mill, Brimscombe Port
Stroud, Gloucestershire, GL5 2QG
www.thehistorypress.co.uk

British Library Cataloguing in Publication Data.
A catalogue record for this book is available from the British Library.

ISBN 978 0 7524 5942 4

Typesetting and origination by The History Press
Printed in Malta

Contents

Preface

The story of William Paulet, 1st Marquis of Winchester, is an extraordinary account of political survival during the turbulent years of the Tudor dynasty. Born into a gentry family, probably in 1484 as the Wars of the Roses came to an end, Paulet served under four Tudor monarchs, rising to the position of Lord Treasurer and becoming the most senior peer in the realm by his death in 1572. With his long and varied career at the heart of the Tudor court, Paulet serves as the archetype for the successful courtier.

This biography sets out not only to describe the life of William Paulet set against the politics of the time but also to explain his role at court and to look in detail at how he lived. The book includes several short, descriptive accounts of daily life at both home and court – all based on detailed research – that are intended to throw light on the many routines and rituals that shaped everyday life during this period. Covering such events as christenings and funerals, together with descriptions of activities such as dressing and dining, this study hopes to provide a vivid picture of the life of a Tudor courtier.

William Paulet has been a part of my life for many years and this book only came to fruition with the help of many people. However, I would like to express my especial thanks to my husband, Geoffrey, and to Valery Rose for their many hours of proof reading and for their invaluable comments and encouragement.

CHRONOLOGY

of the Life of William Paulet	*of* Wider Events
1484 *6 June* Probable date of birth	
	1485 Henry VII defeats Richard III to become King of England
1509 Married Elizabeth Capel	**1509** *April* Accession of Henry VIII Henry marries Catherine of Aragon
1511 / 1518 / 1522 Sheriff of Hampshire	
1514 First appointment as Justice of the Peace	
	1516 *18 February* Birth of Princess Mary
1523 Knighted	
1525 Death of Sir John Paulet	
1526 *5 February* King's Councillor for law *3 November* Joint Master of the King's Wards	

1529

3 November Member of Parliament

1530

Death of Cardinal Wolsey

1531

January Surveyor General of all possessions in the King's hands by the minority
of heirs, also Surveyor of the King's
widows and Governor of all idiots and
naturals in the King's hands

1532

May Comptroller of the Royal
Household
October Member of King's entourage to
France

1533

Joint Master of the King's Woods
Surveyor of Woods in the Duchy
of Lancaster
June Travelled to France with the Duke
of Norfolk

1533

25 January Henry marries Anne Boleyn
April Act in Restraint of Appeals
May Henry's marriage to Catherine of
Aragon declared invalid
   Marriage of Henry and Anne Boleyn
pronounced legal
7 September Birth of Princess Elizabeth

1534

Act of Succession
Act of Supremacy

1535

1 July One of the judges to try Sir
Thomas More

1535

6 July Execution of Sir Thomas More

1536

12 May One of the judges to try men
accused of consorting with Anne Boleyn
October Organising supplies for King's
army during Pilgrimage of Grace

1536

7 January Death of Catherine of Aragon
19 May Execution of Anne Boleyn
30 May Henry marries Jane Seymour
October Pilgrimage of Grace

1537

Sole Master of the King's Wards
October Treasurer of the Royal Household

1537

12 October Birth of Prince Edward
24 October Death of Jane Seymour

1539
9 March Created Baron St John

1540	**1540**
July Master of the Court of Wards	*6 January* Henry marries Anne of Cleves *13 July* Annulment of Henry's marriage to Anne of Cleves *28 July* Execution of Thomas Cromwell Henry marries Catherine Howard

1541
Master of the King's Woods
December One of the judges to try
Thomas Culpeper and Francis Dereham

1542	**1542**
Master of the Court of Wards and Liveries *19 November* Privy Councillor	*13 February* Execution of Catherine Howard

1543	**1543**
6 May Installed Knight of the Garter *16 May* Lord Chamberlain of the Royal Household	*12 July* Henry marries Catherine Parr

1544	**1544**
Organising supplies for King's army during Boulogne campaign	War with France and the capture of Boulogne

1545	**1545**
Governor of Portsmouth *November* Lord Great Master of the King's Household Lord President of the King's Council	French invasion threat and sinking of the *Mary Rose*

1547	**1547**
January Executor of Henry VIII's will *March–October* Lord Keeper of the Great Seal	*28 January* Death of Henry VIII Accession of Edward VI

1549	**1549**
October Involved in the overthrow of the Duke of Somerset	First Edwardian Book of Common Prayer Rebellion in west and east of England *October* Coup against Duke of Somerset

1550
19 January Created Earl of Wiltshire
3 February Lord High Treasurer

1551
11 October Created Marquis of Winchester
1 December Lord High Steward at the
trial of the Duke of Somerset

1552
January Duke of Somerset executed
Second Edwardian Book of Common Prayer

1553
6 July Death of Edward VI
10–19 July Lady Jane Grey proclaimed
Queen of England
Accession of Queen Mary I
Repeal of Edwardian religious acts

1554
25 July Witnessed marriage of Mary I to
Philip of Spain

1554
January/February Wyatt's Rebellion
November Parliament agrees to the
restoration of Papal authority in England

1558
25 December Death of Paulet's wife,
Elizabeth

1558
17 November Death of Mary I
Accession of Elizabeth I

1559
Act of Uniformity
April Elizabeth declared Supreme
Governor of the Church in England

1561
4 June Fire at St Paul's Cathedral

1562
October Elizabeth nearly dies of smallpox

1566
5–25 October Speaker in the House of
Lords

1566
Parliament asks the Queen to name a
successor

1572
10 March Death of William Paulet

1

The Early Years

The long procession moved slowly along the track towards the distant church tower. Above the banks on either side the first blackthorn blossom heralded the approach of spring and early primrose flowers nestled amongst the clumps of grass. The sun was shining but the earth was hard from recent frosts and the ice on the puddles in the cart ruts splintered beneath the walkers' feet. At the front of the procession thirty poor men, dressed in black gowns and walking two by two, were followed by a singing choir and priests, while stretching away into the distance behind them came a long line of over 100 knights, gentlemen and esquires all attired in black and riding two abreast. One rider held aloft an embroidered standard that fluttered overhead displaying the motto 'Love Loyalty' with a crest of a golden falcon, its wings outstretched and with a ducal coronet around its neck. Completing this first part of the procession rode three men, each carrying a white stick, the symbol of their offices as Comptroller, Treasurer and Steward in a great house.

The heart of the procession was led by five men riding on horses caparisoned with black cloth. The leader carried a large banner displaying a coat of arms of three black swords, points downwards and with gold hilts, set within an ermine border. The other four riders, all heralds, wore tabards embroidered with coats of arms and amongst them they carried a helmet and crest, a coat of arms, a sword and a shield. These men preceded an oak coffin draped in a black pall and carried aloft by pallbearers. It was a third of a mile to the village church from the palatial house where the procession had begun, too far for the six men who bore the coffin but they were accompanied by another six to take their places. Beside the coffin walked four men holding banners displaying the ancestral marriage alliances of the deceased and following behind rode the four sons of the dead man with other male relations and friends. Above the distant toll of the church bells they could just hear the sound of the choir of men and priests whose soft chanting drifted back to them and to the many knights, esquires and yeomen who walked at the rear of the procession. It was apparent to any onlooker that this funeral cortège was for a man of great importance.

As they approached the church some of the mourners talked of the life of the deceased. There was disagreement about his age. Some believed he was 87 while others said he was older, more than 100 – but all agreed that he was ancient. They spoke of his remarkable achievements, of how, born the son of a country gentleman, he died as the foremost noble in England, next in rank to Queen Elizabeth herself. They recounted how he had begun his career in royal service during the reign of the Queen's father, Henry VIII, and had maintained his place at Court to serve under three more monarchs – Edward VI, Mary and eventually Elizabeth. His contemporaries were all dead and he was the last of the men who had advised Henry VIII during the great events of that reign. The mourners marvelled that he had managed to survive the dangers of Court life, the factional struggles of ambitious men and the ever-changing religious demands of each monarch. Like a sturdy oak, William Paulet had weathered all the storms of Tudor rule.[1]

The family background and upbringing of William Paulet, 1st Marquis of Winchester, were not extraordinary and did not mark him out for a brilliant career. Paulet inherited a family name that can be traced back to the reign of Henry II in the second half of the twelfth century. Hercules, Lord of Tournon in Picardy, had accompanied the King's third son, Geoffrey, to England and was granted land at Powlett in Somerset. Following the custom of the time he assumed the name of the place where he settled and became Hercules de Powlett. By the sixteenth century the most common usage was Paulet. Although Paulet's ancestors did not hold influential positions at Court they did manage to consolidate their position as gentry, largely by the acquisition of property through financially beneficial marriages. The first of these took place around 1320 between Sir John Powlett, sixth in descent from Hercules, and Elizabeth Reyney who inherited her father's considerable fortune. Sir John's grandson, William, brought further land into the family with his marriage to Eleanor de la Mare, who was heiress to her father's property at Nunney Castle in Somerset and Fisherton de la Mare in Wiltshire. Later their son, Sir John, inherited his father's properties in Somerset and Wiltshire together with those of his mother, and then substantially increased his fortune in 1427 by his marriage to Constance, the grand-daughter and co-heiress to Thomas Poynings, Lord St John of Basing.[2]

Sir John Powlett and Constance Poynings were the great-grandparents of William Paulet, the future marquis. When their son John died in 1492 William's father, another Sir John, inherited an extensive portfolio of lands and property, which included his principal estate at Basing in north Hampshire, the manor of Fisherton de la Mare and several other manors in Hampshire, Wiltshire and Somerset. Sir John served as one of the King's army commanders at Blackheath in 1497, when the Cornish rebels were subdued, and in 1501 he was created a Knight of the Bath on the occasion of the marriage of Prince Arthur to Catherine of Aragon. He married his cousin, Alice, the daughter of Sir William Powlett of Hinton St George in Somerset, a family connection that was strengthened when his sister Margaret married Alice's brother Amias.[3] Sir John and Alice had six children – four sons, William (the future 1st Marquis of Winchester), Thomas, George and Richard, and two daughters, Eleanor and Catherine. While William was rising to prominence at Court his siblings appear to have led ordinary lives. Only his brother George features briefly in William's story in an incident that resulted in George spending a short time in the Tower.

Revered as he was for his longevity, establishing the exact year of William Paulet's birth is almost impossible. Suggested dates of birth have been 1465, 1473, 1474, 1483 and 1484, meaning that Paulet could have been as much as 107 years old when he died.[4] Prior to the middle of the sixteenth century written records of place and date of birth are very sparse and the only available documented evidence suggests 1484. An inquisition post mortem (an inquiry to establish legal rights over land after a death) in January 1525 described Paulet as 40 years and more, placing his birth at 1484 or earlier.[5] This date accords well with his grandfather's birth in 1428, his father's birth sometime before 1460 and his marriage by 1509.[6] The only record of Paulet's place of birth (and the day) is found in a poem written as an encomium on the man's life and death. This tells us that 'At Fisherton, hight Dalamer, this subject true was borne' on Whitsun night, which in 1484 fell on 6 June.[7] Paulet's family owned a manor at Fisherton de la Mare in Wiltshire, a hamlet ten miles north-west of Salisbury on the River Wylye.

Paulet's grandfather, John, died in possession of the manor in 1492 and it is entirely feasible that William Paulet's parents could have been at the manor at the time of his birth and may indeed have used the manor as their home.[8] Therefore Paulet was at least 87 when he died in March 1572. Any earlier date supposes that Paulet's father was rather young when his son was born and Paulet rather old when he married.

There is no record of Paulet's childhood but it is probable that in common with other children of the time he was baptised soon after birth. Due to a high infant mortality rate, many babies were presented for baptism within days of being born because of the belief that only those who were baptised could enter heaven. Members of church congregations were encouraged to memorise the baptism service so they could recite the prayers and baptise a newborn infant who might not survive long enough to be attended by a priest. Godparents were chosen with care to enlarge the family's social network and to provide opportunities for the future advancement of the child.

For the three days since his birth, the infant had been cocooned within a warm stuffy chamber; now he was being carried by his godmother to his baptism. His two godfathers and his relatives, together with family friends and neighbours, had all come to witness this important event. The only people missing were the baby's parents who had remained within the manor. They had no part in the ceremony since the godparents would speak on behalf of the child.

The party came to the door of the church and waited until the priest came out to them – before the baby could be taken into the church he must be exorcised of all evil.[9] The priest asked the name of the child – 'William' replied the godparents – and whether he had already been baptised, to which his godmother answered 'no'. She moved to stand on the right-hand side of the priest (she would have stood upon the left side if the baby was a girl) who began to perform a series of ceremonies to purify the young William Paulet. He made the sign of the cross on the baby's forehead and breast to free him from the power of Satan. The priest recited prayers over him and then placed a small trace of salt on his tongue. The salt was to be the 'salvation of body and soul', purifying his body and driving out the devil. The priest read a passage from the Gospels in Latin, and then those who were able joined him in reciting the Lord's Prayer and the Creed. After he had made the sign of the cross on the infant's right hand the priest led the baby with his godmother into the church by that hand while the rest of the party followed behind.[10]

They gathered around the font where, in answer to questions from the priest, the godparents renounced the devil and affirmed their belief in Christ, and were then admonished that they should ensure that their godchild was brought up to lead a virtuous and Christian life. The priest took the child and after asking the baby's name again he dipped the child's head into the cold water in the font. Three times he lowered the baby, each time with the child's face turned to a different direction, while he recited: 'William, I baptise you in the name of the Father, and of the Son, and of the Holy Ghost'. He raised the child up and passed him back to his godmother then, taking a small jar containing chrism, a mixture of oil and balm, he dipped his finger into the liquid and marked the sign of the cross on the child's head. William was baptised, he was a member of the Catholic Church and, as a token of his innocence, was wrapped in a white linen chrisom cloth. Finally, taking the lighted candle which stood on the edge of the font, the priest placed it within the child's open hand before passing it to one of William's godfathers.[11] The ceremony was finished and the group thanked the priest and moved out into the sunlight.

The formal part of the day was over and now the christening party could look forward to the feasting and drinking that awaited them back at the manor. William's father was at the door waiting for them. The three godparents went upstairs to take William to his mother and to congratulate her on the birth of her son. Alice was sitting in bed and took the baby who was starting to fret. She removed the chrisom cloth and cuddled him but when he began to cry she passed him to the wet-nurse who waited by her side. The wet-nurse had been carefully chosen. She came from a good local family and led a clean and sober life, important factors because it was thought that some of her characteristics might flow into the baby during breast feeding. The nurse carried William into her small chamber next door and sat feeding him. When he was old enough to be weaned she would feed him sops of bread soaked in milk or water, perhaps with a little sugar, and when he was teething the leg of a chicken with most of the flesh cut off would serve as a dummy for him to chew upon.[12]

At last he was finished and she laid him on her bed to change his nappy. She unwrapped the long linen cloth from around his body. The nurse was always careful not to swathe him too tightly. Although the binding would help William to grow with a straight spine and reduced the risk that he might break his legs by kicking too hard, the binding could crush his ribs if too tight and pull his spine out of alignment, leading to a mis-shapen back and shoulders. She removed the wet napkin, replaced it with a clean one and took the swaddling cloth. It was about six inches wide and ten feet long. Starting at William's shoulders she wound the cloth around his body, wrapping his arms to his side, and down to his feet until he was a neat little bundle, easy to carry – he could even be hung on a hook out of harm's way.[13] *With his head protruding from the top he resembled an insect emerging from a chrysalis. As the summer weather got hotter she might leave his arms free from the bands, beginning the swaddling at his armpits, so that he was a little cooler. She lifted up the baby and going back to Alice's room placed the little bundle in the cradle, a decorated wooden box on wooden rockers, and tied strings across the top so that he could not fall out while being rocked.*[14] *The godparents were taking their leave of Alice. The merrymaking to celebrate the birth of John Paulet's first son and heir had begun down below and they were keen to join the other guests.*

After six months the swaddling bands were removed from the baby and the young Paulet was dressed in the unisex attire for boys and girls. This comprised full-length bell-shaped skirts or petticoats, with a top possibly styled as a doublet, all worn over a shift. Young children sometimes wore a 'black pudding', a narrow padded ring of black silk or satin that was tied horizontally around the head, to protect them in case of a fall.[15] At the age of six Paulet was ready to be 'breeched', a proud family occasion on which he first wore hose and breeches. From then on he ceased to wear children's clothes – except perhaps for play when he might have worn a smock over loose trousers – and instead would have worn garments that were smaller versions of men's clothes. The style during the reign of Henry VII was for linen or flannel drawers under hose similar to tights, with a shirt and a top garment of a doublet, like a close-fitting jacket that reached only to the waist. For extra warmth a gown was added, which could be either short or to the floor. Shoes were flat with a wide, round-toed shape.[16]

Childhood was short. Children were dressed to look like adults and were encouraged to grow up quickly in a world where infant mortality was high. Young boys were cared for and educated by the women in the household but after a few years they started to move into the world of men. In 1543 the future monarch Prince Edward was moved to his own suite of rooms at Hampton Court at the tender age of six; the women of his household were dismissed and a household of gentlemen and tutors appointed. Children were taught to be well-mannered and polite and to be respectful towards others. It was important to understand who had precedence over whom. The young Paulet would have learned which people were above his parents in society and those who were below.

By the time of Henry VIII's reign the government of England and the management of the Royal Court employed the services of a decreasing number of clerics and nobles and an increasing number of officials with an academic education. This provided an opportunity for young educated men who might not previously have gained a place at Court to seek a position, usually through a sponsor. To this end the young William Paulet would have been taught all those skills and attributes that were considered essential for a young Tudor gentleman and which would enable him to socialise with and impress those people who were ranked above him in society.

Although some courtiers received little academic education – in 1550 the Imperial ambassador commented that Sir William Herbert, the Master of the Horse, could speak only English and could neither read nor write – Paulet's impressive administrative skills were only made possible by his good education.[17] This would have begun at the age of seven or eight when attendance at school generally commenced. While most girls continued to be educated by their mothers, it was usual for boys to start attending lessons either at home with a tutor or in a school run by a priest or at a grammar school, so-called because its primary purpose was to teach Latin grammar. Latin was an essential part of an ambitious schoolboy's education. It was the language of church services and of written law and was used by clerks for official documents and accounts. It was even useful as a common conversational language. In 1533 the Imperial ambassador, Eustace Chapuys, during a discussion with several councillors including Paulet was asked to speak in Latin as the councillors did not all understand French.[18]

Boys' earlier instruction in social and musical skills continued but was supplemented by the teaching of French, arithmetic, geometry, scripture and handwriting. Much of the teaching was oral and in some subjects the emphasis was on learning by rote. For those at school the day was very long and the boys attended six days a week. The day began at 6am with prayers, and lessons continued until 11am or noon, with a short break for breakfast at around 9am. After a midday meal and recreation, studies resumed and continued until 5 or 6pm.[19] Holidays were short but the children usually celebrated the many church festivals and saints' days with a day off. On St Nicholas' Day many great churches chose a 'boy-bishop' from amongst the choristers to preside over the service and to give a sermon. The local schoolchildren were encouraged to attend this service and one can imagine their delight to see one of their own as 'chief cleric'. Shrove Tuesday was another holiday when the boys were spared lessons and allowed to spend the day in ball games and cockfighting.[20]

School resources were sparse and in 1518 John Colet ordered the boys of St Paul's in London to provide their own candles. Paper was of poor quality and very expensive and so a 'payre of tabullys' (or tablets) were more often used for writing on with chalk. Pencils were almost unknown and boys used pens of sharpened goose quills, carried in a small 'penner' or sheath, with ink made from oak apples and green vitriol (a mixture of iron sulphate mixed with fish-glue and water). The first Latin grammars were printed in England in 1483 as pamphlets costing one penny or so and some pupils had these to supplement the few books owned by the schools. School regimes were harsh; an early woodcut shows a schoolroom with the pupils sitting on forms and the schoolmaster at a high chair with a cane in his hand.[21] Sir Thomas Elyot, in 1531, exhorted parents to choose a good master for their boys because 'by a cruell and irous maister the wittes of children be bullied'. He desired that they should be encouraged to learn through praise and with 'such pretty gyftes as children delite in', and was a great advocate of exercise by which 'the helthe of man is preserved and his strength increased'.[22]

Between the ages of 14 and 18 the boys might enter university at either Oxford or Cambridge, although some sons of the nobility and gentry were first sent to live and work in the houses of other noblemen. One such was Sir Thomas More, a contemporary of William Paulet, who at the age of twelve was placed as a page in the household of Cardinal Morton for two years. The primary purpose of this was the quest for patronage. It was hoped that the host would act as patron to his charge and, when the time came, endeavour to help him acquire a good position, preferably at Court. In a large household there might be several young men in attendance and, if Paulet did follow this route, he would have found himself in the company of boys from both noble and gentry families. The pages' chamber at Hampton Court shows how pages lived together in one room, sleeping on straw mattresses, close at hand in case they were needed. The boys continued to receive tutelage in academic subjects while they worked as pages, serving at table and attending to the diners' needs. Their education included the social skills considered necessary for a gentleman. They learned to show courtesy to women, respect to those above them and politeness to those below. Their instruction included how to care for themselves and how to dress well and make entertaining conversation.

Instructions on good manners and behaviour in company were given in publications such as the *Boke of Nurture* and *The Babees' Book*. From these, young men learnt the rules of social precedence, the complicated rituals which accompanied the preparation of the table before a meal and how they should wait upon their lord. They were instructed not to rush to him but to use smooth actions and gentle words, to offer clean water and towels for him to wash his hands at meals and to stand before him until bidden to sit. When cutting a loaf of bread they were to offer the 'upper crust' to their lord – the bottom crust would be dirty from the burning faggots placed in the oven to heat it before baking commenced.

Great emphasis was placed on not offending one's neighbour at table. Etiquette demanded that you did not 'claw your head or your back as if you were after a flea, or stroke your hair as if you sought a louse'. Pages were instructed not to 'pick your nose … sniff … blow it too loud, lest your lord hear' and neither 'retch not, nor spit too far'. And there was the rather indelicate advice to 'alle wey be ware of thy hyndur part from gunnes blast-ynge'. Because of the communal style of eating, diners were encouraged to 'keep clear of soiling the cloth' and not to lean on the table – wise advice for people eating off trestle tables. They were to 'touch no manner of meat with thy right hand, but with thy left, as is proper' and to wipe their mouth before drinking from a communal cup.[23] There was advice 'against taking so muckle meat into your mouth but that ye may right well answer when men speak to you'.[24] The books also gave very precise instructions concerning the different methods of carving various joints of meat and an aspiring young courtier would have given these special attention. It was considered an honour to be asked to carve the meat at the top table and was the mark of a gentleman to be able to do so properly.

In a large house with many visitors the young aspiring courtier would be able to identify a person's rank by the clothes he wore. Sumptuary laws prescribed certain levels of dress to create a distinction between the classes; for example, only the King and his family were permitted to wear purple silk. The young page learnt how to address each man properly and where he should be seated at table according to his rank. The seating plan was very rigid and a person would be offended if he was placed in a lower seat than was his right. The most important guests sat at the top table on the right-hand side of the host. Other guests were seated in descending order down the 'legs' of tables, with the lowest ranking visitor placed at the bottom of the left-hand table. A large salt cellar was often placed in the middle of the table – thus those of lower rank found themselves eating 'below the salt', away from the family and important guests. Whether Paulet entered a great household or remained at home, by the age of fourteen he would have learned many of the social skills that would later mark him out as a gentleman at Court.

'After having studied at the University of Oxford, [Paulet] became a student in Thavies Inn three years; after that in the Temple.'[25] Although his name does not appear in the University records it is possible that he was a student there because names of students who did not graduate were not always recorded. To attend university at Oxford or Cambridge prior to studying law in London was not unusual. Sir Thomas More spent two years at Oxford and then moved to an Inn in London without taking his degree.

At Oxford and Cambridge the student was admitted to a college or hall where he would live and study. These were run on the lines of a household where the students lived, ate and studied in a large hall and slept in shared bedrooms. The day was long, beginning with prayers at 5 or 6am which were followed by lectures and debates. Paulet would have spent many hours taking part in 'disputes' and discussions, and during the first two years at university much time was devoted to learning the skills of logic and rhetoric. This was essential for prospective lawyers but was also considered necessary training for any ambitious young man. Courtiers were expected to be able to converse and debate on any topic and for men in power the ability or lack thereof to sway others by argument could have momentous outcomes. The universities taught other subjects such as philosophy and theology, Greek, mathematics and astronomy, medicine and law. The law offered was canon and civil law, from which the lawyers became known as 'civilians', but for those hoping to work in the service of the King it was advisable to move to London and study common law in the Inns of Court.

Attending an Inn of Court in London was an accepted route to follow for many sons of noble and gentle birth who aspired to be courtiers. The Inns were seen as centres of education in the same way as universities, and students were taught not only English law but history, scripture, music, dancing and other noblemen's pastimes. Society was becoming more litigious and the Inns attracted students who had no intention of becoming lawyers but who wanted enough knowledge of the law to be able to protect their own property. As today, the Inns of Court were Gray's, Lincoln, Inner and Middle Temple but there were also about ten Inns of Chancery, one of which was Thavies Inn in Oldbourne (Holborn) where Paulet studied. The Chancery Inns each had about 100 students and here the young student barristers would learn basic law before becoming members of an Inn of Court. They learnt to understand legal procedures and precedents and were instructed in the use of writs and the meaning of statutes. They attended court to hear and see how a case should – or should not be – presented and afterwards discussed the arguments they had heard. Much time was given to debating to allow the students to practise and improve their skills of oratory, which would be so vital should they themselves appear in court. While at Thavies Inn, and later in the Temple, Paulet 'applied himself so well, Inclined to learned skill, Till Utter Barrister he was, He there continued still'.[26] He probably spent three years at Thavies Inn before moving to one of the Inns of Court.[27] Here his lifestyle would have been similar to that at Oxford. Each Inn had up to 200 members living together as a community, eating meals and studying in the hall and attending communion in their own chapel.

The training Paulet received in the Temple continued that of the Chancery Inns. Highly practical, it involved committing to memory points of law he had heard in lectures and during argument and discussion. Starting at 8am, the students would gather in the hall to listen to the opinions and judgments of barristers as they argued over legal points, and after supper they took part in the moots. This was the most useful part of Paulet's training. The moot was a practice court where the senior members – the benchers – of the Inn sat as judges to listen to the students argue a case. Initially the students were known as 'inner-barristers' and took part in the proceedings from within the bar, the physical barrier which separates the judges from the rest of the court. When they were deemed sufficiently competent they were called to the bar as 'utter-barristers' and allowed to argue points of law standing outside the bar at moots.[28] Paulet reached this stage of competence and probably belonged to Inner Temple.

Admissions records are scarce and there is no record of his entry to the Inn but from 1505 to 1507 a 'Paulet' is listed as marshal for the Christmas festivities at Inner Temple.[29] The marshal was one of three members of the Inn elected to oversee the Christmas festivities that stretched from Christmas Eve to Twelfth Night and included banquets, music and dancing, plays and masques. The marshal seated the company at dinner according to their rank and took part in the ceremonies that accompanied the meals.[30] Later, in 1535, Sir William Paulet was responsible for his son Chidiock's admission to Inner Temple. Chidiock was then no more than eighteen and gained entry for two years on favourable terms, surely on account of his father.[31]

By his early twenties Paulet was qualified as a barrister and set to embark on a career in law. He had learned the skills necessary for a young gentleman in Tudor society and knew how to be agreeable in company and how to dress and carry himself to make a favourable impression. He came from a respectable family and was well prepared to make his way in the world. It is probable that after his training he continued to live in London and practise at the bar since he was later called as an adviser in law to the King.

Paulet's connection with London is strengthened by his marriage to Elizabeth, the daughter of Sir William Capel.[32] They were married by 1509 though we do not know the exact date of his wedding. It is possible that the marriage took place at the church of St Bartholomew-the-Little at the end of Bartholomew Lane where Sir William Capel and his wife, Margaret, were buried in the chapel he built. Sir William started as an apprentice in London, was knighted in 1482 and served as sheriff, MP for the City and was twice Lord Mayor. He had three children – Giles, Elizabeth and Dorothy.[33]

As the son of a landed family, it would have been quite usual for Paulet's marriage to be arranged by his parents. Since he married in London so far from his family home perhaps he selected his own bride. The choice of partner was very important to both families as marriage joined together not only the couple but also their relatives, bringing each the possibility of new contacts and opportunities in their social and business lives. Perhaps most important was the financial situation of the bride, and the discussions concerning her dowry and long-term support could make the marriage agreement seem more like a business proposal. Husbands were advised that 'when himself is departed, his bounty must be present with her, even after death'.[34] Should the husband die first, his wife should have sufficient property to support her for the rest of her life. Often a piece of land was held jointly by the couple and then solely by the wife if her husband died first. We can see an example of this within Paulet's own family when, in 1468, land was settled upon Paulet's father to be passed after his death to his wife Alice.[35]

The bride Elizabeth was wearing a new gown of blue damask and, since she had not been married before, she wore her long hair loose down her back. One of the men went inside the church and soon returned with the priest. Elizabeth moved to stand to the left of her bridegroom – a woman's correct place beside a man because the Bible told them that Eve had been formed out of a rib in the left side of Adam. William took his bride's right hand and they exchanged vows: 'I, William, take thee, Elizabeth, to my wedded wife...', and then 'I, Elizabeth, take thee, William, to my wedded husband...'

After the priest had blessed the ring William slipped it onto the thumb of Elizabeth's right hand as he said the words: 'In the name of the Father', then onto her index finger as he continued: 'And of the Son', then onto her middle finger 'And of the Holy Spirit' and finally onto her fourth finger 'Amen'. This finger held special significance for it was said that a vein ran from the finger direct to the heart.[36] Paulet had chosen a gimmal ring made of two rings which interlinked to form one, symbolising the joining together of two people. It was given as a token of love and commitment but it was also a mark of ownership and a statement of the status Elizabeth had now accepted. The couple moved into the empty church after the priest, as the rest of the party followed behind them. Standing at the altar step William and Elizabeth listened as the priest prayed for their future together, that they should be blessed with the joy of children, and they accepted the bread as he administered the nuptial Mass. After a final blessing William turned to his bride and led her to the back of the church. Upon a table were laid out small drinking cups with jugs of hippocras, a spiced and sweetened wine drink. The wine was poured out and passed around and the wedding guests pressed around the newly married couple, drinking to their future health and happiness. The cups were soon empty and the party made its way out of the church. The party walked the short distance to Elizabeth's family home to continue the celebrations. William's father-in-law was a wealthy man and would want to impress his guests so a great feast awaited them there.

The marriage was not truly formalised until consummation had taken place and great importance was placed on the ceremonial bedding. The couple was accompanied by the wedding party into the bedchamber where, if the priest was present, he blessed the bed and sprinkled holy water over the newlyweds. Amidst much ribaldry and mirth the couple was helped to prepare and the guests left after having seen them into bed. Written advice was available to help couples enjoy happy and successful marriages. Guidance for men suggested that every good husband should 'afford his wife allowance of all necessary comforts for this present life; for attire and food, for necessity and delight, that she may live a cheerful and a well contented life with him'.[37]

William and Elizabeth had eight children. Their dates of birth are unknown but the wills of Elizabeth's parents indicate that six of them were born before the end of 1516.[38] There were four sons – John, Thomas, Chidiock and Giles – and four daughters, Alice, Margaret, Margery and

Eleanor. All eight children survived into adulthood and married, and Paulet saw some of his great-grandchildren 'grown to man's estate', so there may be some truth in the assertion that he lived to see 103 of his own descendants.[39] John inherited his father's title of Marquis of Winchester but never achieved the acclaim of his father and only held county appointments. Chidiock was prominent in Hampshire and from 1554 to 1559 he served as Governor of the town and castle of Portsmouth. He was twice elected to Parliament. Giles was chosen to be a playmate of the future King Edward VI. Of the other children's lives few details are known.

2

Growing Influence in Hampshire

At some date close to Paulet's wedding his father, Sir John, was taken ill and was unable to run his estates or carry out his duties in Hampshire, and Paulet was summoned home to Basing to take charge. Unsuccessful nominations for him to be sheriff in Hampshire in 1509 and 1510 and many later appointments within the county indicate that he may have spent the next fifteen years or so resident at Basing.[40] In his will in 1525 Sir John made a point of expressing his gratitude to William for the diligence and kindness he had shown towards both his parents and his brothers.[41] This suggests that he had been looking after the family for some time and it is probable that his father had never fully recovered from his illness and that William continued to remain at Basing attending to his family's care and the upkeep of his future inheritance.

From 1511 to 1526 Paulet was one of the King's men in Hampshire. England had no police force and the monarch maintained control of the country through local men appointed to positions of authority. In each county the upholders of law and order were local landowners who were the sheriffs and justices of the peace and, later in the century, the Lords Lieutenant. The King relied on the support and loyalty of these men. In return for the local power and authority gained from their position, they were expected to offer unconditional service to the Crown. They not only maintained the laws of the land but executed the King's orders, collected his taxes and kept him informed of the state of his kingdom. In the event of any serious disturbance they could be ordered to raise and lead an army to quell an uprising, so they had to be trustworthy. A landowner in control of an army was a potential threat to the King and there was always the risk that an ambitious noble could turn that force against the monarch.

Paulet was appointed as sheriff in Hampshire (Southamptonshire) for terms of one year in 1511, 1518 and 1522.[42] The term 'sheriff' came from 'shire reeve' – an officer who oversaw and kept order in the shire – and the office of sheriff originated during the Middle Ages as the Crown's fiscal and judicial representative in the counties. His primary roles were concerned with ensuring the local populace obeyed the law and paid their taxes. The sheriff, usually a prominent landowner, was the chief administrative officer in each county and was aided in his duties by an under-sheriff and clerk, and by constables and bailiffs who were the local officials within villages and hundreds of the county. Towns such as Southampton and Portsmouth were self-governing and were controlled by the aldermen and councillors, carrying out the King's instructions. By the sixteenth century many of the sheriff's duties with regard to maintaining law and order had been passed over to the justices of the peace but he was still responsible for keeping the King's peace. He proclaimed the Quarter Sessions, summoned juries and carried out sentences. He presided over county elections and was responsible for the collection of debts due to the Crown, such as revenue from Crown lands in the county and fines at the County Court. He also had the authority to raise a '*posse comitatus*' – a group of armed men over the age of fifteen whom he could summon to quell any civil unrest. Paulet's grandfather and father had both been appointed as sheriff before him, and his brother George and son John would follow suit.

During his first appointment as sheriff Paulet was instructed by the Privy Council in May 1512 'to review captains, mariners and soldiers at Southampton and elsewhere, to certify number of same and arrest and punish rebels', prior to the soldiers 'proceeding to foreign ports'.[43] This was the Council's method of assessing manpower and of ensuring that the force was ready. Paulet would have been provided with the numbers of the available local men by the constables and local landowners. The country had no regular army and all men who owed allegiance to the monarch had a feudal duty to supply a certain number of armed men to fight in time of war. During January 1514 the Earl of Surrey was mustering an army at Portsmouth in preparation for an anticipated attack by the French. The local nobility and gentry received the order to provide men to fight and to gather with their retainers at the port. Most, including Paulet, arrived with 'good companies' of 20–100 men but nobles such as Lord Arundel sent 300.[44] On that occasion the expected invasion never materialised and Paulet, with the men he had raised from amongst his tenants, was not called upon to fight.

Justices of the peace, or magistrates, were central figures in the government of the counties. The position was held in very high esteem and gave an indication of a gentleman's social standing. Paulet's sons, John and Chidiock, also served as justices, which helped to enhance the power and control the Paulet family held in Hampshire. Removal from the post was a social disgrace and the King used this threat to ensure that the magistrates used their local knowledge to further his interests rather than their own. The inclusion of members of the King's Council as justices outside their own shires ensured that each county had some justices with no local interests to give an impartial view on the King's behalf.

To qualify for consideration as a magistrate, a landowner or his son had to hold land worth at least £20 per annum. The post was unsalaried as it was considered that the landowning classes had a responsibility to maintain the law in their locality. While many justices were members of the nobility, Henry VIII also appointed knights and squires of country families in order to reduce the power of the nobility. A growing number of lesser country gentry and townsmen were increasing their wealth – either by commercial enterprise or from patronage at Court – and were then able to buy large areas of land in the country, thus making them eligible for the position of magistrate.

John Paulet was a justice of the peace and it is possible that William was initially nominated to replace his father during the latter's illness. His first appointment in Hampshire was made on 24 January 1514, and he was reappointed on 18 October and twice the following year when he was one of about two dozen magistrates in the county.[45] Commissions were renewed annually and men often remained in post for many years. Paulet was also appointed as justice of the peace for Wiltshire and Somerset where he owned further estates, and his training as a lawyer was to prove invaluable for his work. In Hampshire all justices were expected to attend the Quarter Sessions held in Winchester, where citizens accused of serious crimes were tried. These were held at Easter, Midsummer, Michaelmas and Epiphany. At other times Paulet dealt directly with persons accused of minor crimes, either sentencing them to jail, allowing bail or committing them to the next Quarter Session. He had the power to order the arrest of suspects and to examine them, and was able to inquire into charges against the sheriff on matters such as jury corruption. Paulet was dependent on the local officials (the bailiff and the constable) to keep the peace and to bring offenders before him. These men were empowered to arrest vagrants and beggars, attend to the upkeep of the roads and maintain general law and order in their area. They passed information to Paulet and he issued orders to them. Since there were many justices at any time within Hampshire, Paulet would have been particularly responsible for maintaining the law in the parishes closest to his own estates.

Throughout the sixteenth century, government involvement in citizens' lives grew and the responsibilities of the justices increased as their judicial and administrative duties widened. For instance, in 1531 an act of Parliament made a distinction between the two kinds of poor – those capable but unwilling to work and those too old or sick to work. The new act provided for the former to be whipped and for the latter to be allowed to beg under licence. In 1536 the first Poor Law was passed, which gave justices responsibility for ensuring that each parish employed those capable of working, collected alms for those unable to work and cared for those in need. They were given increased responsibility for the regulation of wages and prices, weights and measures, the holding of fairs and markets, the licensing of ale-houses and playhouses, the administering of laws against unlawful gambling, the maintenance of religious observance and the upkeep of the highway.

The senior justice of the peace in each county was nominated as *custos rotulorum* (the keeper of the shire records) and Paulet may have held this title during his father's lifetime. The King's commissions and letters regarding any actions to be carried out within the county were issued by the Privy Council and sent to the *custos rotulorum*. It was his responsibility to call the justices of the peace together 'for the execution of the King's commandments'.[46] These commissions were generally enacted for a limited time and carried responsibilities such as collecting subsidies or inquiring into the imparkation, or enclosing, of land in Hampshire. Hampshire, being a southern coastal county, was always at risk of invasion, and commissions were often issued to examine and improve the coastal defences and ensure the maintenance of warning beacons. With the two ports of Portsmouth and Southampton in the county Paulet was also frequently involved in the muster of troops and the manning and provisioning of the ships. He described how 'many times came commandments to gather men to be conducted to the sea-side to defend the coasts' and that 'everie castle and fort were furnished with armure and weapon'.[47] Paulet was notified of one commission in the autumn of 1523, concerning the collection of a subsidy in aid of the Duke of Suffolk who was marching with an army towards Paris. England was at war with France but there was no money in the royal coffers to pay for it and the funds for Suffolk's expedition were raised through taxes. All persons in each county owning £40 and upwards in goods or lands were required to pay, and it was the responsibility of the justices to co-ordinate the collection. The commission document, dated 2 November 1523, lists Paulet as commissioner to collect taxes in three areas – Hampshire, the town of Southampton and the city of Winchester. Here, for the first time, he is styled as Sir William Paulet, although only on the commission for Southampton.[48] The title is given again the following April in an account of the money collected for the cost of the French war.[49] So it appears that during 1523 the King had knighted Paulet during his father's lifetime, Sir John's title not being hereditary. Paulet's knighthood must have been bestowed for services rendered in Hampshire, which suggests that he had already been brought to the King's notice.

Paulet had another responsibility in Hampshire, which he held for many years, that of steward of the lands of the bishopric of Winchester. He took on the office before 1516 during the episcopacy of Richard Fox and continued when Thomas Wolsey was confirmed in 1529 following the death of Fox. Winchester was one of the wealthiest sees in England and the revenues from the bishopric lands would have been very welcome to Wolsey, who enjoyed an extravagant lifestyle. As steward, Paulet oversaw the administration of the bishop's manors and lands, examined the way they were run by the bailiffs, held hundred-courts and attended to any business the bishop had in that area. A letter from Paulet to Wolsey in June 1529 concerned a survey that Paulet was making of the castles, manors and lands in the bishopric, possibly an initial inventory for the new bishop. He referred to there being only a few deer in one park – 500 instead of 1,000 – and suggested that certain hunters and fishermen should be punished as an example. He finished by saying that he would be in Taunton on Monday – a long ride from Hampshire but probably not unusual because the bishopric lands were widely spread.[50] The appointment was a part-time one. At Christmas 1541 he was paid £10 for the year and received his travelling expenses. His brother George also received £10 for working as auditor.[51] Paulet continued as steward until at least 1541 by which date he was devoting much time and energy to his many roles at Court, and some of his responsibilities as steward must have been assumed by an assistant.

Paulet records that after his father's death in 1525 the King commanded Wolsey to send for him to come to Richmond where he was appointed, with Sir John Mordante, to the office of Surveyor of the King's Woods throughout the realm, 'with such fees and allowances as were necessary for them'.[52] Although there is no formal record of these appointments, during 1526 Sir John Mordante was appointed with Roger Wiggyston to be 'surveyors of woods' and on 28 February of that year these two men and Paulet were named together in a commission to inquire into the state of some of the King's manors with particular attention to be given to the condition of the woods and the possible sales of felled timber.[53] Certainly Paulet did work with John Mordante in some capacity in 1526. By 1533 he and Thomas Cromwell had been appointed as joint Masters of the King's Woods and Surveyors of Woods belonging to the Duchy of Lancaster, and in February 1536 Paulet became Keeper and Governor of Pamber Forest, north-west of his estate at Basing.[54] Finally, on 23 June 1541, he took the position of chief official for the King's woods – the sole Keeper or Master of Woods in England and the Marches except for those in the royal parks and in the custody of the Duchy of Lancaster and the Court of Augmentations.[55] As with so many appointments in Tudor government, the office of Keeper of Woods brought with it perks. In 1548 when Paulet was granted the office of Keeper of Alice Holt and Woolmer Forests in Hampshire he received the right to all fallen trees and branches of felled trees, all honey and wax found in the woods, pasture for two horses, the right to fish in the forest waters, the authority to hold a 'wodecourte' and take fines, and permission to take a stag and a buck in the summertime and a hind and a doe in winter.[56]

Timber was an essential commodity in Tudor England and great attention was given to the management of the King's woods, which were the source of most of the country's timber. Wood was used for building and fencing, furniture, fuel and shipbuilding, and careful management ensured that woodland was treated as a renewable resource. Large numbers of trees were coppiced every four to eight years to provide smaller, more pliable lengths of wood for fencing and fuel, especially charcoal. Regulations guaranteed that certain trees were allowed to mature to a suitably large size before being cut for use in houses and shipbuilding. The Officers of the Woods oversaw the husbandry of the trees, their felling and the sale of timber. They organised the planting of new trees and the erection and repair of fences to protect saplings and new coppice growth from animals, as well as controlling the numbers of animals such as deer within the woods. During felling, some trees were to be left standing on each acre and were then to be fenced for seven years to keep out grazing animals and some woods were not to be converted into tillage or pasture. Much of Paulet's work was routine, dealing with legal matters, and would not require his constant attendance. Orders to certain men to 'desist from spoiling woods' or assigning trees for repair of a stable and building a hay-house or giving instructions to sell coppice woods at the best price but 'suffering no timber or great trees to be felled or sold' could equally well be carried out by clerks.[57] However, the necessary documents would have carried his signature and the men who were called to 'account for their wood sales' would have appeared before him.

This appointment marked the point at which Paulet made the change from being a local county official to that of a government administrator. Positions of responsibility were frequently awarded either to people who already exerted some influence or to those who had important family connections. Paulet appeared to have neither of these when his father died in 1525. As the son of a member of the gentry and not the aristocracy, he could not expect to be called to Court on the basis of his lineage alone. Patronage was the most practical route; for example, in 1509 Thomas Wolsey was made Royal Almoner and a member of the King's Council through the patronage of the Lord Privy Seal, Bishop Fox. Fox could see that Wolsey had great potential and, in return for his help, Wolsey kept the Bishop informed of news in London when Fox was away from Court.

It is possible that either Bishop Fox or Wolsey might have brought Paulet to the notice of the King. Fox's naming of Paulet as an executor of his will reflects the regard the Bishop held for him, and he left him a bequest of a couch with its covers together with a tapestry.[58] Fox resigned as Lord Privy Seal in 1516 and left Court to retire to his diocese at Winchester. It may well be that 'when about to take his farewell of the Court, Bishop Richard Fox recommended Wolsey his Chaplain and William Paulet, steward of the estates belonging to the see of Winton'.[59] Both Paulet and Wolsey worked for Fox and were well acquainted with one another. In 1517 Fox recommended to Wolsey that Paulet should sit on a commission on unlawful assemblies, and letters from Fox to Wolsey around Christmas 1526 indicate that Paulet carried letters and messages between the two men.[60] In 1525 Wolsey was very influential with the King and would have been in a position to recommend Paulet for the office of Surveyor of Woods. Interestingly, when Wolsey fell from royal favour in 1529 and was ordered to Esher for a few weeks he was short of money; Paulet was one of those who stood by him and offered to lend him funds.

Paulet may also have come to the King's notice through the monarch's familiarity with his brother-in-law, Sir Giles Capel. Giles was a courtier, a soldier and jousting partner of the King. He took a prominent part in the celebratory jousts for Henry's coronation and was one of seven gentlemen companions to the King in the jousts at the Field of Cloth of Gold in 1520. He held a position as Knight of the Body to the King and accompanied Henry to France to meet Charles V in 1520 and again in 1532 when the King took Anne Boleyn to meet Francis I.[61] Giles spent a lot of time in the company of the King and had ample opportunity to seek preferment for members of his family.

Paulet's legal training had made him an ideal choice to operate the machinery of the law within Hampshire, and he had begun to acquire the position and influence that would eventually lead to the Paulets being the dominant family in the county. The years he spent at home, working as sheriff and justice of the peace, gave him a valuable insight into how the King controlled the country and provided the opportunity to learn the administrative skills he would later put to even greater use. His own ability, perhaps with the assistance of a patron, had put him on the threshold of a long career serving his sovereign and country.

3

Master of the King's Wards and the Royal Divorce

Paulet stood before the fire with his arms held out while his servant tied the points to attach the sleeves to the armholes of his doublet, the front of which was already tied together. It needed deft fingers to thread these laces on the sleeves through the eyelet holes in the doublet and then to tie them securely. The garment looked like a short and close-fitting jacket reaching to his waist. Paulet was impatient to be on his way to attend a meeting of the King's Council but dressing could take a long time. He had already donned clean undergarments which the servant had warmed before the fire – linen breeches which had a drawstring waist and a linen shirt with black-work embroidery on the cuffs and collar, decoration his wife Elizabeth had stitched. On his feet and lower leg he wore knitted woollen stockings secured in place by a garter above each knee. The servant finished tying the points and lifted the black silk hose that matched the fabric of the doublet. Paulet stepped into them and then waited again while the servant tied more points to attach the hose to the bottom of the doublet at his waist and to tie up the flap of the codpiece. After checking that the hose reached to the knee, hiding the garters, the servant helped his master into his leather shoes. Flat soled and with square toes, they were low cut and needed the buckle and strap to secure the foot.

The servant laid a cloth around Paulet's shoulders before combing his hair, then, after setting down a basin of warm water, he stood ready with a towel while Paulet washed his hands and face. The cloth was removed and the servant placed a black linen coif on his master's head, covering his hair and coming down over his ears. Next Paulet was helped into a close fitting sleeveless jerkin of fine black wool, the box pleated skirt reaching down to his knees. He fastened a belt on which hung a leather pouch around his waist and waited as the servant lifted the heavy gown onto his shoulders. Falling almost to his ankles, with short sleeves and a wide fur collar, which exaggerated the width of the shoulders, the gown would be cumbersome to wear for any physical activity but it was well designed and did not feel unduly ponderous. The servant placed a black velvet bonnet upon the coif and, with the addition of a gold chain about his neck and some rings upon his fingers, Paulet was ready. His appearance was sombre but by the fine quality of the fabrics it would be apparent to onlookers that he was a man of status and wealth.

By the end of 1526 Paulet's position was firmly established with two new appointments to add to that of Surveyor of the Woods. On 5 February his name had appeared on a list, which included that of Sir Thomas More, of King's councillors who were to act in the capacity of legal advisers.[62] The King's Council was a group of men who acted as advisers to the King in all matters legal, civil and military. They included not only the most important and powerful nobles, clerics and lawyers but also administrators such as Paulet who were retained 'for matter in law'. The Council was under Wolsey's control so he may have had some influence over Paulet's appointment. A core of the most influential councillors acted as advisers on a regular basis but it is probable that Paulet only attended council meetings when his legal advice was sought. To be a member of this august body, working with the men who ran the country, was a measure of the esteem in which he was held.

The second appointment had followed on 3 November when he became Joint Master of the King's Wards with Sir Thomas Englefield.[63] From their offices at Westminster Palace they were responsible for managing the estates and finances of heirs who were underage (men came of age at 21 years and women at 14). The post carried a certain amount of power and meant contact with wealthy and influential courtiers. It also provided the opportunity to line one's purse, honestly or otherwise, and for an ambitious courtier it could lead to promotion. But it brought Paulet under the scrutiny of the King and to retain the position he would have needed to demonstrate his ability to deliver sufficient funds. The office of the King's Wards provided a valuable source of revenue.[64] A constant supply of money was needed to replenish the King's coffers (which were kept in strong-rooms at the Tower and in the King's private chambers). Parliament was responsible, through the raising of taxes, for the financing of national matters such as war but it was Henry's responsibility to fund the Court and the government. Income from Crown lands and feudal fees provided much of this revenue, together with customs duties, and fines and fees from the courts. The medieval system of feudal dues that Henry VIII inherited benefited him greatly as the principal landowner and overlord of many tenanted estates. When a tenant died his land reverted to the landlord and the tenant's heir could only take control of the property on payment of a fee. If the heir was a minor the lord was granted wardship of his body and entitled to claim the income from the lands until the ward came of age and paid a fee to release the property into his own control. The lords paid dues to the King for the land they held and they in turn received fees from their tenants and wards. Paulet and Englefield were responsible for the administration and collection of the fees payable to the King.

The collection of any monies in Tudor England was a difficult process and securing the revenue from wardships had been inefficient during the reign of Henry VII. By concealing his assumption of property a tenant avoided the payment of fees and, in the case of a minor, the loss of estate income. It was difficult for the Crown to identify those people who should be paying dues in an age when there was no formal registration of death. Henry VIII was determined to improve the system of wardship to increase the income it generated. Occasional commissions were established to 'inquire touching concealed lands' in an attempt to identify land which had changed owner-ship without payment of fees, and in 1521 Paulet had been named to such a commission within Hampshire and Wiltshire.[65] The two Masters were assisted by an auditor who recorded the accounts presented to him by a receiver-general or finance officer, an attorney and a clerk of wards who kept records and acted as co-ordinator. But Paulet relied especially on the work of the feodaries whom he appointed in each county. Their role was to ensure that the Crown received all the revenue to which it was entitled and that Crown lands were valued as highly as possible at inquests.

The primary source of revenue was from the rents and profits from the wards' lands but further income was raised from the sale of wardships. This was a highly competitive business as wardships were a valuable commod-ity. A ward's family would pay handsomely to retain control of the estates rather than let them fall temporarily into other hands. Wardship conferred the right of the lord to control the marriage of an heir or heiress. This right could be sold on for a fee or used, especially in the case of an heiress, to bring the ward's lands within the estate of the guardian. He was responsible for the education and upbringing of his ward and often the heir or heiress was raised alongside the lord's own children, later marrying one of them. Paulet was able to purchase grants of wardships for himself, and though we can only speculate on whether he paid a fair price, he was certainly in a position to have first-hand knowledge of particularly lucrative wardships. Amongst others, in 1527 he was granted the wardship of Richard, son of Richard Waller, for £133 6s 8d but without the right to the income from his lands.[66] And 26 years later, in 1553, Paulet took custody of William, the younger Richard's son, but this time he received £40 per year and the right to choose William's bride.[67] Even as late as 1570 he appealed to William Cecil, who was by then Master of the Court of Wards and Liveries, to be allowed to continue as guardian for three daughters of a Mr Andrews.[68]

To buy a wardship was a very complex and lengthy business which could leave a petitioner severely out of pocket after paying fees to the officers. All the officers of the Wards received salaries out of the revenues but these were relatively small and constituted only a small part of their total income for their work. Paulet and Englefield received an annuity of £100, paid quarterly, and the clerk received £10 a year.[69] The real financial reward for their work came from the official fees they collected at each stage of an inquiry. An inquisition was set up to examine the value of the ward's property and to set the 'fine' for purchase of the wardship. Every document that was drafted and every entry that was made in the clerk's record books required the payment of a fee to the officer concerned. There were many such actions and often one officer would receive several fees for different aspects of the same inquisition. If schedules were of great length the clerk was to receive 'more as the partie is willinge to give', and if the heir was female or a nobleman the fees were doubled.

Paulet was responsible for creating an administrative system that could cope with the increasing workload as the scope of his responsibilities increased. In 1537 Englefield left his position and Paulet continued alone as Master. Earlier, in January 1531, he had received two further appointments as Surveyor-General in England, Wales and Calais of all possessions in the King's hands by the minority of heirs, and Surveyor of the King's widows and Governor of 'all idiots and naturals' in the King's hand.[70] Widows were entitled to inherit one-third of their husband's lands as a dower but this was granted only after the payment of monies to instigate an inquisition, and on the agreement that she would not re-marry without a licence from the King – for which she would pay another fee. In the case of 'idiots and naturals', the crown took control of their land and provided for the family from the profits of the land. To define an idiot, it was accepted that a man was not an 'idiot' if he knew his own age and the names of his mother and father and could count money up to 20 pence.[71]

As Henry's reign continued his need for money increased and reforms by Cromwell resulted in finance being controlled by six departments. The Exchequer collected customs duties and taxes, the Duchy of Lancaster administered the lands it controlled and the Crown lands were administered by the Court of General Surveyors. Two new courts were established: the Court of Augmentations to oversee the transfer of monastic lands to the Crown and their resale to the nobles, and the Court of First Fruits and Tenths that collected the payment of one year's income from every new benefice incumbent together with an annual tax of one tenth of the annual value of every benefice. Finally, in July 1540, the system of wardship was formalised with the setting up of the Court of Wards. This was a court of records with its own seal, kept in the custody of the master, which handled its own accounts rather than passing them through the Exchequer as previously, and which had an attorney to hear legal cases. With his new status as master of a court Paulet saw his salary rise to £133 6s 8d a year.[72] He was now overseeing an increasing amount of business and two years later his responsibilities increased again when the office of Master of the Liveries came under his control. His appointment as Master of the Court of Wards and Liveries combined all aspects of wardship and livery.[73] Paulet did not see a rise in his salary as a result of this larger empire. Although now couched in terms of marks (not a coin but the money of account used in transactions and valued at 13s 4d), his annual salary remained the same at 200 marks; but the opportunities to receive fees increased.[74]

A man was entitled to 'sue out his livery' – to gain possession of his property – by bringing a suit in court when he reached the age of 21, or in the case of a woman when she reached the age of 14 or was married. A payment would be made for an inquisition to establish whether he was the rightful heir and for him to prove his age. In earlier days he would have brought witnesses or 'proves' – people aged at least 42 who could confirm the heir's date of birth by connecting it with some memorable event such as a storm or personal accident. From 1538, when Thomas Cromwell ordered that parish registers should be kept to record dates of baptisms, marriages and burials, it became easier to provide accurate proof of birth date. If the heir was found to be of age and the rightful claimant to the land, he began the complicated procedure of suing out his livery. As with the grant of a ward-ship, this involved the payment of sums of money to each official involved in every stage of his claim, whether for drawing up a document or for just entering the details in the record books. Gaining possession of land to which you were entitled was a long and expensive business and it is not surprising that some tried to avoid this formality.

Although the officers of the court were paid salaries from the court's revenues and continued to receive fees for each stage of an inquiry, there were also many opportunities for bribery and corruption. A payment to an official might help to secure an especially profitable wardship against competition. There is no evidence that Paulet was involved with any cor-rupt dealings although, interestingly, he appears to have been ignorant of a spectacular example of corruption between 1545 and 1550 when John Beaumont, receiver-general of the Court of Wards and Liveries, embezzled £11,823.[75] To put this sum into context, the income to the King from the court during this time was between £7,000 and £13,000 per annum – Beaumont was creaming off a large part of the King's income.[76]

The position of Master of the Court of Wards and Liveries was a public role. Relations of an heir or those people wishing to buy wardships would all be keen to make the acquaintance of the Master in the hope of prefer-ential treatment. Positions within the Court were lucrative and men hoping to secure such a place would approach Paulet in the hope of his patronage. Paulet's brothers, George and Richard, probably acquired their positions in the Courts of Wards and Liveries and Augmentations through his influence.[77]

While the purpose of the Court of Wards and Liveries was still primarily to supply funds for the King, the inclusion of the business of livery increased the amount of judicial business. Cases involving both wardship and liveries were predominantly concerned with finance – most commonly the avoid-ance of or non-payment of fines by actions such as taking possession of lands without suing. Paulet, together with the other officers, sat as judges to oversee proceedings in such matters, but they also handled cases involving the mistreatment of wards and the misuse of their lands. Many people saw the sale of wardships as being akin to a trade in children and their transfer from one guardian to another as being enormously disruptive. Paulet had a responsibility to safeguard the well-being and interests of the wards. Sir Nicholas Bacon wrote that 'the chief thing and most of price in wardship is the ward's mind, the next to that his body, and the last and meanest his land.' In reality, more consideration was often given to control of the land than to the care of the heir's body and mind.

As Master of the Court of Wards and Liveries, Paulet now had a team of eight men working for him and, as time passed and he was given more posts at Court, he relied increasingly heavily on these men to perform well in his absence. He and his officers were the equivalent of modern civil servant administrators and many of them held their appointments for many years. Paulet's appointment as the first Master of the Court of Wards, after having been Master of the King's Wards for fourteen years, gave continuity to the office and the policy that it followed. He retained the post until 1554, when he was succeeded by Sir Francis Englefield, the grandson of the earlier Thomas Englefield with whom Paulet had begun as master.

For nearly 30 years Paulet witnessed his role as Master of the Wards expand and change as he tried to modernise a system based on medieval feudalism. He established an administrative system that increased revenue, and then managed the merger of wardships and livery and the absorption of the resultant increase in workload. Together with his responsibilities for widows, idiots and naturals he oversaw the collection of revenue from the estates of all those people who were in the King's care. With his administrative skills, legal training and experience Paulet was eminently suited to his work in the Court of Wards and Liveries. He was a most accomplished government servant and his long tenure in this position indicates his success. While in the post he had the opportunity to increase his wealth and he was appointed to even more influential positions alongside his mastership.

Paulet's appointments in London did not prevent him from being involved in commissions within Hampshire, and in April 1528 he was ordered to supervise a muster of foot soldiers to accompany Lord William Sandys to France.[78] Towards the end of the year there was a threat of disturbances among the citizens of London and on Thursday, 3 December Paulet was one of the commissioners involved in midnight searches in and around the city. Details of the searches were kept very secret. Suspect parties were to be apprehended and questioned. The commissioners were to remove from alehouses, inns and other suspicious houses all gaming tables, dice, cards and bowls, which were to be openly burnt next day, and all crossbows and hand guns which were found were to be broken in two pieces.[79] These searches were repeated the following November when Paulet is listed again for the Lambeth and Lambeth Marsh area.

In August 1529 writs were issued for the election of members to sit in the Parliament which was to meet on 3 November and to which Paulet was elected, with Sir Richard Sandys, to represent Hampshire.[80] The writ for their election was sent to Windsor so it is possible that the King intervened to secure their selection for the candidates list. Elections were held between 8 and 9am at the County Court at Winchester, when men with freehold land to the value of 40 shillings or more per year were eligible to vote.[81]

Thomas Cromwell also sat in this Parliament and it may be that Paulet played a part in his selection. Bishop Fox had died in October 1528 and was succeeded as Bishop of Winchester by Cardinal Wolsey – although he was not to hold this position for long. As Bishop of Winchester Wolsey had control of several boroughs, including Taunton in Somerset, and held some influence in the outcome of elections. Thomas Cromwell was secretary to Wolsey when, on 9 October 1529, the latter was charged with praemunire – that is, of asserting his power in England on the authority of papal bulls from Rome. He was sent in disgrace to retire to his house at Esher on 20 October. Wolsey's supporters fell away from him causing Cromwell, who continued to serve him, to tell George Cavendish, Wolsey's servant, that 'I am in disdain with most men for my master's sake.'[82] In an attempt to rescue his own career Cromwell tried to find a seat in the new Parliament and Paulet, using his powers as steward of the bishopric lands, was able to enter Cromwell's name as one of those returned for Taunton. Whether he did so out of friendship for Cromwell or on instructions from Wolsey we do not know. We can only wonder whether English history might have been different if Cromwell's name had not been submitted for Parliament at the last moment.

As Wolsey's friends deserted him Paulet stayed loyal. In December Wolsey was stripped of the bishopric of Winchester and the following Easter he travelled to York where he intended to be enthroned as Archbishop of York. A letter from Paulet to Wolsey on 6 June 1530 gives a glimpse of the relationship between the two men with the former offering advice to help Wolsey reclaim the King's good grace. He tells Wolsey to sign and seal a new patent for the Duke of Norfolk: 'Do it freely, with as gentle letters as you can, as it will do you much good', and 'The more you content the King and Norfolk, the better speed you will have.' He then confirms that he will always be ready to lend Wolsey the £100 he promised.[83] The wording of the letter suggests that this was more than just a master–servant relationship and that the two men were friends. If Wolsey had helped to secure him a place at Court, Paulet may have been trying to repay the debt. The following month on 14 July Paulet was named in a commission to inquire into the property Wolsey held in six counties, including Hampshire, prior to its being confiscated by the King.[84] Did Paulet find this a disagreeable task, helping in the downfall of the master he was still serving? It was to be a role he would play again, dismantling the lives of men he had known and worked with after their fall from favour. But it was a facet of Tudor court life and the commissioners must have hoped that the same fate would never befall them.

On 1 August Paulet wrote to Wolsey from London, again referring to the money he had promised to lend. He said that he would still be glad to lend £100 but could not do so all at once. He sent £40 then with a promise to send the rest as soon as possible. It sounds as if he could not raise sufficient cash, even on pledge, since 'people here are so scant of money'.[85] Wolsey remembered his debts and after his death in November 1530 his will listed Paulet as a creditor 'for ready money lent to the Cardinal, £40'.[86]

During the 30 years following Wolsey's death, the power of the Catholic Church in the country fluctuated wildly until eventually Catholicism ceased to be the authorised religion and was replaced by the Anglican Church of England. Paulet not only witnessed this evolution but, as a member of the Reformation Parliament, was instrumental in introducing the legislation that paved the way for the changes.

The Catholic Church which Paulet knew as a young man was a powerful force at the beginning of the sixteenth century. Its influence in every facet of life is difficult to comprehend today. Existence was a daily battle for many people and the Church offered an eventual escape – a route to salvation and eternal life. Their time on earth was a brief interlude between birth and death, a period through which they had to struggle as best they could, following the Church's instructions to ensure a better life after death. The populace attended church on Sundays and Holy days and took communion on Easter Day. They made confession to their priest and fasted or ate fish on the prescribed days. They prayed to God and the saints, especially their own 'personal' saint – the saint on whose holy day they were born or whose name they went by, or the saint adopted as patron of their trade. Their prayers were for the souls of those in purgatory and for their own salvation. They prayed that death would not take them suddenly, that they would be allowed time to repent and confess their sins. The rich built chantry chapels where priests could say masses and pray for them after death, speeding their souls through purgatory and on into heaven. On the eve of the Reformation the city of London had over 100 churches, a cathedral and 39 religious houses. The skyline was punctuated by spires and towers. In church courtyards stood tall stone preaching crosses from where priests delivered sermons, at street corners crosses were set up and statues of saints were displayed in niches on buildings.

The Catholic services Paulet would have attended were mystical and almost secretive, conducted in churches where little light entered through the stained glass windows and the walls were decorated with large, colourful paintings of Bible stories. Many churches had a Doom painting depicting the terrors of hell above the arch leading into the chancel. Crucifixes and images of the saints and the holy family were erected on altars and pedestals. Incense permeated the air, choirs sang and bells rang. In larger churches the congregation gathered in the nave standing or kneeling, since there were no chairs, as they listened to the rhythmic chanting of the priests from the other side of the rood screen that separated the people from the choir. Overhead hung the rood, a large cross supporting the image of the crucified Christ, which towered above the people.

The Catholic Mass on the eve of the Reformation was primarily a cleri-cal service involving the priests alone, with the congregation as witnesses – rarely participants. The priest and his attendant ministers stood in the sanc-tuary at the far end of the choir, facing away from the congregation towards the altar and so shielding most of the ceremony from them. The congrega-tion was sometimes able to view the proceedings through the screen if it was of open-work – otherwise the only view was through the door which led into the choir. The prayers and responses in Latin were unintelligible to many but they added to the mystery of the ritual which was being enacted before them and yet out of sight. They made 'courtesy' when the priest did, kneeling on one knee, and stood again when they heard the Gloria and the Sanctus. As they listened to the words of the priest those who were able recited the confession. The climax of the Mass was the elevation of the host. The priest raised the consecrated bread above his head, where all could see it. They were witnessing a miracle where bread and wine were to become the body and blood of Christ. Candles were lit to illuminate the act and the sacring-bell was rung. The kneeling people raised their hands, praying and looking towards the priest. It was considered a blessing to see the lifting of the host and members of the congregation would move around for the best view of the elevation, some even arriving at church just for that moment. For a while the town outside became a part of the church as passers-by, advised of the solemnity of the moment by the tolling of the church bells, were expected to be suitably reverent.

This was the Church Paulet had always known – a Church which held power over people through mystery and through their fear of the future and at the same time offered the hope of eternal salvation. Religion dictated almost all aspects of life. Many popular celebrations and festivities arose out of holy days such as Whitsun when towns held games or processions, and even the dates of events were recorded by the church calendar. In 1535 the trial of Sir Thomas More was noted to be held on 'Thursday next after the feast of John the Baptist'.

As Wolsey died the Church was about to come under attack from the people, from Parliament and from the King. The people believed implicitly in what the Church taught, and to question these teachings was to condemn their souls to eternal damnation. The Latin translation of the Bible was read by the clergy and scholars and there had been no reason for others to question the Church's interpretation of its meaning. But as men such as Erasmus and Luther read the original Greek texts and developed their own interpretations, they disagreed with some of the established teachings. The new English translations of the Bible enabled more people to enter into discussion of its real meaning. Interpretations which paid more attention to preaching and teaching than to relics and supported belief in the redeeming power of Christ's words did not fit with the ritual of 'bells and smells'.

There was concern about both the power the Pope exerted in the daily and political life of the country and the large sums of money the Church in England sent to Rome. Many people were tired of the rule and law of the Church, the courts of which gave judgements on moral law and heresy, on wills and matrimonial cases. They resented paying tithes and the payments collected by the courts for fees, probate on wills and the mortuary payments due before a body could be buried in consecrated ground. The Church, especially the monasteries, had great wealth but had lost the esteem of the people, and higher clergymen such as Wolsey were seen as overly wealthy and ostentatious. Wolsey's power and the lifestyle he and others of the clergy enjoyed were viewed as unacceptable for men of the cloth. This all contributed to a growing lack of respect for the clergy, many of whom displayed a lack of morals, were ill-educated and often absent from their parish.

Whilst this dissatisfaction with the Church resulted in a wave of anti-clericalism amongst the people, the King was increasingly beginning to see the Church as an obstacle in his endeavour to divorce his wife, Catherine of Aragon. Lack of a son and heir had caused Henry to question the validity of his marriage. Was God punishing him for marrying his brother's wife even though that marriage had reportedly not been consummated? His approaches to the Pope for an annulment had been rebuffed and it became apparent to Henry that he must either force the Pope to give in or reduce the pontiff's power in England. The way forward was to be through a series of parliamentary acts.

Parliament was summoned irregularly, usually when the King needed money for war. When it was called in 1529 it had not sat for six years and this Parliament's main actions paved the way for the royal divorce and gave the King greater control over the Church. As a member, Paulet witnessed legislation which led to profound and long-term effects on the Church in England. Parliament was called eight times before it was dissolved in 1536, by which time the Church had ceased to regard the Pope as its head.

The Commons had 310 seats, all English members who were generally lawyers, wealthy merchants, members of the gentry, councillors and court officials who were influential in their own counties. Each of the eight sessions met for a few weeks at a time with the members sitting between 8 and 11am. Voting on an issue was initially done by each participant shouting out 'Aye' or 'No'. However, if the decision was unclear, the Ayes moved to one side and the Nos remained in their place while each man was counted. On Wednesday, 3 November 1529 Paulet took his place for the first time in what was to become known as the Reformation Parliament. In the parliament chamber at the monastery of Blackfriars the proceedings were opened by the Lord Chancellor, Sir Thomas More, in the presence of the King. From his chair the King looked along the chamber towards the members of the Commons who stood behind the bar at the opposite end while the Lords were seated along the walls on either side of him. When the opening proceedings were finished, Parliament was adjourned to sit at Westminster Abbey on Saturday, 6 November, the Lords sitting in the Great Hall and the Commons in the monastic refectory on the south side of the great cloister.[87]

By the time this first session was prorogued on 17 December Paulet had heard Wolsey denounced and the Commons had made the first tentative moves against the Church with bills against pluralism (control of multiple parishes) and non-residence of priests, and to limit the fees charged for the proving of wills and for mortuaries. There were also 18 statutes concerned with economy and trade and with changes to the legal system, and a bill which cancelled the huge debts the King had incurred by borrowing money from his subjects seven years earlier.

Between January 1531 and April 1533 Paulet attended four further sessions of Parliament, ranging in length from five to ten weeks. There he witnessed the King and Parliament start to bring their full weight to bear against the Church, with Parliament acting to reduce the large sums of money paid to Rome and the King using Parliament to increase his power over the bishops and priests. The clergy agreed to his demand that they should recognise him as their Supreme Head but only with the qualification of Supreme

Head 'as far as the law of Christ allows'. The Act in Conditional Restraint of Annates stopped the payment of annates (one third of a year's income) to the Pope by bishops and archbishops when they succeeded to a new see, and allowed for their consecration to take place without a Papal Bull. After the King declared that the clergy had dual loyalty since they gave an oath of obedience to the Pope and so were only 'half our subjects', the Church submitted to royal authority by agreeing to the contents of the 'Submission of Clergy'. This document granted Henry the right of approval of existing and future canon laws. It gave him control over the laws of the Church including those concerned with divorce and remarriage. Unable to accept the implications of the submission, Thomas More resigned as Lord Chancellor the day after the document was accepted by the King. More's conscience was to trouble him for the next three years and would eventually lead to his trial by a group of peers, of whom Paulet was one.

Early in April 1533, during its fifth session, the Commons passed the Act in Restraint of Appeals. This ended the right of appeal to Rome by those dissatisfied with the outcome of a case heard in the Church courts. This avenue of seeking justice had been very slow and involved large sums of money leaving the country but, of most concern, it had given Rome legal jurisdiction over matters in England. Significantly, the new Act made possible the settlement of the King's divorce by the Church in England. Queen Catherine would not be able to appeal to the Pope if the case for the divorce was heard in England and the marriage found to be invalid. The bill faced opposition in the Commons and a list compiled by Cromwell gives the names of 35 opponents. Paulet's name is not there, suggesting that he was at least not a strong opponent and indeed may have been a supporter of the bill. Either way he was a witness to the King's increasing use of his power. The bill went on to the statute book in April and on 23 May at a church court the new Archbishop of Canterbury, Thomas Cranmer, declared the marriage of Henry VIII and Catherine of Aragon to be void. The marriage which Henry had made with Anne Boleyn earlier that year on 25 January was declared lawful and Anne was crowned Queen on 1 June.

Paulet missed the spectacle of the coronation because he was travelling to France for a meeting with the French King. The previous year, in May 1532, he had been appointed to the post of Comptroller of the Royal Household with its associated membership of the King's inner council of advisers, and it was in this capacity that he went on commission across the Channel. An event in 1531 may have had some bearing on his selection as Comptroller. On 14 July Henry had left Queen Catherine at Windsor while he and Anne Boleyn spent a month hunting in Surrey and Hampshire. On 4 August they arrived at the Vyne, the home of Sir William Sandys, Lord Chamberlain of the Household. The Vyne was only four miles from Basing, and Sandys and Paulet were friends as well as neighbours. This relationship is illustrated in the long gallery that Sandys had recently built. The carvings on the wooden panelling show the arms and emblems of his family and friends including the arms of Paulet – three swords angled downwards with their points together. On 6 August Paulet received the first visit to his house by the monarch when Henry and Anne spent the day hunting in the park at Basing. The reason for this hunting trip may not have been entirely for pleasure. Catherine surmised that Henry's real intention was to 'accustom the lords and governors of the counties … to see her with him', and to try to ensure their future support when he divorced Catherine. Both Sandys and Paulet were religious conservatives and it was important to Henry that he should retain the goodwill of such people. The position of Comptroller may well have been a reward for Paulet's loyalty.[88]

4

Comptroller of the King's Household and the Act of Supremacy

Paulet swept off his bonnet as he bent low towards the floor. He looked up and felt a sense of relief to see that the King was smiling and signalling to him to rise. It was Sunday morning and after Mass many of the King's councillors had gathered in the Presence Chamber where the King, sitting on his throne, had been in conversation with the Duke of Norfolk. Suddenly, the Duke had approached Paulet and indicated that the King wished to speak to him. Walking towards the throne, Paulet tried to remember if there was any reason why the King might be displeased with him but he could think of nothing. Perhaps he was just going to inquire about a wardship.

Paulet approached closer to the throne as the King began to talk about how pleased he was with Paulet's work as Master of the Wards. He believed that Paulet would be of great use to him within the Court and was minded to make him Comptroller of the Household and so he would leave the office of Master of the Wards. Paulet felt a rush of elation. His position as Master of the Wards was an eminently respectable post for a member of the gentry and a knight, but to be Comptroller of the Household was a real promotion. The Comptroller worked with the Lord Steward and the Treasurer overseeing the workings of the below-stairs departments in the royal palaces, employing and disciplining the enormous number of servants, organising the acquisition of food and the preparation and distribution of meals. He would be placed prominently in the royal household with a position at Court, under the scrutiny of the King and working alongside members of the nobility. He would live, sleep and work within the palaces and, since positions were often filled from within the household, he was well placed for further advancement. He had been noticed by the King and was set to begin a career at Court – but he knew that he must appear somewhat reticent about accepting the post, as was traditional when offered a position, so he replied that he believed he had as yet done no great service as Master of the Wards but that he trusted he could do so and asked the King to allow him to continue as Master.

Paulet was very aware that he had little experience of the royal household, unlike the two previous Comptrollers, Sir Thomas Boleyn and Sir Henry Guildford, who had just died. Both had accompanied the King during the early years of his reign, while the Treasurer, Sir William Fitzwilliam, had been taught to hunt by the King himself. All these men had previous experience of court life. Paulet continued to portray himself as unsuitable for high honour when he 'desired his grace to bestow the Comptroller's office upon one bred and brought up in the house, for he should do best service'. Smiling broadly the King explained to Paulet that he believed he was the man most suitable for both posts and thus he would appoint him as Comptroller to hold together with the position of Master of the Wards. Paulet was overwhelmed and, proffering his thanks, he bent low to the floor again as the King called to an usher to bring a white staff that lay upon the cupboard. Commanding Paulet to rise, the King presented this staff of office to him and announced to all those present in the chamber that henceforth Paulet was to be Comptroller of the Royal Household. Paulet bent low yet again and then walking backwards he moved away, hardly able to believe what had just happened. To hold both posts concurrently enhanced his status enormously. He would spend much of his time with the Court, close to the King, rather than at the office of the Wards at Westminster. He would have influence at Court and the power to grant positions to servants in the household, while still being able to dispose of wardships. The opportunities for him to offer patronage and to receive payment in return were many and could result in a substantial increase in his income. As he looked at the staff he held he smiled in anticipation at the thought of sharing the good news with his wife, Elizabeth.

As Comptroller, Paulet became one of the three 'white sticks', joining the Lord Steward and the Treasurer of the Household as the managers of domestic life within the royal houses. Their sobriquet of 'white sticks' came from the white staff which they each carried as a symbol of their authority. As in the house of all wealthy nobles, the royal household was divided into 'above and below stairs' departments – known as the *Domus Regie Magnificencie*

and the *Domus Providencie* respectively. The former, under the control of the Lord Chamberlain, comprised the many nobles, gentlemen, ushers, grooms and pages who attended the King and staffed the chambers where he might appear. The *Domus Regie Magnificencie* was where Henry's magnificence was displayed and it was in support of this that the below-stairs departments and staff of the *Domus Providencie* worked, under the control of the 'white sticks', to sustain the King and his image.

Image was paramount. A successful monarch inspired respect and loyalty from his subjects. The magnificence of the buildings, the conduct of the courtiers and the paraphernalia of Court life around the King all contributed to the impression of majesty and power. Surrounded by a huge retinue supported by hundreds of servants, Henry VIII created a court to rival that of King Francis of France. But Henry needed more than this. His father's claim to the throne had been tenuous, based on his descent from Edward III's son, John of Gaunt, and his mistress Catherine Swynford. It was therefore even more important that Henry be seen as majestic, surrounded by a splendid court, to overcome any doubts in the people's minds as to his right to be King of England.

The Court consumed vast resources and the Lord Steward – assisted by the Treasurer and the Comptroller – was responsible for providing everything necessary for feeding and lodging the servants and courtiers. This was an enormous task, in sixteenth-century terms comparable to supplying a small town. The Court of Queen Elizabeth I is estimated to have consumed in one year 1,240 oxen, 8,200 sheep, 2,330 calves for veal, 760 'stirks', 310 'porks', 53 boars, 560 sides of bacon, 13,260 lambs, 33,000 chickens, over four million eggs and 60,000lbs of butter, while up to 300 casks of wine and 600,000 gallons of ale were drunk, a quantity described by one Spanish gentleman as 'enough to fill the Valladolid river'![89] This was housekeeping on a grand scale. Together the three men controlled the housekeeping at all the King's houses when he was in residence, organising the kitchens, ensuring the supply, preparation and distribution of food and drink, and the provision of household items. Henry VIII probably visited about half of the nearly 70 houses he owned during his reign.[90] While some of them, such as Nonsuch and Langley, were small and used only for short periods by small hunting parties, others could accommodate the entire Court, which numbered between 800 and 1,500 people.[91] These principal establishments – Whitehall Palace, Greenwich, Windsor and Hampton Court – were where the King and his courtiers spent most of their time.

Paulet's responsibilities as Comptroller were set out in the *Book of Household Ordinances* which detailed job descriptions for all the principal officers and servants. Ordinances were issued from 1445 to 1604 to regulate the workings of the Court and increase efficiency in accounting and budgeting. Wolsey and Thomas Cromwell both made amendments to the Ordinances in 1526 and 1540 respectively. Although these stipulated that the Lord Steward, the Treasurer and the Comptroller should be in attendance at daily meetings, in practice the three men were often busy about other business for the King and so attended only when necessary. In their absence the daily business of the household was carried out by the Cofferer assisted by the clerks. However, it was expedient for all three officers to be fully aware of the workings of the department. Any failure on their part to manage the household competently would have been noticed and it is doubtful if the King would have allowed them to remain in such positions of authority if they were ineffective. Although much of the routine daily business was carried out on behalf of the Comptroller by the Cofferer and clerks, the fact that Paulet moved on to hold a further three important posts within the Household implies that he was viewed as an effective Comptroller.

Carrying his white staff of office, Paulet walked the few paces to the Counting House from his chambers where he had been busy studying lists of accounts. The Household Ordinances stated that the Board of Greencloth should meet between 8 and 9 o'clock each morning and when he entered the chamber the other members were already there waiting for him. Glancing through the large window which looked down the road towards the bakehouse he saw a cart trundle through the gateway beneath him and into the courtyard. This was a good vantage point from which to watch goods and people arrive at or leave the kitchens at Hampton Court. Paulet turned his attention back to the chamber. There was none of the wooden panelling or tapestries found in the state apartments. Here the walls were painted white with lime-wash and the room was furnished with two high-backed settles on opposite sides of a large trestle table, a side table and two stools. This was the nerve centre of the household, where a small group of men made the decisions and issued the orders necessary to ensure that up to 800 people were fed and accommodated with the minimum of disruption.

Paulet greeted Sir William Fitzwilliam, the Treasurer of the Household, and the Cofferer and slid in beside them on one of the settles. Sitting opposite them were two Clerks of the Greencloth and one of the three clerks who worked for Paulet. Each day these men organised the purchase of food and oversaw the preparation and serving of up to 1,600 meals a day. On this particular morning

Paulet and Fitzwilliam were in attendance to listen to proposals for future purchases of provisions, and to agree new prices to be paid to the poulterers. With so many people to feed attention must be given not only to calculating the correct quantity, so there should be no excessive waste, but also to the quality and cost of the food.

The trestle table which stood between the two settles was covered with green baize – hence the Board of Greencloth. Parchment rolls and counters were laid out before the clerks and Paulet watched as they finished copying details of the previous day's accounts from each kitchen department onto some of these sheets of parchment before rolling them up and tying them with narrow strips of cloth. Paulet paid more attention when they reached for a large thick bundle and, untying the ribbon, opened out the long list which they had drawn up. Later in the year the King and Court were to move to Greenwich for two weeks and this was a list of all the food and household items that would be needed during their visit. The responsibilities of the officers of the Counting House were wide-ranging and the list ran to several pages. It covered every conceivable food that might be consumed from the routine staples of the whole Court – bread, stewing beef, mutton, eggs, ale – to the luxuries served to the King and his courtiers – swan, lark, pheasant, sugar and wild strawberries. But they also ensured the supply of all other household goods – items such as furniture, kitchen implements, linen, candles, and firewood.

As Comptroller it was Paulet's responsibility, with Fitzwilliam as Treasurer, to check the lists and authorise the purchases. It was a massive task but the Cofferer was a very competent man and Paulet had no doubt that this shopping list was well thought out. The lists were perused, Paulet asked a few questions and quantities were changed but finally all were satisfied and the Cofferer was instructed to pass the lists to the purveyors who would visit the area around Greenwich to find suppliers and negotiate prices. With such a quantity of food to be found, preparations needed to begin early. Paulet then turned his attention to the increase in prices of poultry. William Gurley sourced various birds, rabbits and eggs from other suppliers in London but he had been complaining that they were charging him higher prices and he could no longer sell to the King at the old price. Gurley was a reliable poulterer and Paulet proposed that the prices paid to him for some birds should be raised, 2d extra could be paid for large birds, so a peacock would be 16d and a heron 20d. For one dozen larks they could pay 6d and for one dozen sparrows 4d. Rabbits could be charged at 3d each and eggs at 20d for each 100 in the winter but only 14d in summer when the hens were laying better.[92] The business was finished and Paulet rose to leave. It was 10 o'clock and dinner was soon to be served.

Much of Paulet's work was concerned with the kitchens. In the larger houses these comprised the great kitchen, where most of the cooking was done, and as many as eighteen departments or offices, each one dedicated to carrying out a particular kitchen activity or preparation of one variety of food. The Household Ordinances give instructions for the bakehouse, pantry, cellar, buttery (ale and beer), spicery, confectionery (sweetmeats), wafery (biscuits), larder, acatry (meat and fish), sea-fish, poultry (fowl and rabbits), pastry, saucery, boiling house, scalding house, scullery (pots and pans), chaundry (candles) and ewery (water vessels) plus the support departments such as the laundry, wood yard and coal house. With a total staff of about 200 people, and each office under the control of a sergeant, a clerk and a purveyor, the kitchens were the largest and busiest department in the household. Their constant noise and bustle, and the heat and smoke as the fires were stoked to work at full blast, caused a visiting Spanish gentleman to describe them as 'veritable hells'.[93]

In such a large organisation there were countless opportunities for theft, and a system of cross-checking was established to try to minimise this. Paulet was instructed to apply 'good guiding and oversight of all charges and expenses' and had particular responsibility for checking the accounts of the Treasurer of the Household, aided by the three Clerk Comptrollers.[94] The daily accounts for each kitchen department were recorded and cross-checked against the annual departmental accounts and against the record of Board of Greencloth decisions regarding the quality, quantity and cost of food to be ordered. With this information Paulet was able to monitor any discrepancies between quantities of food ordered and delivered and meals prepared, allowing him to identify instances of waste and pilfering and any attempts to falsify the accounts. Any dishonest staff member was subject to punishments meted out by the members of the Greencloth. Dishonest trading by purveyors could incur a penalty of loss of wages for a first offence, imprisonment in the Marshalsea for a second and dismissal for a third offence. Checks were made to ensure that no unauthorised people were eating at the King's expense and that wasted food was disposed of in accordance with regulations.

Certain members of the Household were allowed to keep food and household items as 'perks' of their position; the Sergeant of the Bakehouse kept all the crusts cut off bread before serving.[95] However, selling these food remnants could be very lucrative and the 'chippers' might be tempted to cut off rather more of the bread crust than was necessary. Dishes that were untouched at table could be eaten by the chamber servants. At the marriage banquet of Queen Mary to Philip of Spain in 1554 Edward Underhill, a Gentleman Pensioner, carried in 'a great pasty of a red deer in a great charger, very delicately baked' which others refused to carry because of its great weight. It was apparently untouched after the meal and Underhill sent it to his wife and her brother in London. One wonders how fresh it was by the time of its arrival![96] However, no respectable person would have eaten a dish if it had been 'broken' or partly consumed and these dishes were given to the poor people who gathered at the palace gates. Shakespeare used the term 'eater of broken meats' as an insult.[97]

In common with most members of the Court, Paulet's wages included the cost of all his meals. Those in constant attendance on the King and anybody in an established post in the household were entitled to 'Bouche of Court' and many more also received a 'diet' of two full meals a day. 'Bouche of Court' was a supply of bread and drink, with wood and candles for heat and light in the winter – the necessities, although the quantities each person received were dependent on their rank and position. As Comptroller, Paulet received bread and one gallon of ale each morning, afternoon and evening together with a pitcher of wine after supper and, each day during the winter, one torch and candles for light and four faggots for heat, all to a total annual value of £35 12s.[98] The quantity and variety of food which each person received, together with where they should eat, was recorded on a list in the Counting House. Kitchen staff ate in their workplace while other servants, the Yeomen of the Guard and junior household officers ate in the Great Hall. Those of higher rank – senior household officers, courtiers and nobles – took their meals in the Great Watching Chamber, close to the King's own apartments. The kitchens provided two meals each day, the first sitting for dinner being served at 10am and the first supper at 4pm.[99]

Paulet took his place for dinner at the table appointed for him in the Great Watching Chamber. The table was laid with fine white linen and at each place was a small, shallow silver plate, a trencher, with a smaller wooden trencher placed inside it as a surface upon which to cut. A silver spoon and drinking cup were set to the right-hand side and a folded napkin and manchet loaf to the left. Paulet carried his own small knife for cutting pieces of meat. Since the diners shared bowls of food the meal was a sociable event.

He looked around the chamber to see who was seated at the tables allocated to the Lord Chamberlain, Lord Sandys, and the Treasurer, Sir William Fitzwilliam. Men were placed according to their rank so nobles and high-ranking councillors sat with the Lord Chamberlain. Other councillors below the rank of baron, together with some gentlemen, were at the tables of Paulet and Fitzwilliam. Paulet took the napkin and, after folding it lengthways, draped it across his left shoulder ready to use for wiping his lips. He picked up the manchet. Here in the Great Watching Chamber the diners were given these small bread rolls made of white flour rather than the wholemeal cheat loaves eaten by the servants dining in the Great Hall. He cut through the manchet horizontally then, as was customary, he sliced the top half into four strips and the bottom half into three before replacing them at the side of the trencher. The servants brought the first course of dishes to the table. Since it was not a fish day there was a selection of meats – boiled pieces of beef, stewed mutton, a piece of roast veal, capons and rabbit – accompanied by potage, fritters and a custard (an open pie of cooked meat in an egg batter). There was plenty to choose from although not as much variety as the Lord Chamberlain would be feasting upon.

The whole menu was laid out in front of Paulet and he chose those dishes he most enjoyed. He was not expected to taste everything. All the food was served as 'messes', portions sufficient for four men, and Paulet was sharing with Sir Nicholas Carew, Master of Horse, who sat to his left and Sir Brian Tuke and Sir Francis Bryan who sat opposite. He used his spoon to help himself to potage directly from the bowl, then cleaned his spoon using a piece of bread before helping himself in the same way to the stewed mutton in sauce. To serve himself with a slice of the veal Paulet held the piece of meat he would eat, using the thumb and two fingers of his left hand, and carved this off holding his own knife in his right hand. He placed the cut meat upon his trencher, cut it into bite-sized pieces and placed the pieces in his mouth using his right hand. In this way he never used fingers which had been in his mouth to touch meat that might be eaten by somebody else. The juices upon his trencher he soaked up using pieces of bread which he then ate. Any food around his mouth he removed using the napkin across his shoulder and he took great pains not to drop food as he passed it to his trencher.

When they had eaten enough the bowls were carried away and the second course arrived. Again there were several dishes – roast lamb, plovers, rabbits and larks with a pie and a tart of fruit, more fritters, baked quinces and cooked eggs in sauce, and all the while servants supplied the diners with wine or ale. It was a reflection on the King's honour that he was able to feed his courtiers so well and that expense was not an issue. The Comptroller and Treasurer together were *allocated four messes, sufficient to feed sixteen people, at dinner and supper and Paulet knew that the annual allowance for this food was more than £350.*

The diners rose to leave and Paulet made his way back to his chambers near the Counting House. At 4 o'clock he would return to this chamber to eat his supper. While the food would be similar to that which he had just eaten, there would be fewer dishes to choose from but after such a full dinner he would have little need of more. Tomorrow the menu would be completely different. It was a Friday, a fish day and, as in Lent, the meat would be replaced by a great variety of fish, which might include ling, salmon, plaice, gurnard, conger, pike and bream.[100]

If Paulet was away from the Court on the King's business he still received an allowance for his food. While in France in 1533 this was about 15 shillings a day but by 1540, in line with his increased status, it had risen to 20 shillings.[101] Paulet's wages, which included an allowance to pay for his winter and summer robes, were calculated to take account not only of his free meals but also his accommodation and stabling for twelve horses. If the King stayed in a property that was not large enough to accommodate everybody, rooms were provided in houses surrounding the residence, but as Comptroller Paulet needed to be close at hand and so was provided with rooms within the King's house. When his predecessor Sir Henry Guildford died, a letter reporting the new appointment stated that: 'Sir Henry Gylford Controllar was, ys dyssessyd. Mr. Pawlet has his roome.'[102] Later in his household career Paulet had his own house in London at Austin Friars and it is likely that when the Court was at Westminster he would have slept and eaten at home whenever possible. As with the eating arrangements, where it was considered most prestigious to eat in a chamber as close as possible to the King's dining room, a courtier would also aspire to sleep as near as possible to the King's apartments. Although the Comptroller was allocated rooms next to the Counting House and near the kitchens at Hampton Court, it is likely that Paulet used these for administration and slept elsewhere in the palace, away from the smell and activity of the kitchens. The King often supplied beds for courtiers, decorated according to their rank, but Paulet was responsible for the other furnishings in his rooms. He would have provided rushes or mats for the floor, tapestries to hang on the walls, a chest for his belongings, perhaps a table and chair for writing and candlesticks and linen. He was allowed five servants to attend him and 'keepe his chamber' and they were to be 'honest persons, and of good stature, gesture and behaviour'.[103]

The courtiers' rooms had fireplaces and some had running water. The larger residences and some of the smaller such as Nonsuch, had piped spring water to the kitchens, the King and Queen's bathrooms and to some of the courtiers' rooms although there was no provision for the latter to have personal bathrooms. Their baths were taken in a wooden tub in front of the fire. Some courtiers' chambers had a garderobe, the seat made of a plank of wood with a round hole positioned over a vertical shaft which emptied into a drain. This could be smelly and unhealthy and an alternative was for courtiers to use either a chamber pot or their own close stool, a large wooden box with a hole in the top and a removable pewter pot inside. For greater comfort the top could be padded and upholstered.

After overseeing all the matters in the counting house and kitchens, Paulet was expected to be in attendance in the Presence Chamber each day at 10am and 2pm. The senior household officers were members of the King's council and were on hand not only in case the King should wish to talk with them upon any matter 'but also for the hearing and direction of poor men's complaints on matters of justice'.[104] Often other business took Paulet away from Court but when present he joined the throng of people waiting in the chamber, playing out his role as courtier and councillor. Courtiers spent many hours waiting, passing the time by discussing business and personal affairs, or just in casual conversation, but always ready to attend the King.

Life at Court was not very settled because the King and his household frequently moved to cleaner, fresher accommodation. Henry VIII was very concerned about the cleanliness of his houses, and the presence of so many people made the atmosphere stale and the house 'waxed unsavoury' and needed to be aired.[105] Efforts were made to prevent dirtiness and smells. No dogs were kept in Court apart from a few small spaniels for the ladies, and other dogs were kept in kennels so 'the house may be sweete, whole-some, cleane and well furnished, as to a prince's honour and estate doth apperteine'.[106] The kitchen boys or scullions were ordered to sweep and clean the courts and outer areas twice a day, and to 'not goe naked or in garments of such vileness as they now doe'.[107] There was a problem of courtiers relieving themselves against the walls in the courtyards and at Greenwich red crosses were painted on the walls, on the assumption that the men would not desecrate a cross, and urinals made of stone and lead were positioned around the courts.[108] In 1547 it was necessary for the

Privy Council to issue a proclamation 'forbidding nuisance in the Court' whereby 'no persons of what degree soever, shall make water or cast any annoyance within the precinct of the court'.[109] At Hampton Court a house of ease, or communal lavatory, was built in 1536, which provided 28 lavatories side by side in rows.

Rooms and furnishings constantly needed cleaning and repairing but the presence of so many people made it very difficult to carry out these activities properly. The best opportunity was provided when the Court moved out of a building and Paulet would have quickly become accustomed to the routine of the King moving to a new residence every few weeks. Once a house was empty, servants could remove rush mats and rubbish, sweep and wash the floors, wash the walls and repair and replace both the fabric of the building and the contents.

The threat of plague would send the Court away from London and into the country at any time, but even when there were no cases of plague or sweating sickness the King still spent the winter months travelling between his houses around London and in the summer left the city to progress and to hunt. The purpose of the progress was to enable the King to see his country and, more importantly, to allow his people to see him, and by travelling in the summer the opportunities for hunting were at their best. It made a grand sight for the villagers – the royal standard and the pennants of the accompanying lords fluttering in the breeze, the King and his friends all on horseback, the Queen with her ladies-in-waiting and the rest of the household following behind. When the roads were dusty the progress would be strung out to allow the dust to settle between the groups of travellers. The progress was a major logistical exercise involving the removal on horseback and by cart of several hundred people together with furniture, wall hangings, household items and personal belongings. Many courtiers and servants would return to their own homes while the King was travelling but, as an officer of the Household, Paulet was always in attendance.

The details of each progress were planned months in advance and recorded in 'giests' or lists. The King visited not only his own houses but also those of his favourite courtiers. The giest set out which houses were to be visited, for how many days (anything from one to fifteen) and the length of the journey between each house, usually between five and seventeen miles.[110] Once these points were established, the household officers could plan how to transport, accommodate and feed the enormous entourage. Before the progress Paulet and the Lord Steward and Treasurer organised the provision of food and supplies at each house to be visited. The houses were checked and any necessary repairs and alterations carried out. A carpentry bill for a visit of Queen Elizabeth to Paulet's house at Basing in 1569 records the making of 'presses in the Robes' and partitions for the 'squiers for the bodye' as well as 'dyvers other necesseries'.[111] The presses, or cupboards, were probably used to hold the Queen's clothes although large presses were also provided for hanging tapestries and carpets. On the moving days the three 'white sticks' oversaw the removal of the kitchen staff and their equipment, so that when the King arrived at the next residence everything was in place for the Court to operate as usual.

A visit from the monarch to a private house was a nightmare for the host. To provide accommodation, food and entertainment for so many people, even for just two days, involved an enormous amount of planning and money. Having already travelled on progress with the King, Paulet was well prepared for what to expect when Henry stayed at Basing House for two nights in October 1535. Considering the upheaval of moving every few days for up to ten weeks it is probable that many courtiers were not very enthusiastic about going on progress. These perambulations around the countryside disrupted further what was an already unsettled lifestyle and one estimate suggests that Henry VIII moved between properties over 1,100 times during his 38-year reign.[112]

Paulet's involvement in the organisation of progresses and routine moves between palaces gave him invaluable experience that could be called upon when the King went to war. When Henry travelled to France in 1544 for the war against the French at Boulogne he was accompanied by many of his household. Paulet was given responsibility for victualling, supplying not only the Household but the soldiers and garrison with food and drink – a mammoth task but one at which he was very skilled. To win a war, an effective system of victualling and moving troops was as important as the fighting and Paulet played a vital part in Henry's efforts.

Paulet's appointment as Comptroller lasted for five years. His life became focused upon the court. His wife, too, spent more time at court and was allocated lodging in the King's houses.[113] In 1538 Elizabeth received 10 shillings for attending upon Princess Mary as a servant, most probably to wait upon her rather than carry out menial tasks.[114] It was considered a great honour, even for nobles, to wait upon the King or a member of his family. Paulet's position offered status, power and influence, with the opportunity for bestowing and receiving patronage and the possibility of the ultimate prize of being accepted into the intimate circle of the King's friends. But court life was fraught with its own peculiar problems and dangers. It was expensive to maintain the appearance of wealth that the King expected his courtiers to display in their clothes, servants and houses. Their behaviour was constantly under scrutiny and Paulet saw many contemporaries move in and out of royal favour. His predecessor as Comptroller, Sir Henry Guildford, had openly criticised the proceedings against Queen Catherine to achieve the King's divorce. Anne Boleyn's threats to deprive him of his office when she became Queen caused him to resign his post but the King refused to accept the resignation, 'saying that he ought not to mind women's talk'.[115] Guildford, however, insisted on returning to his home in Kent for a time although he did retain the office until his death a few months later. But on the whole, living in the shadow of the monarch was beneficial for those who moved with care and, while others might come and go, Paulet continued working at Court until his death in old age.

The position of Comptroller was a springboard for promotion within the King's household and many of those appointed moved on to other more prominent positions. Sir William Fitzwilliam, later Earl of Southampton and John Russell, 1st Earl of Bedford, each served as Comptroller and both went on to become Lord High Admiral. Sir John Gage was appointed to the positions of Comptroller, Vice-Chamberlain and Lord Chamberlain. However no-one was to hold as many offices within the Court as Paulet and by the time he became Lord Great Master in 1545 he knew better than anyone how the King's house operated. His household career spanned eighteen years during which time he held the four senior posts. He was never a close personal friend of the King and it is safe to assume that he achieved his appointment and subsequent promotions through competence and not through favouritism. The post of Comptroller needed good administrative skills, a knowledge of finance and a personality that commanded respect and obedience from others. As Joint Master of the King's Wards he had already shown he possessed the first two attributes, and the third was well tested in the royal household.

When the King travelled his household moved with him, even overseas, and Paulet oversaw the organisation of these removals. On 11 October 1532 he was part of the entourage of over 2,000 men and women who attended the King when he journeyed to Calais with Anne Boleyn to meet the French King, Francis I. This meeting was to renew the Anglo-French alliance and to confirm that Francis would support Henry in his plan to marry Anne, against the objections of the Pope. For four days the French King entertained Henry and his entourage at Boulogne and then both companies rode to Calais where Henry lodged and entertained Francis, the cost of which Cromwell and Paulet recorded as £939 6s 3½d.[116] By 15 November the King had returned to England but Paulet and Cromwell, together with Henry Norris, Henry Heneage and Robert Foulier, remained in Calais for another three weeks to purchase land and property on behalf of the King. Land was needed for new fortifications and Paulet was also commissioned to review the drainage of the land around Calais to see if it would hinder the new constructions.[117] The property was to be for the use of men on the King's business in Calais.[118]

Paulet was regularly appointed to commissions and attended events as a witness or representative on behalf of the King. At the time of Queen Anne's coronation in 1533 he was part of the large suite accompanying Thomas Howard, 3rd Duke of Norfolk, on a mission to join the French King. Francis supported Henry in the matter of the divorce and Norfolk's retinue left England at the end of May to accompany him when he met Pope Clement at Nice to insist that the King's new marriage was valid by scripture and supported by theologians. Paulet kept Cromwell informed of events and wrote to him on 15 July from the Auvergne, giving details of their meeting with the French King five days earlier and of their journey with Francis en route to Nice for the meeting with the Pope. However, Paulet doubted whether the Pope would keep it 'otherwise it is an advantage to the King'.[119] Before the meeting could take place, the combination of the introduction of the Act in Restraint of Appeals, the eventual enforcement of the Annates Act and the news of Henry's marriage forced the Pope into action. On 11 July he threatened the King with excommunication if he did not give up Anne and return to Catherine by September. This threat, which was never actually implemented, caused great fear at the time amongst those who knew of it. The proposed meeting between the Pope and the delegation did not take place and on 28 August Norfolk's company returned to England.

While some of the events Paulet witnessed as a councillor were to be of historical interest, many were just routine although they still provide an insight into the workings of the Court. In January 1533 he witnessed the formality of the holding and return of the Great Seal to Thomas Audley as Chancellor of England. Audley had been Lord Keeper of the Great Seal since Thomas More's resignation. This seal was used to authenticate important documents in the name of the King, and as a demonstration of the source of the seal's authority the King took the Great Seal from Audley, held it for a quarter of an hour and then returned it to Audley's custody, signalling his appointment as Chancellor of England. Audley then returned the Great Seal to its bag which he secured with his own seal.[120]

Paulet was also often present when the King received visitors or as part of a delegation to meet visitors in the King's absence. He was amongst the councillors who met the Imperial ambassador, Eustace Chapuys, at Westminster on 7 May 1533 to inform him that he would lose his diplomatic immunity if he attempted to bring in letters from the Pope.[121] Chapuys was a regular visitor to court at this time, making representations on behalf of the Holy Roman Emperor, Charles V of Spain, in support of Queen Catherine. Over the next few months Paulet was closely involved with Queen Catherine and the Princesses Mary and Elizabeth, the daughter born to Anne Boleyn on 7 September 1533. Three days later, as the new heir to the throne, Elizabeth was baptised in a grand ceremony at Greenwich.

Paulet had returned from France with Norfolk just a few days earlier, in time to witness the event as a member of the procession that accompanied the baby from the palace to the church. The walls along the route were hung with arras and the floor strewn with rushes. The church too was hung with tapestry and a crimson satin canopy fringed with gold was placed over the silver font. The procession was a very grand event, although protocol dictated that the parents should not attend. The Dowager Duchess of Norfolk carried the baby, wrapped in a mantle of purple velvet with a long train held by Thomas Boleyn, Earl of Wiltshire, Edward Stanley, Earl of Derby, and the Countess of Kent. About them walked dukes, earls and lords and they were followed by a procession of gentlemen, squires, chaplains, more lords and their ladies, the Lord Mayor of London, the King's Council, barons and bishops. At the door the Bishop of London with other clergy welcomed the baby and received her into the church for the baptism. Trumpets were blown after the christening and gifts were presented. Wafers, comfits (sweetmeats preserved in sugar) and hippocras (spiced red wine) were then brought in for the refreshment of the guests, and the baby and her gifts were borne to the Queen in her chamber, lit along the way by 500 torches.[122]

Paulet's involvement with Queen Catherine and her daughter, Mary, was not so happy. After the King's marriage was declared void on 5 July 1533 Catherine of Aragon was ordered to style herself as Princess Dowager and Princess Mary to be the Lady Mary. Despite a commandment delivered by Lord Hussey and letters from Paulet informing her of her new title, Mary refused to use the new style and attempted 'arrogantly to usurp the title of Princess, pretending to be the heir apparent'.[123] In October 1533 she complained to the King, asking if he was aware that a letter to her written by Paulet had contained no reference to her as princess but as 'the lady Mary, the King's daughter'.[124]

Two months later, on 2 December, instructions were given to Charles Brandon, Duke of Suffolk, Robert Radcliffe, Earl of Sussex, Paulet and Richard Sampson, the Dean of the Royal Chapel, to attend upon Catherine at Bugden for the 'diminishing of her house' and to remove her to Somersham House near Ely, an unhealthy site surrounded by marsh-land. [125] On Wednesday 17 December, after dinner, the four commissioners met with Catherine in her great chamber where she protested that she was Queen and refused to use the title of Princess Dowager, also refusing to accept servants sworn to her service under that title rather than as Queen. Her servants were loathe to take a new oath, having already sworn alle-giance to her as their Queen, and some were removed. The commissioners did allow John de Atequa, a Spanish bishop, to remain so that she would have a confessor who could speak Spanish, but they avoided a difficult situ-ation by not asking him to swear an oath to the 'Princess Dowager'.

Catherine's refusal to move to Somersham on account of her health was reported to the King and they added that she might 'keep [to] her bed' or refuse to put on her clothes in order to prevent her removal. The commis-sioners wrote a similar letter to Norfolk and Cromwell. They referred to Catherine as the 'most obstinate woman that may be' and advised that they might need to move her by force. [126] On 27 December Chapuys reported to Charles V what happened when the four men tried to move Catherine. They stayed for six days to close the house and to observe the effect of the loss of her servants upon the Queen. Only two gentlewomen were left to wait upon her but the Queen remained steadfast in her determination to stay, causing Chapuys to describe her as 'constant'. The commissioners loaded her baggage and prepared a litter and horses for her but she locked the door of her chamber and refused to leave. They dared not break down the door for fear of the assembled people and so left, leaving her where she was. [127]

From 15 January to 30 March 1534 Paulet sat in his sixth session of Parliament during which the members agreed to the Act of Succession. This stated that the marriage of Catherine and Henry was contrary to the law of God and that the marriage with Anne was legal and her heirs were to succeed. It required all adult male subjects to swear an oath to uphold the Act or face life imprisonment and confiscation of property. On 30 March Paulet was present when both Houses of Parliament took the oath. [128] Catherine and Mary were also instructed to swear to the Act of Succession but this necessitated renouncing their titles. This they would not do. In April and again in July, Paulet with Thomas Boleyn visited Mary at Hatfield to hear her swear to the oath and renounce her titles. She refused on both occasions, replying 'so wisely that they returned quite confounded'.[129]

Paulet was frequently amongst the council members who spoke to Chapuys concerning the behaviour of Catherine and Mary. One morning in May 1534 the Council called the ambassador to Westminster to inform him that if the women persisted in refusing to take the oath, the King would be compelled to proceed against them. Chapuys replied that, on behalf of the Emperor, he could not accept the invalidity of Catherine's marriage and thus the denial of Mary's right to the crown. He was later informed that Mary's position in the line of succession would be after Anne's sons and Elizabeth.[130] Henry sent a message to Catherine warning her that the penalty for refusing to take the oath was death, whereupon Chapuys returned again to Westminster to discuss the threat against her. The King, who was preparing to go hunting, was surprised at his unexpected arrival and demand for an audience. Chapuys was invited to take dinner with the Duke of Norfolk after which he met the attendant group of councillors, including Paulet, who relayed the King's message that the matter of whether Catherine and Mary should swear the oath was still to be decided.[131]

Paulet did exhibit some sympathy for Mary's plight. In August he arrived at Hatfield Place where Mary was acting as lady-in-waiting to the baby Princess Elizabeth. They were to remove to Greenwich but Mary argued that she should not travel behind Elizabeth. Paulet agreed to this and allowed her to ride ahead. The Spanish ambassador noted that she reached Greenwich one hour before the baby and 'secured the most honourable place in the barge'.[132]

Queen Catherine died on 7 January 1536. Her disembowelled body was embalmed and sealed in a lead coffin containing spices before it was buried in the Benedictine Abbey at Peterborough.[133] The funeral was not the great occasion usual for a Queen of England. Paulet was sent there to 'order all things' for her burial and he was the only man of status, apart from four bishops and four abbots, who attended with the chief mourner Lady Eleanor, the King's niece.[134] A sermon was preached against the power of the Pope and the marriage of Henry and Catherine, and after the Mass her body was buried in a grave at the lowest step of the high altar. Paulet's final task regarding the Queen was to dismantle her household.[135]

By 1534 Paulet was Comptroller of the Household, sole Master of the Wards and a member of both the King's Council and of Parliament. By the end of his seventh session of Parliament in December that year the power of the Pope in England had been destroyed and the Crown was in control of the Church. The passing of the Act of Supremacy acknowledged that the King ought to be regarded as the 'Supreme Head of the Church in England', though it did not state that he was so in fact. It also gave him the power to carry out the visitations which would soon lead to the Dissolution of the Monasteries. The Act for Payment of First Fruits came as a blow to the clergy. Having ceased the payment of annates to Rome they were now ordered to pay first fruits and tenths to the Crown. First fruits were the payment of one year's income by the new incumbent of all livings from archbishop down to the priest of a chantry, and tenths were an annual 10 per cent tax of the annual value of every benefice to be paid at Christmas each year. These payments to the Crown were to be far more onerous than those previously paid to Rome.

Parliament extended the Treason Act to include writing or talking against the King and Queen in addition to threats to their persons and denial of their titles. Two Acts of Attainder were also passed, one against Bishop Fisher and five other men and the second against Sir Thomas More. The Act of Attainder registered More's conviction for treason and declared all his property forfeit to the King and his blood 'corrupted'. As a consequence his heirs would not be able to inherit his goods or titles. The previous April, More and Fisher had refused to swear the Oath of Succession and had been imprisoned in the Tower. More explained to his daughter Margaret that he accepted the right of Parliament to determine the succession but not to invalidate a Christian marriage and he could not swear the oath without putting his soul in peril.[136]

Early in 1535 Henry took the title 'Supreme Head of the Church in England' and all ecclesiastical and lay officials were ordered to swear in support of the Act of Supremacy and against papal power in England. On 5 May 1535 the first executions took place. Four Carthusian monks and one priest who had refused to swear the oath accepting the King as the Supreme Head of the Church in England were burnt at Tyburn. This was such a momentous event – death as the penalty for not swearing an oath – that nearly all the Court was present at the execution.[137] Fisher and More also refused to take the oath and on 17 June Paulet was one of seventeen judges commissioned to sit in Westminster Hall to try Fisher and three others. The men were condemned and executed that month. A few days later on 1 July the scene was repeated as Paulet again sat in Westminster, this time to try More. He too was found guilty and beheaded at Tower Hill on Tuesday, 6 July.[138] More's manors and estates, which were forfeit to the Crown, passed to other courtiers. On 20 April 1536 Paulet received 'custody of the estate of Sir Thomas More, deceased, at Chelsea' and in 1547 he was granted the property outright by Edward VI.[139]

Paulet witnessed Parliament's ratification of the Acts of Succession and Supremacy. He may have been only one man amongst many but these men together were responsible for authorising statutes that were used to dismantle the power of the Pope in England. Swearing to the oaths – denying the Pope and accepting the King as all powerful – was an enforced public acknowledgement of their personal approval of what they had done. The Commons took the Oath of Succession without dissent. Paulet must have sworn both this oath and the Oath of Supremacy. However, although he had spent his adult life working to promote the supremacy of the Crown over the state, for 50 years he had also held an allegiance to the Pope as head of his religion – obligations which he denied when he swore the Oath of Supremacy. How did the new attitudes to the Church and Pope sit with his religious beliefs?

In the early sixteenth century the populace believed that obedience to the King was paramount. Indeed the Church taught that it was a sin for subjects not to obey the King in all matters – including religious beliefs. But never before had a King disagreed with the tenets of the Church. Henry's denial of papal authority went against the Church's teaching but many people believed their souls would not be jeopardised. If they held the wrong religious beliefs, as prescribed by the King, and carried out the wrong religious practices it was the King who would be answerable to God and not them. The sovereign was all-powerful and for many the idea that the King might be wrong was inconceivable. But for those men who understood and disagreed with the politics of Henry's decisions, the threat of the death penalty may have persuaded them to swear the oath. Paulet certainly did not feel so strongly about the place of the Pope in his religion or the sanctity of the King's marriage that he felt obliged to make a stand like Sir Thomas More. But then very few people did. Paulet fell in line with the other councillors, obeying his King by swearing to the oaths and condemning More to be executed. It was, of course, possible to accept the religious leadership of the Pope even if the King did not acknowledge his eminence, to display public conformity but to hold private beliefs.

5

The Dissolution of the Monasteries and the Pilgrimage of Grace

In January 1535 Paulet was appointed to two commissions. The first, a commission of sewers, was routine. It was to survey and repair sea-banks and sea-walls in Hampshire, and ensure the cleaning of rivers, streams and ditches whereby water was carried away.[140] The second was not routine and, while having a huge effect on the country, was also to lead to benefits for many courtiers, including Paulet. This commission was to assess the annual value of every monastery, priory, hospital, parsonage and clerical living in the county. His son, John, and brother, George, were also involved.[141] All through England the value of the Church was being assessed and recorded, ostensibly so that tenths could be calculated. But the King wanted money and the monasteries and other church buildings were a rich source of land and goods. Distribution of these lands to gentlemen who were able to pay for them would create wealth for the King and increase his supporters. The survey was completed within six months. The following spring Paulet sat in his eighth and final session of Parliament when the Suppression of the Monasteries Bill was passed. This allowed for the dissolution of all those religious houses which had been assessed with an annual income of less than £200, on the alleged grounds that they were corrupt and decayed. It also established the Court of Augmentations to handle the transfer of the church lands to the Crown. The value of £200 was only a temporary limit and very soon all monasteries would be dissolved.

Once the King had control of the lands and buildings he redistributed many of them to his courtiers; some were given as gifts but the majority were sold to swell the royal coffers. In April 1536 the Duke of Norfolk wrote to Cromwell asking him to speak to the King on his behalf regarding Norfolk being given stewardship of certain suppressed lands. Norfolk's comment 'Where others speak I must speak too' shows that it was common practice for courtiers to request land from the King, either through an intermediary such as Cromwell, the King's secretary, or, in the case of monastic lands, by submitting an application and 'particulars' to the Court of Augmentations.[142] The particulars were a detailed official survey and valuation of the land and properties. If the court granted the petition, the recipient might receive the land as a gift from the King. Otherwise the purchase price was calculated from the valuation and the buyer paid this sum, either in money or by the exchange of land. Paulet too had written to Cromwell asking for property. A letter in 1532 refers to a house at Tottenham 'which you promised me' and later, in February 1535, he refers to the parsonage of Hatfield, in the diocese of Ely, 'which I should have had of you and should be glad to have it now'.[143] In August 1536 Paulet received his first rewards from the Dissolution. The King granted him Netley Abbey near Southampton 'with the grange, mill and lands in the parish of Netley, and the manors and lands of Hound, Shetsea, Shalling, Townehill and Shamulhurst belonging to the abbey and Waddon and Aisheley in Dorset'.[144] Two of the commissioners who reported on Netley were his brothers, George and Richard – perhaps they reported the state of the abbey to Paulet and he then petitioned the King for the property.

Paulet converted the church and cloister buildings of the abbey into a large house. The piers and arcades of the church were removed to leave the outer walls, and a hall and chambers were constructed within the nave and south transept. The buildings on two sides of the cloisters were converted into private apartments, the monks' dormitory possibly being used as a long gallery. Little remains of the mansion today, indeed the ruin resembles that of a church rather than a great house.

Netley was ideally placed for Paulet to use when he was inspecting the south coast defences but generally, when he was in Hampshire, he stayed at his estate at Basing in the north of the county. Basing House was built of flint and stone and was set inside the earthworks of an ancient motte and bailey castle surrounded by 300 acres of land. In 1531 he was granted a licence to 'build walls and towers' and fortify the manor.[145] This licence to crenellate was one of the last to be issued. As the country became more peaceful, fortified houses with battlements were seen as being unnecessary and land-owners built houses which offered comfort and privacy rather than security. However, in the case of Basing the fortifications later played a major part in the house's history. During the Civil War Oliver Cromwell's men razed the house to the ground, but only after a siege lasting two years. Paulet enlarged the building to become one of the finest houses in the country, renowned for its magnificence and worthy of a visit from the King. He made altera-tions to the existing house and added a substantial new building of red brick set around two courts. Basing House was described as 'the greatest of any subject's house in England, yea larger than most of the King's palaces'.[146] Engravings show the remains of a palatial building which was reputed to have had 380 rooms and reached to five storeys in parts. With its turrets and towers, gatehouses and battlements, chimneys and gables the building may well have resembled the palace at Hampton Court.[147] While he was building his own house, Paulet spent much time at Hampton Court and it is likely he copied features he saw there.

Paulet also built a grand mansion at Austin Friars in London, one of many religious houses surrendered to the King. On 22 April 1539 Paulet paid a fee of over £2,000 for several pieces of land, manors, rectories and buildings, all proceeds of the Dissolution. They included property at Browne Candover, Itchenstoke and Itchen Abbas in Hampshire and Fisherton Delamare in Wiltshire, and a grant of the 'great messuage' recently built by Paulet within the walls of the priory of Augustine Friars.[148] It would appear that this grant regularised the position regarding a house that Paulet was already build-ing. It was a popular residential area. Thomas Cromwell, Sir Richard Rich and Sir Thomas Wriothesley also lived there and in January 1541 Paulet was given further property there which had formerly belonged to Cromwell and to Rich.[149]

Two mid-sixteenth-century maps show Winchester House, as it was known, on the corner of London Wall and Broad Street, well situated for Paulet to reach Westminster, Whitehall and the Tower.[150] The site was bounded by a high stone wall that enclosed one of the largest gardens attached to a house in the city – most other large gardens generally belonged to the churches or merchant guild halls. The garden was laid out as a par-terre, with dwarf hedges and a large fountain. The presence of the fountain indicates that the house probably had a supply of running water. Water was piped from springs to conduits in the streets but it was rare for water to be piped directly to private homes. Only two other fountains are marked on the 'Agas' map, these being at the Palaces of Westminster and Whitehall. In

1567 Paulet was granted control of both a spring, which rose at 'Stebenheath' in Middlesex, and the water course through which it ran into London and to Austin Friars.[151] Since the flow of water to a building could not be switched off, the provision of a fountain helped to regulate it. The house, of dark red brick with stone dressings, was built to replace the Augustine Friars house and cloister but Paulet did not pull down the church; rather he repaired it at his own expense.[152] In 1550 Edward VI granted the church to be the 'preaching place' for Dutchmen living in London although their use of the church was restricted to the nave and aisles.[153] Paulet enclosed the east end of the church including the transepts, choir and chapels and reserved this area for his own use for the storage of corn, coal and other household goods.[154] Nothing remains of Austin Friars House apart from a piece of carved oak panelling in the Victoria and Albert Museum. But the evidence of items such as the garden fountain and a classically styled stone roundel at Basing, both of which were also found in royal palaces, indicate that Paulet was not only a man of great wealth but also one with a taste for what was considered to be the very best in architecture – or possibly just a man who was trying to emulate the King.

As the years passed and his wealth increased he lived in great style. Stow records that he kept 220 gentlemen and yeomen in a livery of Reading tawny, and provided 'great relief' for the poor at his gate.[155] Paulet was not alone. The Venetian ambassador wrote that the English nobility reside in mansions with a 'great abundance of eatables' and 'numerous attendants' and 'they seem wholly intent on leading a joyous existence'.[156] Paulet's household staff would have been organised in a similar way to that of the King, with a steward, a comptroller and a treasurer to oversee and control his many servants.

Paulet rode out through the gate of his house at Austin Friars into Broad Street, followed by two servants, and turned towards Westminster where he was to attend the Court of Wards and Liveries. The journey was nearly three miles and he knew the route well although he was aware that if he turned off the main thoroughfares, into the rabbit warren of small streets and alleys, he could soon become disorientated. London was densely populated and buildings were crammed closely together. Even London Bridge, which connected the city with the borough on the south side of the River Thames, had houses and shops built along each side. The three men rode down the street, passing the well as they turned

into Threadneedle Street. A constant babble of talking and shouting surrounded them together with the noise of cart wheels and horses' hooves, the din of an iron foundry and the occasional ringing of church bells. The city was never completely silent and the air was full of the sounds – and smells – of over 150,000 people.[157] *Although some rubbish was carried out of the city on dustcarts much was left decaying on the roads and the stench of human sewage that ran in the gutters mixed with the odour of horse dung.*

As he saw the tower of St Bartholomew Church, Paulet offered up a silent prayer for his wife's parents who were buried there, just before his nose was assailed by the smell of meat and fish coming from the Stocks Market, some of which was perhaps not as fresh as the purchasers might have wished. With so many traders together, buyers were hopeful of competitive prices. He proceeded along Poultry. Peering into the shops, he could see chickens, ducks and geese held in wicker baskets for sale. Many of the shops were just a single workroom in a small house opening onto the street. The shutters over the unglazed windows were let down during the day to become counters on which goods could be displayed and over which the transactions took place. A sign depicting what each shop sold swung out over the road but at a height of about nine feet so that a horse and rider could pass beneath.

Hanging under the eaves of one house was a long pole with an iron hook on the end, a common sight in a town where fires could spread so quickly between such closely packed buildings. The hooks were used to pull thatching off the roof to try to prevent the fire spreading. Many houses were timber-framed but those men who could afford to do so used stone or brick with tile roofs so that their houses were more likely to withstand fire. The smell of meat and poultry was replaced by the sweet smell of baking bread; he was passing Bread Street. Many shopkeepers gathered together in their trades so that streets became known by the name of that trade – Milk Street, Beer Lane, Cornhill, Butcher Row, Old Fish Street, Shoe Lane, Ironmonger Lane.

As he moved along Cheapside the road widened and people passed along on either side of the Standard and of Eleanor's Cross. Two water carriers were busy filling tall wooden vessels at the tower of the stone Standard. A pipe inside the tower fed taps from which people could collect water to carry home, or have it delivered for a fee by water carriers. The Eleanor Cross was one of the twelve memorials erected by Edward I to mark the stopping places of the funeral procession of his wife Eleanor; Paulet would pass the final cross when he reached Whitehall.

As he rode he peered into side streets. Although this main thoroughfare was well paved with stone some of the alleyways were rough ground. They were narrow and where the upper rooms of houses overhung the street they looked dark as the buildings appeared to meet in mid air to make a tunnel. These streets were the haunt of thieves, especially at night when the only light came from lanterns on the houses of the wealthy and outside inns. Even on busy roads Paulet and his men wore swords. He rode down Paternoster Row, under the steeple of St Paul's Cathedral, surely the highest building ever seen, and on towards Ludgate.

Paulet led the way across the stone bridge over the Fleet River and on through Temple Bar, a wooden gateway which marked the western edge of the city. The crowds thinned out and the Strand was quieter. Here, behind many of the houses, were large gardens rather than close-packed houses and to the north lay fields. They soon covered the distance from Charing Cross and along King Street, beneath the two great gatehouses and into the yard at Westminster Palace. Beside the fountain Paulet handed the reins to his servants and strode off into the Hall, leaving them to stable the horses. Many people found it easier to travel to Westminster by river. Watermen were constantly rowing up and down the Thames and the cost for such journeys was just a few pence, although the price was higher if the boat was rowed against the tide. Perhaps next time he would walk the half-mile from his house to the river and hire a boat above London Bridge to bring him to Westminster Stairs.

Paulet would have travelled between London and Basing House by horse, probably accompanied by several retainers who would have provided some protection against robbers, as well as attending to their master's needs. On long journeys riders travelled at between three and five miles an hour, depending on the weather, enabling them to cover 30–40 miles a day.[158] Basing House was about 45 miles from London and could have been reached comfortably by Paulet on a two-day ride. However, most people did not travel far and then only for a purpose. Official correspondence was moved more quickly by post-horse but generally travel and communications were slow; in 1558 the inhabitants of Much Wenlock, in Shropshire, did not learn of the death of Queen Mary and the succession of Queen Elizabeth for eight days.[159]

One critical factor in the speed of travel was the quality of the roads. Within towns some of the streets were paved but in the country the road surface was dependent on the underlying ground. Stone gave a hard foundation, clay was slippery when wet and loose soil could turn into deep mud in the winter. Each parish was expected to maintain the roads within its boundaries. When highways became 'very noisome and tedious to travel and dangerous to all passengers and carriages' the parishioners were ordered to bring their tools and carts and spend a certain number of days repairing them.[160] Even just filling potholes could greatly improve the comfort of riding in a cart. Coaches were introduced in the mid-sixteenth century but, with no springs and only leather flaps or curtains at the windows, they provided limited comfort. One of the earliest references to a 'coche' is to one owned by Sir Philip Hoby in 1556. Bearing in mind Paulet's age (he was then in his seventies), it is highly probable that he too would have owned one of these vehicles.[161]

The King stayed at Basing House during the summer of 1535. Paulet and Sir William Fitzwilliam were preparing to travel to Calais with a retinue which included Paulet's brother, George, to examine and fortify both Calais and Guisnes against the French.[162] In August, while they were still waiting to leave for France, Fitzwilliam informed Cromwell that Paulet wished to have a fortnight 'to see his buildings which he has to do at home'.[163] This referred to the building work at Basing that Paulet was keen to oversee in preparation for a possible visit from the King and Anne Boleyn. On 16 October, while on progress, the King changed his itinerary on hearing of the death, probably from plague, of four people at Farnham and of one near Guildford. Paulet wrote to Cromwell that the King is to visit 'my poor house of Basing'.[164] Three days later the royal party moved from Lord Sandys' house, the Vyne, to Basing House where they spent two nights. During the stay Sir Francis Bryan described the King as 'merry' but this happy state was not to last for long.[165] In April 1536, six months after entertaining the Queen at his home, Paulet was named in a special commission with Lord Chancellor Audley, the Dukes of Norfolk and Suffolk, the Earl of Wiltshire, Thomas Cromwell, Sir William Fitzwilliam, Lord Sandys and other councillors and judges to find evidence against Anne.[166]

Henry had tired of his wife and was desperate for a son. His eye had alighted on Jane Seymour and he wanted freedom to re-marry. The commissioners moved quickly and, on 1 May 1536, Mark Smeaton and Henry Norris were sent to the Tower, charged with being the Queen's lovers. Next morning Paulet was one of the men who met Anne at Greenwich to inform her that they were to inquire into her relationships with Norris, Smeaton and several other men. Anne denied any impropriety but after her interrogation the commission ordered her arrest and she was moved to the Tower.[167] Sir William Kingston, the Tower Constable, reported to Cromwell that Anne said she was 'cruelly handled' at Greenwich by Norfolk and the Council but she 'named Mr Comptroller to be a very gentleman'.[168] Her brother George, Lord Rochford, was charged with incest and also imprisoned in the Tower as were Sir Richard Page, Sir Francis Weston, William Brereton and Sir Thomas Wyatt. On Friday 12 May Paulet was in Westminster Hall as one of twenty men who were to try those accused of consorting with the Queen. Weston, Norris, Smeaton and Brereton were all found guilty of treason and condemned to a traitor's death.[169] Wyatt and Page were freed. Three days later Anne's trial took place in the Tower watched by an audience estimated by Chapuys at 2,000.[170] Her uncle, the Duke of Norfolk, presided and her father was among the 26 peers of the realm who were her judges. Since her so-called lovers had already been found guilty, the verdict was a foregone conclusion and, once her guilt was decided, Rochford was found guilty of incest and executed. On 17 May, Anne's marriage to the King was declared invalid due to Henry's previous liaison with her sister, Mary, and on 19 May her execution took place in the Tower, witnessed by members of the Council. Henry waited just eleven days before marrying Jane Seymour.

Soon after, in July 1536, came the first moves to reform the accepted doctrines of the Church. The 'Ten Articles' declared what these beliefs should now be. They maintained that only three sacraments – communion, baptism and penance – were necessary, and they diminished the value of images in churches and of prayers to saints and for the dead. It was ordered that a Bible in English should be placed in all churches. The removal of images was met with resistance in some parts of the country and in the north of England it was one of the factors which led to an uprising. There was a feeling of resentment against increasing government interference, a problem which had intensified under Cromwell. Different groups had different concerns. The aristocracy and gentry resented the Statute of Uses, passed by Parliament early in 1536, which reasserted the King's right to feudal dues. The commoners were against enclosure and increased rents. But what united them all was their shared fear of what was happening to the Church. Concerns about the Dissolution of the Monasteries and the attack on the old religion increased with rumours that many parish churches were to be pulled down and even that licences would be needed for the consumption of certain foods.

That autumn, Paulet was involved in the chaotic attempt to provide men and supplies to subdue rebellion. He and Sir William Kingston were sent to Ampthill as general overseers of war supplies, procuring and distributing ordnance, weapons, horses and men and paying wages.[171] But lack of funds and the time taken for letters to pass to and from the Council in London resulted in confusion. The King's army, heavily outnumbered, would have been defeated if the rebels had been set on fighting rather than on using peaceful means to achieve their demands.

On 1 October, a riot at Louth in Lincolnshire was the precursor to the county rising up. Within days the gentry had taken over leadership of the cause and submitted demands for the suppression of the monasteries to cease and for Cromwell to be removed from power, all the while declaring their loyalty to the King. The King immediately summoned men to form his army. Orders went out instructing noblemen and gentry to assemble with their retainers at Ampthill from where they could be sent north to oppose the rebels or south to defend London.[172] Paulet's quota was to provide 100 of his own men, and his brothers Thomas and Richard were summoned to attend with six men each.[173] Paulet left Windsor, where he was organising provisions, in time to present himself with Norfolk, Henry Courtenay, Marquis of Exeter, and Sir William Kingston for the musters on 16 October.[174]

The Duke of Suffolk was sent to Lincolnshire with a small army but the rising collapsed when the King refused to negotiate with men who had taken up arms against him and by 15 October the gentlemen of Lincoln offered to submit. Meanwhile there were risings in other northern counties. In Yorkshire the rebels followed a lawyer, Robert Aske, whose description of their cause as a pilgrimage led to the risings being known as the Pilgrimage of Grace. These rebels took York and were joined by Thomas, Lord Darcy who surrendered Pontefract Castle to them on 21 October. By 17 October one estimate numbered the rebels at 40,000. Suffolk could not yet safely leave the collapsed rising in Lincolnshire, George Talbot, Earl of Shrewsbury, had 7,000 men to hold the River Don and, on 18 October, Norfolk and Exeter set out on their way north with 5,000 men. Paulet and Sir William Kingston remained at Ampthill overseeing the movements of men, weapons and money.

A series of letters illustrate how poor communication and lack of funds seriously hampered their efforts, and contradictions in orders resulted in near chaos. On 17 October Norfolk, Exeter, Sandys, Paulet and Kingston wrote to Henry saying that a 'good store of money must be sent'. The following day they wrote to the Council asking again for more money, saying that the £10,000 they had received for Norfolk's army was scarcely enough, that the soldiers complained they could not live on 8*d* a day and would not advance further. On 20 October the King ordered Paulet, Kingston and Sandys to send 2,000 soldiers on horseback and foot from Ampthill to the Duke of Suffolk in Lincolnshire, making up the number with footmen if necessary. They replied immediately to the Council that most of the men remaining at Ampthill had been discharged because of the expense of keeping them, but that they would try to get horsemen since 'footmen shall in this deep time of winter make little speed'. They also pointed out that guns and ammunition had been handed over to the Master of Ordnance to be returned to the Tower and to Windsor, and that £2,000 had been received and already used. That same day Norfolk wrote to the Council complaining that he had not received certain letters they had sent to him. He also reiterated that men had been sent home, that there was not as much ordnance as the Council thought and that he needed more money to pay the troops. [175]

On 21 October the Council wrote to Paulet and Kingston with thanks from the King for their diligence and desiring them still to furnish 2,000 men. They were sent 1,000 marks (£666 13s 4d) with the exhortation to 'be careful in spending it and the remainder if any to be delivered to the King'. They were also ordered to recover the ordnance if possible, otherwise they were to send bills, bows, arrows, javelins and ten pieces of ordnance to Suffolk. There was a further £3,000 reportedly on its way. The next day, Sunday, 22 October, Paulet and Kingston replied again that the men had returned home after the musters to save money and that it would take time to reassemble them. They estimated that there should be 600 men in the area and that the rest would have to come from far away, and reminded the Council that since Norfolk had taken sufficient ordnance for Sir Anthony Browne and himself the remaining ordnance had been returned, as per the King's earlier order. They pointed out that Suffolk had no need of either men or ordnance but that they had ordered Sir Anthony to go to Suffolk with his men and artillery if necessary. Meanwhile the Council were already writing to tell them to send just 600 men to Suffolk and ten pieces of ordnance – even though he said he did not need either! The time taken for messengers to ride between London, Ampthill and the North was so long that when Paulet received instructions from the Council circumstances had already changed. However, their problems were not confined to men and money. On 23 October they reported that the countryside was barren of victuals where the army had passed through and many soldiers had taken 'horses and mares from the plough' without any agreement or restitution. Paulet and Kingston had to deal with the local justices to try to resolve the problem. [176]

It was some weeks before the rebels dispersed. On 27 October Norfolk met Aske and his supporters at Doncaster Bridge. With his lack of military force, the Duke was able to do no more than talk with them and a truce was called while their demands were considered by the King. On 8 December, after Norfolk had offered pardons and terms acceptable to the rebels, they began to return home. The King, however, made no move to ratify the terms, and when there were minor riots in January and February, Henry used these as an excuse to release himself from the promises made to Aske. The King and Privy Council supported Norfolk's executions in the north in order to intimidate the inhabitants. Paulet was named in the commissions to try the rebels. Nearly 200 of the perpetrators were hanged, including Darcy and Aske.[177] The King's men had been heavily outnumbered and the rebels might have had sufficient strength to overcome the army but they had no real desire to fight. They were loyal to the Crown and had hoped that talk would convince the King that their grievances were justified and remediable.

Two references to Paulet during the rebellion give an insight into the contemporary perception of him. Firstly, while Darcy was at Doncaster, some of his servants were heard to say of Norfolk, Sussex, John de Vere, Earl of Oxford, Fitzwilliam, Paulet and Kingston: 'God save the King and them all! for as long as such noblemen of the true noble blood may reign or rule about the King all shall be well.'[178] The second came in Henry VIII's response on 2 November to the rebels' petition in which they demanded that unpopular statutes should be repealed and that the King should maintain the true faith. Countering their complaint that not many of his councillors were nobles, the King listed those whom he considered to be noble 'both of birth and condition'. Paulet's name appeared alongside the Dukes of Norfolk and Suffolk, the Marquis of Exeter, the Earls of Shrewsbury, Oxford and Sussex, Lord Sandys and Sir William Fitzwilliam. Although from the gentry, Paulet was perceived by both King and servants as having noble qualities.[179]

6

Treasurer of the Household and the Fall of Cromwell

A year after the rebellion, in October 1537, Paulet was appointed to the position of Treasurer of the Household, following in the footsteps of Sir William Fitzwilliam who had been made Lord Admiral and elevated to Earl of Southampton. Known as Mr Treasurer to distinguish him from the Lord Treasurer, this new position was nominally a promotion, giving Paulet 'second estate next the Steward' but his life carried on much as before.[180] He still had the same seniority at court and his entitlement to meals and accommodation was unchanged. He was still involved in the meetings of the Board of Greencloth, passing judgement on offenders, checking expenses and budgets, and making decisions on food and supplies, but he now had more involvement with accounting and the issue of money in the Counting House. The source of funding for the Counting House changed over time with its revenue being drawn variously from the Exchequer, the Treasurer of the Chamber and the revenue courts, including that of the Wards and Liveries that Paulet controlled. This money was used by the Cofferer to pay the wages of the officers and servants of the Lord Steward's department, and to provide the prests, or advances of money for the purveyors to make their purchases.

Efforts were made to control household spending and to stop the drain on the royal coffers. With his 'grete charge of policy and husbandry of all this household' Paulet took a special interest in the operation of the purveyors and the costs of food.[181] Letters from Paulet to Cromwell illustrate the vast sums of money spent on feeding the court and the forbearance of the local suppliers. In 1535 he asked for £2,000 for the King's provisions and a year later, when the King's suppliers were exasperated at waiting for outstanding money, Paulet wrote asking for £1,000 'else we can have no longer provision from brewers and purveyors; for they have borne with the King as long as they may.'[182]

Paulet assumed his position as Treasurer at a time of great national celebration which was soon followed by tragedy. On Friday, 12 October 1537 the Queen, Jane Seymour, gave birth to Prince Edward at Hampton Court Palace. The King had a son and heir and the populace rejoiced. Great fires were lit in the streets and there was 'goodly banqueting and triumphing cheer with shooting of guns all day and night'. The following Monday the baby was christened in Hampton Court chapel in a grand ceremony echoing that of Princess Elizabeth. A long procession wound its way through the corridors, the Great Hall and the courtyards as the baby prince was carried under a canopy from his chambers to the chapel. Gentlemen bearing unlit candles led the way followed by the choir and clergy. The King's councillors came next, two by two with Paulet walking beside Sir William Fitzwilliam, followed by the ambassadors and nobles. A gold salt was carried and a richly garnished vessel containing the chrism was held by Princess Elizabeth who was herself carried by Edward Seymour, the baby's uncle. After the baptism, spices, wafers and wine were served to Mary and Elizabeth and the godparents, while all 'estates and gentles' received spice and hippocras and all others bread and sweet wine. Then the baby Prince was carried to the King and Queen, the route illuminated by the candles that had been lit at the christening.[183] No-one was aware at the time that though the Tudors were to rule for another 65 years, this was to be the last baptism of a royal Tudor baby.

The Queen never recovered after the birth of her son and twelve days later she was dead. Norfolk and Paulet were ordered to see to her burial. Firstly the wax-chandler removed her entrails 'with searing, balming, spicing and trammeling' in cloth. Then the plumber 'leaded, soldered and chested' her in a lead coffin and her entrails were 'honourably interred' in the chapel at Hampton Court. Masses were offered daily and on 12 November her corpse was taken in a grand procession from Hampton Court to Windsor Castle. The funeral party set off at 5am with Princess Mary as chief mourner, in the King's absence, and with all the courtiers and their ladies following behind. At the castle the mourners were 'sumptuously provided for', the corpse was buried and all was finished by noon.[184] The King had gained an heir but had lost his third wife; it was to be more than two years before he married again.

On Sunday, 9 March 1539, at Westminster Palace, Paulet was rewarded for his work as Comptroller and Treasurer when the King elevated him to the peerage as a baron with the title of Lord St John. The title of Lord St John was inherited through the descendants of John de St John who had taken his name from a settlement in Normandy and who was awarded lands in Oxfordshire after accompanying William the Conqueror to England. The St John name became connected with Basing in the twelfth century on the marriage of Mabel de St John to Adam de Portu, Baron of Basing. Their son, William, took the surname of St John in recognition of the large inheritance which came to him from his mother and he was styled Lord St John of Basing early in the thirteenth century.[185] The title died out 200 years later with no living male heirs but was re-established as Lord St John for William Paulet.

As Paulet waited for the yeomen usher to push open the doors he acknowledged the gentlemen beside him, Sir John Russell and William Parr. In just a few minutes the three men would be elevated to the peerage. Ahead of them Garter Knight, one of the heralds, carried three sheets of vellum, the letters patent announcing their new titles. The three men had followed him in procession from the small chamber where they had gathered with their assistants after attending High Mass in the chapel. Paulet walked with Lord Cobham and Lord Dacre on either side of him, behind Lord Clinton who carried Paulet's new parliament robe. Russell and Parr were similarly accompanied by other lords. As they stood in the Guard Chamber the doors into the Presence Chamber were pushed open. Paulet could see into the large room, richly hung with tapestries. At the far end, beneath a canopy of cloth of gold, stood the King smiling amiably on all those around him. On either side of the chamber, against the wall so as to leave a large clear space in the centre, stood many nobles who all turned to face the party waiting at the door.

Paulet stepped into the room and, with Russell and Parr beside him, the three men made their first obeisance, bowing low to the King. Their assistants stepped up to place the robes about their shoulders. Paulet and the other two processed towards the King, pausing on the way to make another low bow, and knelt down when they came to the monarch. Garter did not read aloud the patents but one by one handed them to Thomas Cromwell, Lord Privy Seal, who stood beside the King and who in turn passed them to Henry. Paulet took the vellum scroll which confirmed his investiture as Lord St John and, after the King had said many gracious words to him, he gave the King thanks for bestowing such a great honour upon him. Russell and Parr went through the same ritual, being created Lord Russell and Lord Parr, and the three men rose from the floor and stood before the King. The trumpets blew to announce their creations and, bowing again, the three lords retreated, bowing yet again before turning to follow the trumpeters into the next chamber.

Paulet was now a peer of the realm, entitled to sit in the House of Lords. Behind him he could hear the other nobles leaving the Presence Chamber and following them to dinner. The meal was a celebratory affair as his friends congratulated him on his new title. The cooks had worked hard and Paulet thought upon the rewards that he and Russell and Parr were expected to give them for their efforts, together with all the others who had been involved in the day's proceedings – the heralds, musicians, gentlemen ushers, sewers and workers in many of the household departments. It was exhilarating to receive honours but it was also very expensive. The trumpets sounded and as he listened he heard the herald proclaim his new title for the first time in public – the noble Lord St John, Sir William Paulet.[186]

The post of Treasurer was always held by a knight and Paulet now relinquished this position to Sir Thomas Cheney. Four years later he returned to the Royal Household as Lord Chamberlain but in the meantime his many other roles kept him well occupied. Paulet retained his position as a councillor and, as Lord St John, he had a seat in the Lords in Parliament. His elevation to the nobility had made him a member of a very select group. There were only 43 nobles when he entered the Lords – two dukes, one marquis, 13 earls and 27 barons. Although some titles were extinguished when their holders died without producing an heir and others were forfeited when nobles were executed as traitors, the King did create new peerages and award lapsed titles; the title of Earl of Essex passed through three families between 1540 and 1575. In 1540 Thomas Cromwell held the title for less than three months before being executed for treason. Three years later William Parr was honoured with the title when his sister, Catherine, became Queen and after his death, he having no heir, the vacant title was awarded to Walter Devereux. When Henry VIII came to the throne there had been 42 nobles; when he died there were 51, over half of whom he had created or promoted to higher titles. Many of these men spent only limited time at Court; their role was to maintain the King's control within their own localities. Nobility did not give them an automatic right to a position on the King's Council. When Henry died, only seven of his eighteen councillors were titled and most of these also held posts at Court.

A few days after his ennoblement Paulet experienced a little excitement in his relatively calm life during an inspection of defences on the south coast. In June 1538 the King of France and the Emperor had signed a ten-year truce. Later that year Pope Paul III prepared to issue a Bull of Excommunication against Henry. The Bull had been drawn up as a threat but never used at the time of the King's marriage to Anne Boleyn. The Pope also called on the Emperor and the monarchs of France and Scotland to 'persuade' England to return to the Catholic Church. England was seized by the fear of war on her own soil with potential attackers invading on several fronts. Defences were improved at Calais after movements of horsemen in northern France raised fears, and the military defences on the Scottish borders and in southern England were ordered to be improved. In February 1539 Paulet was put on a commission to take musters in Wiltshire and to check defences on the coast in Hampshire.[187] Along the south coast ditches were dug and barricades and palisades set up as the country prepared for an invasion.

On 19 March the Earl of Southampton and Paulet put to sea with three boats to view defences at Southampton Water, Calshot Point and the Isle of Wight. They saw a Spanish vessel take on-board grain, and suspecting it was 'uncustomed' they tried to intercept it. The Spaniard slipped anchor and made all sail to get away but there was no wind and Paulet divided the three boats to approach her, calling to her to yield. The Earl of Southampton wrote 'when the Spaniards manned their top as if to say "come and you dare" ... this stirred my choler something.' The two men were enraged at the nerve of the Spaniard and, although it was dangerous to go on since the Spaniard had ordnance and Paulet and the Earl had only hand-guns, they continued until she struck sail and Paulet boarded the ship. They took the captain and a Southampton merchant to the Isle of Wight, impounded the ship and continued with their inspection of the island, surveying the roads and coastal approaches, viewing Carisbrook Castle and devising a defensive tower for East Cowes.[188] The invasion never came. By July the threat was receding as both Francis I and Charles V were reluctant to go to war against England, and the threat to excommunicate Henry was never carried out.

Paulet remained in Hampshire after his sailing adventure. On 1 April he attended the burial of Lady Sandys at the Vyne where he was described as being a 'great doer' who will be 'herrode and condytore of everything himself'.[189] Perhaps he was using his organisational skills in the planning of the funeral. By 28 April he had returned to London to be summoned to the House of Lords for the first time to take part in the King's seventh parliament. The members sat in Westminster Hall, the lords sitting on benches along one wall facing the bishops on the other. At the end of the long chamber the King's seat, under a cloth of estate, faced between the benches towards the lower end of the room where a bar marked the point past which members of the lower house and visitors could not pass. In the middle of the floor between the benches were great woollen sacks covered in red cloth on which sat the Lord Chancellor, his two clerks and members of the King's Learned Council. The Parliament sat on 39 occasions between 3 May and 28 June and Paulet was assiduous in his attendance, missing only one sitting. Members passed the Act of Six Articles which was an attempt to clarify some of the points of contention between Catholics and Reformers. It stated that: the body and blood of Christ were present in the form of bread and wine in the Sacrament; it was not necessary to take both bread and wine; confession through a priest was to be encouraged; masses for the dead were permissible; vows of chastity were unbreakable; and priests could not marry. The Act was never fully enforced, unlike the one introduced for the dissolution of the remaining monasteries, abbeys and hospitals. This Act prescribed that all those religious houses which had already been 'voluntarily' granted to the King were to be his property, and all those which might 'hereafter happen to be dissolved, suppressed, renounced' were also to pass into the King's possession.[190] Receivers, one of whom was Paulet's brother Richard, were appointed to confiscate religious foundations and lands and to assign pensions to the displaced nuns and monks.[191]

1540 began with the arrival of Henry's new Queen, Anne of Cleves. On Saturday, 3 January Paulet was in the King's entourage when Henry received Anne at Blackheath.[192] The King was horrified by the appearance and bearing of his new wife but the wedding went ahead three days later. After only six months the marriage was annulled and Anne, who was happy to become the King's 'sister', lived a life of relative comfort away from the Court until her death in 1557. Just nineteen days after the annulment, in July, Henry took one of her maids of honour, Catherine Howard, as his fifth wife. The same month saw the downfall of Cromwell who had engineered the failed marriage to Anne.

Catherine's uncle, the Duke of Norfolk, was a strong supporter of Catholicism and one of the leading opponents of Cromwell. The latter's enemies outnumbered his friends and by 1540 they had finally gained the upper hand, talking against Cromwell to the King and accusing him of supporting heretics and blaming him for the King's disastrous marriage to Anne. Although in April 1540 Henry favoured Cromwell with the Earldom of Essex, Cromwell's influence with the King may have already begun to weaken, a fact which Paulet's brother George had spoken publicly about in 1538. George, who had been serving as one of four commissioners establishing order in Ireland after the rebellion led by Thomas Fitzgerald, returned to England in April amid accusations that he had made slanderous comments about Cromwell.[193]

Cromwell attempted to find evidence against George by taking depositions from witnesses who had heard him speak in Ireland. John Alen, a member of the King's Council in Ireland, remembered George speaking freely against Cromwell and saying: 'As for my Lord Privy Seal ... the King beknaveth him twice a week, and sometime knocketh him well about the pate; and yet when he hath been well pummelled about the head and shaken up, as it were a dog, he will come out into the great chamber shaking of the bush with as merry a countenance as though he might rule all the roost.' George, standing at the lower end of the chamber, had witnessed Cromwell come out from the Privy Chamber and was able to 'perceive these matters well enough and laugh at his fashion and ruffs, and then my brother and my lord Admiral must drive a mean to reconcile him to the King again.' Other witnesses confirmed these words. Leonard Gray in Drogheda wrote to the King quoting George as saying that the King did 'many times fall out with the Privy Seal in his Privy Chamber' and that Cromwell would then send for William Paulet and ask for his help in regaining favour and that 'the Lord Admiral Fitzwilliam, Earl of Southampton and Paulet should rule all with the King.' Chief Justice Aylmer recalled George saying that when he came home he would 'laugh at this geare with my lord of Norfolk, Mr. Treasurer and my lord Admiral when they were secretly together'.[194]

By 18 May George was imprisoned in the Tower.[195] Four days earlier Paulet, who was at Waltham with the King, wrote to Cromwell on behalf of his brother. He asked him to hear the matter himself and to show pity and favour to his brother and 'henceforth he will no more offend Cromwell or any other nobleman'.[196] This appears to have been the end of the matter and George was released. He may well have been speaking the truth. In September Anthony Budgegode, in a letter to Cromwell, described George 'as true a man to the King as lives' because 'he gave counsel without dissimulation.'[197]

George's allegation that Cromwell needed Fitzwilliam and Paulet to intercede with the King on his behalf certainly suggests that Cromwell was no longer confident of Henry's support. George believed that his brother had some influence with the King. Whether Paulet supported Cromwell is thrown into doubt if he really did laugh at Cromwell behind his back. Cromwell's continued success depended partly on the support he received from his peers. A move against him by some of the councillors could be enough to bring him down if the King's support was uncertain and he may have taken no further action against George because he viewed the Treasurer as an ally.

Paulet spent a month in Calais during the spring of 1540, investigating claims of discontent and heresy and re-establishing civil order.[198] By 17 April he and the other commissioners had finished their work and were ordered to return home. They left on 23 April after being smuggled out of the town by the authorities to catch the tide at 2am, ignoring the strict rules which forbade entering or leaving the town at night after the closing of the town gates.[199] Parliament had been reconvened while Paulet was in Calais and on his return he took his seat for two weeks until it was prorogued on 11 May. However, on 25 May the members were recalled and an Act of Attainder without trial was brought against Cromwell. This condemned him for treason and heresy and denied him an opportunity to speak in his own defence. On 19 and 29 June Paulet sat in the Lords when two readings of the Bill were heard without opposition.[200] Cromwell had been arrested on 10 June and once the Act of Attainder was passed he was considered to be legally, if not yet physically, dead. However, in an age when retribution often followed swiftly, he was allowed to live until he had provided the statements necessary for the King to divorce Queen Anne and he was then beheaded at Tower Hill on 28 July.

Paulet had known and worked closely with Cromwell for many years but, as a member of the House of Lords, he voted to attaint him for treason and heresy. The two men had both started out by training in law but Cromwell had seized career openings and forged ahead while Paulet may in contrast have waited for advancement to come to him. They had worked together as Surveyors of Woods and as councillors, and Paulet's position in the royal household had brought him into regular contact with Cromwell. It appears that when Cromwell was attainted Paulet's name was still on the deeds for some land which he had recently purchased from Cromwell. These lands were seized by the King but Paulet did receive £900 in recompense from the Court of Augmentations.[201]

Wolsey and Cromwell were both dead and no doubt men such as Paulet took heed of their downfall.

The year after Cromwell's execution Paulet condemned to death another Lord, one who had accompanied him at the ceremony for his elevation to the peerage. On this occasion the crime was not treason but murder. One night in April 1541 the 24-year-old Thomas Fiennes, Lord Dacre of the South, and a group of friends had been poaching on land neighbouring his property in Sussex when they encountered three game-keepers. In the ensuing fight one of the gamekeepers was killed and the young Lord and his associates were accused of murder. In June, when the Lord Chancellor, the Earls of Sussex and Hertford, Russell, Paulet and Sir John Baker met in Star Chamber to consider Dacre's case they were not all agreed that he was guilty. They 'made great conscience' to find him guilty, looking hard for any real evidence of his guilt but 'would rather have used some means to make him confess'. On 27 June the jury panel of seventeen lords including Paulet assembled to hear the case. Some were against charging him with wilful murder, but 'suddenly and softly they agreed'. Dacre pleaded not guilty and referred himself to trial by his peers. However, upon hearing that the rest of the group had confessed, he admitted his guilt, pleading for mercy from the King. A pardon was not forthcoming and he was hanged at Tyburn two days later.[202]

Later that same year Paulet took part in the proceedings which brought another of Henry's wives to the block. Young Catherine Howard did not enjoy her time as Queen for long. In November 1541 the King was pre-sented with evidence of her relationship with Francis Dereham before her marriage and with accusations of her adultery with Thomas Culpeper after her marriage. On 1 December Paulet was named on the commission to try Culpeper and Dereham.[203] They were found guilty and executed. Three weeks later Paulet sat again, this time to try the Queen's relatives including her uncle, Lord William Howard, and his wife.[204] They were all found guilty of concealing knowledge of Catherine's infidelity and sentenced to per-petual imprisonment and seizure of their property, although they were later pardoned. The Duke of Norfolk escaped condemnation only by disowning his niece and condemning her actions. Paulet was present in the Lords to hear the reading of the Bill of Attainder against Catherine convicting her of treason.[205] After being Queen for only eighteen months she was beheaded at the Tower at 7am on 13 February 1542. Paulet witnessed the execution with all the Council except Norfolk and Suffolk. The King had lost or dis-posed of five wives in less than nine years.

7

Privy Councillor and Lord Chamberlain

Paulet stood waiting before the doors to the Presence Chamber at Hampton Court. The doors opened and Sir Thomas Wriothesley, the King's Secretary stepped forward beckoning to Paulet to enter the chamber. Paulet walked in and bowed low. He moved forward to bow again and finally stopped before the King as he bent for a third time. Magnificently attired, the King looked majestic and powerful as he sat beneath the canopy of state. He signalled to Paulet to rise and, turning to Wriothesley, announced so that all the men within the chamber could hear that William Paulet, Lord St John, was to be called to be one of the King's most honourable Privy Councillors. Paulet managed to voice his thanks and assured the King that he would do his utmost to serve him and England to the best of his ability. With Wriothesley beside him the two men retreated from the royal presence, bowing as they walked backwards to the doorway and out into the adjoining chamber.

Once the doors had been closed behind them Paulet relaxed and accepted Wriothesley's congratulations as the Secretary led him along the galleries to the council chamber. An usher opened the door and Paulet walked into the oak-panelled room where the Privy Council sat around a large table. He knew all the men present, most of them held appointments at Court. At the head sat the Lord Chancellor, Thomas Audley, and along each side the councillors were arranged according to their rank, those of highest rank nearest to Audley. Paulet moved to stand before him, aware that all the faces were turned his way, as Wriothesley announced that it was the King's pleasure that Lord St John should become one of his councillors. Audley recited the oath and, laying his hand upon a Bible given to him by the Secretary, Paulet swore to maintain it. It was done. Such a simple ceremony but it meant that he was now one of Henry VIII's Privy Councillors with the authority to act in the name of the King.[206]

Paulet was admitted to the Privy Council on 19 November 1542 in conjunction with his appointment as Master of the Court of Wards and Liveries.[207] He had previously been named as a member of the embryonic Privy Council in the King's response to the Northern Rebels in 1536 but had probably surrendered this position when he relinquished the Treasurership. However, in the interim, he had been sitting as a judge in the Court of Star Chamber and his signature on council documents indicates that he continued to play a role in the King's Ordinary Council, remaining with a small group of councillors in London while the King went on progress.[208]

The Privy Council had emerged during the 1530s when Cromwell began reorganising the King's large and unwieldy council into a more streamlined body. As Comptroller and Treasurer, Paulet had been one of the select group of nineteen leading councillors, many of them holders of state and household offices, who formed the inner ring of advisers to the King. They became the Privy Council, their role being to govern the country according to the monarch's instructions while the lesser or 'ordinary' councillors, many of them lawyers and court finance officials, were summoned to give assistance or reports as required. But, although the Privy Council was a collection of the most powerful men in the country, its actions were still controlled by Cromwell and it was not until after his death in 1540 that it started to resemble the precursor of the present-day cabinet. Then the Council began to use a permanent secretary and to keep a register in which a clerk recorded attendees and the proceedings and decisions of meetings. Paulet joined the newly named Privy Council as it developed into a formal entity where, after years of being under the control of first Wolsey and then Cromwell, the councillors were at last free to make decisions as a collective body.

The responsibilities of the Privy Council were wide-ranging, from the defence of the realm against both external threat and internal treason and rebellion to the sending of a man to the pillory for using lewd words. It regulated commerce, set standards for the conduct of individuals within society and authorised political appointments. As a new member of the Privy Council, during the first six months of 1543 Paulet saw warrants issued for the payment of accounts and debts. People were examined for unacceptable religious practices, both in their worship and in matters such as eating meat during Lent without a licence. In one specific example, twenty joiners were committed to the Tower for making a 'disguising' (masque) on a Sunday morning. A charge of piracy was considered, and orders were sent to victual ships and to send ships to join the fleet. Warrants were issued for the arrest and release of prisoners, passports authorised for travellers to enter the country and licences granted to importers of wine and other goods. There were commercial and financial regulations, disputes over pricing were resolved and disagreements between private individuals were heard and settled. Council decisions were relayed to sheriffs, justices and lord lieutenants by letter signed by several councillors, and sometimes accompanied by a proclamation or a commission. The Council made political decisions of both local and national importance but it was itself a centre of personal politics. Dissatisfied and power-seeking councillors would seek factional support in a bid to achieve their own political aims, a situation which would take on particular significance for Paulet during the reign of Edward VI.

After his swearing-in Paulet was next listed as attending the Privy Council on 11 December 1542 at Hampton Court.[209] He remained a member until his death nearly 30 years later and was assiduous in his attendance. In January and February 1543 he attended almost every day and during the first six months of the year he was at 145 Privy Council meetings, missing only sixteen.[210] It was not unusual for the Council to meet every day, including Sundays. During the first six months of 1543 there were only 21 days on which no formal meeting of the council took place, but meeting so regularly was no hardship for the councillors since many of them lived in the same building as the King.

Members met in the council chamber within the King's privy lodgings. Meetings began with the secretary detailing business and reading out letters and, when a matter was to be discussed, it was he who began the debate. The councillors then contributed to the discussion in ascending order of rank.[211] The King rarely attended these meetings and the two permanent Principal Secretaries formed an important link between him and the privy councillors. When the King went on progress the Privy Council split. Some councillors, accompanied by one secretary, travelled with the King while the remainder, and the other secretary, stayed in London as a skeleton council to attend to state business. The 'Council in London' received correspondence which they sent to the 'Council with the King' who took the decisions. These were then relayed back to the London councillors for them to act upon.

Paulet began 1543 at Hampton Court where the King had spent Christmas but, even amidst all the feasting and jollity, the Privy Council still held daily meetings except on Christmas Day itself. The first Privy Council meeting of the new year was attended by fourteen of the nineteen councillors – Archbishop of Canterbury Thomas Cranmer, Lord Chancellor Audley, Lord Privy Seal John Russell, Lord Hertford, Bishops Gardiner of Winchester and Bonner of Westminster, Lord St John (as Paulet was listed), Sir Thomas Cheyney, Sir John Gage, Sir Anthony Browne, Sir Anthony Wingfield, Sir Thomas Wriothesley, Sir Ralph Sadler and Mr Dacres. The King always resided at Westminster Palace, or nearby, during Parliament, and on 22 January Paulet moved with the Court to Westminster in time for the first sitting of the Lords. They remained there until 21 March when they moved to St James's Palace, before returning to Westminster on 16 April where they stayed for four weeks until Parliament finished and the King returned to Hampton Court.

When Parliament was in session Paulet often attended both the House of Lords and the Privy Council on the same day, although his parliamentary attendance was not as regular as at the Council. During the Parliament of 1543 he sat for only half of the 62 sittings of the Lords, yet he attended nearly all the council meetings. Parliament sat in the morning for up to six days a week with occasional afternoon sessions when there was business to finish. Sessions began at 8 or 9am while the Privy Council generally met between 10am and 2pm.

Life at Court started early in the day. The Gentlemen of the Privy Chamber were to be ready by 7am to dress the King, and the Grooms of the Privy Chamber were at work even earlier, making the fire and cleaning the King's chambers.[212] During the hot summer of 1540 the French ambassador, Charles de Marillac, reported that Henry arose between 5 and 6am, heard mass at 7am and then rode until dinner at 10am.[213] Chapuys records arriving to meet the King and councillors at 7 and 8am and on the occasion when he arrived unexpectedly at Westminster at dinner time, probably around 10 or 11am, he was considered to be late.[214] And yet this early start to the day did not mean the court retired to bed early. Sir Ralph Sadler, in a letter to Cromwell in 1536, referred to midnight as 'our accustomed hour in court to go to bed'.[215]

In the spring of 1543 Paulet received the great honour of being appointed a Knight of the Garter, the 311th since the order began.[216] It was an award he had long awaited, having been proposed but passed over on ten previous occasions since 1531. When the Garter Knights met at Westminster on St George's Day, 23 April, he was nominated by Sir Anthony Wingfield, Sir John Gage, Sir Anthony Browne, Sir Thomas Cheyney, Lord Russell, Lord Walden and the Duke of Norfolk – only the Earl of Hertford did not support him.[217] At any one time there were only 26 Garter Knights including the monarch and the Prince of Wales. The honour was instigated by Edward III as the highest reward for loyalty and military merit, but a knight could be deprived of the dignity if he was charged with a crime against Catholicism, attainted of high treason or deserted the battlefield. Lord William Paget was degraded from the Order in 1552, not only for his support of the Lord Protector Somerset but also because he was not born of a family of sufficiently high status, being 'no gentleman of blood', though this had not prevented his elevation in the first place.[218]

The King was not present at Paulet's installation a fortnight later so it is probable that he invested Paulet with his garter at Westminster soon after his election, tying it about his left leg below the knee. Paulet left the Court on 5 May to travel to Windsor for his creation alongside John Dudley, Viscount Lisle and Lord William Parr. The ceremony took place next day in St George's Chapel with the Earl of Hertford representing the King. The Knights processed to the Chapter House where each new recipient, dressed in a crimson gown, was girded with a sword before the procession moved into the quire of the Chapel. Here he took the oath to maintain the Statutes of the Order. A mantle or cloak of velvet of a dark blue 'heavenly colour' lined with white satin was put on him, a crimson velvet hood fastened on his right shoulder and a great collar or chain of gold with an image of St George killing the dragon was placed around his neck. Upon his head he wore a black cap with a feather. He was handed the Book of Statutes of the Order, and bowed to the altar and the Sovereign's stall before being led into his own stall, for Paulet the fifth on the Sovereign's side of the chapel. Above this stall his garter banner and sword with a helmet and crest were set up during his lifetime and his arms and hatchments were engraved on a metal plate and set upon the back of the stall where they remain to this day. After the communion service which followed there was a procession to the King's guard chamber for a magnificent banquet where Paulet's new title was proclaimed to a fanfare of trumpets.

The Statutes of a Knight of the Garter stated that Paulet must attend the annual ceremony of the Garter Knights unless he was out of England, or had a reasonable excuse and permission from the Sovereign. A request by him to Queen Elizabeth to be spared attendance at the St George's Day Feast in 1564 was refused with the response that she could not 'dispense with his attendance'.[219] On the eve, or 'vigil', of St George's Day he was to wear the 'habit' of the order with the gold collar from 3pm until after evensong and supper. On the day itself he was again to wear the 'habit' and collar at the morning procession, mass and evensong and until after supper. The gold collar weighed 30 ounces and was a chain in the style of garters. In the middle of each garter was a double rose, alternately red with a white centre and white with a red centre, and at the end of the collar was fastened an image of the saint. The collar was to be worn at principal and solemn feasts and on other days he was to wear a small chain of gold or a blue riband with the image of St George as a pendant, except in times of war and sickness. Paulet is portrayed in paintings wearing either his collar or a riband with the pendant.[220]

Paulet was riding high in the King's favour. On 16 May 1543, just days after the investiture, he was confirmed as Lord Chamberlain, an appointment that was first recorded in the House of Lords Journal on 4 April when he was described as 'Lord Chamberlain of the King's Household'.[221] The Lord Chamberlain oversaw the operation and ceremonial of all the public rooms leading to the King's privy chambers, rooms such as the Great Hall, the Guard Chamber and the Presence Chamber. Here the majesty of the King was displayed to maximum effect through the magnificence of the rooms and in the ceremonial observed by the nobles, gentlemen and servants who frequented them. The elaborate costumes of the courtiers and the gold and jewels they wore added to the splendour of the court. These were the rooms through which the King walked and Paulet was responsible for ensuring that all the courtiers, visitors and servants who came under his jurisdiction in these chambers behaved in an acceptable manner. Assisted by the Vice-Chamberlain, he controlled a staff of yeomen ushers, waiters, grooms and pages. He issued orders to the Gentlemen Pensioners and to the Yeomen of the Guard through their captain, and to the cupbearers, carvers, sewers, physicians and chaplains as well as musicians and entertainers. The position put Paulet in close contact with the King – he was the man who applied the royal wishes in the court and who also received the King's complaints.

The Court was especially busy during law terms, and when Parliament was sitting and its members were in London, but there was also a fluctuating population of diplomats, men on business and those who just wanted the social prestige of being seen there. The public rooms were always busy. Here the courtiers and visitors waited to catch a glimpse of the King, perhaps to present a petition to him or in the hope that they might be called to attend upon him. For those hoping to make their way at Court it was vital to be seen both by the King and by prospective patrons. 'Out of sight' really could be 'out of mind' when a courtier was away. In these rooms the courtiers lived out their lives, making friends and enemies. They exchanged news, arranged marriages, carried out business and worked for advancement and power.

Hampton Court Palace today still provides an example of how some of these rooms were laid out. Most people could gain access to the Great Hall but only nobles, knights and gentlemen who held posts within the household or others with special permission were allowed further, into the Great Watching or Guard Chamber and then the Presence Chamber beyond. Access between rooms was controlled by ushers who stood on duty at the connecting doors, and movement became more restricted as one moved closer to the King's own rooms. Entry to the King's Privy Chamber, the heart of the palace, was through a short corridor from the Presence Chamber and was restricted to the King's favourites, privy councillors and the staff of the Privy Chamber.

Paulet walked across Base Court at Hampton Court Palace on his way to the King's apartments. He paused to bow to Sir William Paget, making sure that he did not bow as low as Sir William who, as the King's Secretary and only lately knighted, was junior in rank to himself. The two men conversed briefly before Paulet moved into the shadow of the clock tower and turned up the staircase before halting at the entrance to the Great Hall. He always felt overawed by the size and magnificence of this great chamber which had only been built a few years earlier and which was designed to impress. Perhaps most of all he was overawed by the realisation that this Hall and the chambers of state which lay beyond, together with their occupants, were his responsibility. As Lord Chamberlain this was his domain. He walked beneath the minstrels' gallery into the hall where trestle tables and benches were ready for the servants' dinner. The whitewashed walls were bare but he knew how magnificent the hall looked when hung with tapestries for banquets and state events. Overhead the great hammerbeam roof soared above him, intricately carved and decorated with royal emblems and painted carved heads.

As Paulet stepped up onto the dais the usher at the door recognised him and moved to one side to let him pass. The Great Watching Chamber was smaller than the hall but more impressive in its decoration. Around the walls were hung tapestries embroidered with gold thread and depicting Bible stories and historical and mythological characters. On the ceiling gilded batons enclosed colourful badges depicting the King's genealogy. These devices were displayed all around the palace in glass window panes, wood, stone and plaster and woven into tapestries and they served to remind courtiers and visitors of Henry VIII's right to be King of England.

Paulet moved among the men who stood within the chamber, stopping to speak to some of them. Sir Anthony Browne asked Paulet if he could intervene in a dispute over a wardship, and Lord Russell tried to interest him in a piece of land he planned to sell. This was always a good place to do business while people were waiting in hope of seeing the King. Paulet surveyed the men of the King's Guard who stood along the sides of the chamber and were responsible for the King's safety. They were smart in their bright red uniforms, and he sensed that they stood a little taller when they saw him approach. He wondered what conversations they overheard as they waited to perform their ceremonial role of escorting the King and lining his route around the Palace.

Paulet turned towards the end of the chamber and the usher opened the door for him to pass through into the Presence Chamber. The decoration of these rooms became increasingly sumptuous as he moved closer to the King's private apartments although they offered little comfort to the waiting courtiers. They were large and could be cold in winter when people would gather around the big stone fireplaces for warmth. The Presence Chamber was hung with even more expensive tapestries than those in the Watching Chamber and was similarly sparsely furnished with just a cupboard covered by a richly embroidered tapestry. There were no chairs for the courtiers since they were not allowed to sit in the presence of the King but at the far end, beneath a red silken canopy of state, stood a large chair, the King's throne. This chair and the canopy were symbols of the King's authority and, even in the King's absence, Paulet bowed towards it.

Standing by the window the Duke of Norfolk spoke to Sir John Gage, the Comptroller, and Sir Anthony Wingfield, the Vice-Chamberlain. As Paulet greeted them the sound of trumpets echoed through the palace announcing that the King was soon to eat. The King often took his meals in private in his Privy Chamber but today he was to dine in the Presence Chamber. The dining table which stood before the King's chair was covered with fine white linen cloths which reached almost to the floor. A silver spoon lay to the right of a silver trencher and a folded napkin to the left. Fine white manchet loaves wrapped in embroidered linen were placed beside an intricately engraved silver salt. At the side of the chamber a cupboard and a table were covered with cloths, the first bearing gold and silver gilt drinking cups and flagons of wine and ale, the other bowls of water and towels for the King to wash his hands.

When he was satisfied that everything was in its correct position Paulet walked through to the hall-place, a waiting area where Sir John Gage and Sir Anthony Wingfield were already standing, and joined the head of the procession of Gentlemen Ushers who carried in the great silver gilt serving dishes. He watched as they set down the platters in order upon the table, together with small dishes of sauces to accompany various meats. Bowls of vegetable pottage and stewed beef were laid out alongside roasted goose and swan. Delicacies of almond cream, a tart of prunes, fritters and jellied milk stood beside pigeon pie and stewed venison, mutton and capon. When the King had eaten sufficient the remainder would be collected together and given to poor people at the gates of the palace. Everything was ready and Paulet moved into the next chamber. The King was washing his hands in a basin of water offered to him by Lord Chancellor Audley and, when this formality was over, Paulet escorted him into the Presence Chamber to take his seat at the table. Paulet's role in attending the King at dinner was now over and, as the King's carver began to slice and prepare the meat, Paulet and others who were not needed for the serving of the food withdrew to take their own meal.[222]

By the end of May, Paulet had left the Court and was at Westminster with Cranmer, Norfolk, Hertford, Bonner, Gage, Sir Richard Rich and Sir John Baker. The Regent of Flanders, fearing an invasion from France, had asked Henry for help and the 'Council in London' were levying men and supplies to send to Calais. Meanwhile the King and Privy Council were at Harwich from where they sent the King's signet ring so that Paulet could authorise letters with the King's seal.[223] About 5,000 troops crossed the Channel but no major engagements took place; instead plans were laid for an attack on France the following year.

Paulet met the King when he landed at Greenwich on 19 June but returned to London the following day.[224] On 17 June the King, trusting in the 'loyalty, wisdom, integrity, care and industry' of the Duke of Norfolk, Paulet, Audley, Gardiner, Bonner and Gage, commissioned these men to meet the Scottish ambassador to discuss a future marriage between Prince Edward and Mary Queen of Scots.[225] A marriage alliance between England and Scotland would bring Scotland under English control. There had been continuous enmity between the two countries and the negotiations included English control over the Scottish government during Mary's minority and peace between the realms. The discussions were fruitful and Paulet returned to Greenwich by 26 June for the signing of the marriage treaty on 1 July.[226] However, many of the powerful Scottish clans refused to agree to this union of crowns, which they felt had been forced on them, and the treaty collapsed the following December when it was annulled by the Scottish Parliament.

The Court moved to Westminster after the signing of the treaty and then on to Hampton Court for the King's marriage to Catherine Parr on 12 July, but their stay there was very short. On the 15th a plague proclamation was issued from the palace forbidding Londoners to enter the gates of any buildings where the King and Queen were living, and forbidding the return of court servants who had travelled to London.[227] Two days later the Court packed up and set off to Surrey, to Oatlands (near Weybridge) and Guildford, in a move to get well away from London and did not return to the city for over four months.

On Christmas Eve the King and Court travelled from Westminster to Hampton Court for the festivities. The previous day, Sunday, Queen Catherine's brother, Lord William, had been raised to the title of Earl of Essex and her uncle, Sir William Parr, had been created Lord Parr of Horton. Paulet, with Lord Russell, accompanied Sir William at the ceremony, and on 1 January 1544 the three men were together again when they accompanied Sir Thomas Wriothesley for his creation as Baron, Wriothesley being led between Paulet and Russell, and with Parr bearing the robe.[228]

Many courtiers spent time at Court during the Christmas season. Advent, particularly Christmas Eve, was a time of fasting but after mass on Christmas Day the celebrations started and continued until their climax on Twelfth Night – a last day of brilliance and extravagance before returning to the gloom of winter. The Great Hall was probably decorated with holly, as the Inns of Court halls were, and with a large boar's head as the centrepiece of the table. Food and wine were plentiful and the Master of the Revels organised entertainments of music, dancing, masques and plays. Throughout the Christmas season the entertainments were enlivened by the 'Lord of Misrule' aided by his often unruly 'courtiers' and 'servants'. Henry Machyn describes how on 4 January 1553, King Edward VI's Lord of Misrule rode around the streets of London, arrayed in a gown of purple velvet with 'spangles' of silver. The Inns of Court and some nobles selected their own Lords of Misrule to enliven their celebrations. In 1557 Paulet's Lord of Misrule was accompanied by 'a great company of musicians and disguisers, and with trumpets and drums, and with his counsellors and other officers, and there was a devil shooting of fire, and one was like death with a dart in his hand.'[229] But although they were supposed to add to the festivities, their participation could be disruptive, sometimes wreaking havoc. On 27 December 1523 one 'Master of Misrule', William Babyngton, killed Robert Wolfe while he was at Christmas Games.[230]

The first day of January, rather than Christmas, was the time of giving and receiving gifts between friends and family, servants and masters. Courtiers gave gifts to the King and in return they received one from him. The first record of Paulet giving a gift and receiving one from the King is on 1 January 1534, and he would undoubtedly have presented the monarch with a gift each year thereafter.[231] Courtiers' gifts to the King were items such as gilt cups, books, clocks, a decorated tablet of gold or money and these were borne in by their servants to be presented as a fanfare of trumpets sounded. In return, money or a gift of a gilt cup or bowl was delivered to the sender. In 1562 Queen Elizabeth gave Paulet a gilt cup with a cover weighing 33 ounces in return for his gift to her of a purse of crimson satin containing 40 angells, a sum of £20.[232] After the birth of Prince Edward, Paulet was among those courtiers who also exchanged New Year gifts with the young Prince. Although his gifts to the baby were traditional presents, such as gilt jugs with lids, some of the other donors' gifts reflected the Prince's age – a bell of gold with a whistle, a bonnet and needlework – while others, such as two oxen, provided food for the Prince's household.[233]

The New Year was celebrated at Court on 1 January although there was a dual calendar system in England. The civil calendar which began on 1 January was the Julian calendar but state and Church documents were dated according to the Church calendar, which began the year on 25 March, the date of the Annunciation. For many years, monks and clerics had been the clerks of the country and documents had been dated according to the calendar they followed. The calendars were standardised in 1752 when the Gregorian calendar was introduced – eleven days were cut from the calendar that year to compensate for the divergence of the calendar from the solar year and the New Year was fixed at 1 January. However, officials such as Paulet would have also been familiar with a third dating system, used particularly for state documents such as Acts of Parliament, which was based on the reign of the monarch where the beginning of each year was the date of accession.

8

The Siege of Boulogne and Lord Great Master

England began 1544 under the threat of war. In the summer of 1541 France and Spain had fallen out with each other and both sides had courted Henry for his support in the event of a future conflict. The King, meanwhile, had returned to his long-term ambition to conquer Scotland and remove the French faction which ruled the country, but diplomacy and a fruitless invasion attempt led by the Duke of Norfolk in 1542 had failed to bring the country under English control. On 24 November 1542 an attack by 10,000 Scots was defeated at Solway Moss. Three weeks later the Scottish King, James V, died, leaving his country under the rule of his baby daughter, Mary Stuart, and the control of the French faction. With the failure of the negotiations in 1543 for peace allied to a marriage agreement between Prince Edward and the infant Queen, Henry made plans to invade Scotland again.

The King's intention to fight in Scotland and later in France was going to take a heavy toll on his coffers and in March 1544 Paulet was commissioned with Sir Thomas Wriothesley, Sir Richard Rich and Sir Richard Southwell to raise money for the wars by selling lands, lead, captured ships and their cargoes, leases and wards. The preamble to the commission stated that 'the King intends to pass in person into France against his ancient enemy the French King.' He also planned to 'noye, invade or defend the realm of Scotland' whose people from time to time attempt to 'noye and destroy us'.[234] Paulet became involved in the preparations for war in February when he was appointed, with Bishop Gardiner and Sir Robert Bowes, to organise the provision of victuals for the King's army in Scotland.[235] At the time he was unaware that he would be overseeing military victualling for over eighteen months as the army fought against both the Scots and the French and then defended England's shores against invasion.

The Earl of Hertford, Edward Seymour, sailed to Scotland that spring to attack Edinburgh and the surrounding towns but, as with the Pilgrimage of Grace, funding was a serious problem. This was exacerbated by the size of the army – 15,000 men and another 3,000 'men of war' (sailors and the ships' own fighting forces) – together with 7,000 horsemen who travelled by land.[236] Hertford wrote to the Privy Council on 28 April complaining of a 'great lack of money' and that there was not enough to pay a month's wages. There were complaints about the food, that the pipes or casks of beef did not contain the expected quantities and that the pieces were small. Much of the bread was missing and much of what they had was 'mouldy and ill baked'. In explaining the discrepancies in the beef, Gardiner and Paulet blamed the shortages on clerical errors but insisted that there should still be sufficient food and that 'if much dried by salt, the beef must weigh lighter'.[237] The campaign did not last long. After attacks on Leith and Edinburgh in early May Hertford withdrew leaving Scotland still under the control of the French faction.

Meanwhile preparations were underway for war with France. In 1543, after two years of overtures from France and Spain, Henry had sided with Spain against his long-standing enemy. France's enduring hostility to England, and her involvement in the anti-English faction in Scotland, made Spain seem the obvious partner. Henry and Charles V agreed to invade France during the summer of 1544 with the intention of taking Paris.

More money was needed and the clergy and nobility, Paulet among them, were asked by Henry to lend money to pay for the war. [238] They were also ordered to provide the King's army. Muster books were drawn up showing the number of soldiers to be furnished by the gentlemen of England from the King's Council downwards. Paulet, as Lord St John, was ordered to provide a contingent of 100 horsemen and 300 footmen. This was a large contribution when compared with those demanded of other privy councillors. Although the Duke of Norfolk armed 100 horsemen and 500 footmen, the Bishop of Winchester provided only 100 horsemen and 200 footmen, Lord Lisle 100 horsemen, Sir William Paget 100 footmen and Sir William Petre 20 footmen.[239] Paulet's son, John, and his brothers, Richard and George, were also to provide men. Since contributions, whether of money or men, were generally assessed on the donor's wealth it appears that Paulet was already recognised as a man of substance.

Courtiers were making their own preparations for the wars. In March 1543 Chapuys had informed Mary of Hungary, the Governor of the Netherlands, that England was preparing to fight the 'common enemy'. He picked out Paulet in particular from those who had applied to him for a licence to export armour from countries under the Governor's control. Paulet wished to import 100 harnesses for footmen and 100 pikes in preparation for the war in Scotland. 'Certainly he deserves it ... an honourable and wise gentleman ... I most humbly beg your Majesty to grant him permission, which I have no doubt would be immediately granted were your Majesty to know the qualities, virtues and good inclinations of the said knight.'[240] At some point Paulet paid £8 for a complete set of 'harness', or body armour, which was suitable for the battlefield.[241] Others were preparing for the possibility that they might not return from the war. On 30 April 1544 Charles Lord Mountjoy wrote his will in case he was 'slain in war' in France. His father had been the first to nominate Paulet for the Garter in 1531 and Mountjoy's will included a bequest to Paulet. He did return from the war but died later that year.[242]

With his experience of the Pilgrimage of Grace and the war in Scotland, and as Comptroller and Treasurer, Paulet was an obvious choice to be victualler for the army and he earned a reputation for his competency. He and Gardiner 'controlled all the victuallers in the host and who were so learned in arithmetic and geometry and in making accounts that they could show by signs and figures how many pieces of bread would suffice for all the people who were under the King on that side of the sea'.[243] On this occasion the two men were responsible for supplying an army of 40,000 men, not only finding food but also transporting it by land and sea. Their role was absolutely vital to the success of the invading force. Although the soldiers were described as 'men of strength' and showing 'great courage and great presence of mind in danger' the Venetian ambassador believed that they needed to be 'largely supplied with victuals; so it is evident that they cannot endure much fatigue'.[244]

Assisted as usual by the officers of the Greencloth, Paulet and Gardiner found themselves once again facing demands, this time for lower-priced victuals. Throughout June the Duke of Norfolk complained to the Privy Council that there was a scarcity of food and that the soldiers could not afford what was available because the prices were too high.[245] Even members of the Privy Chamber complained that food prices in France were high. Goods were bought with the King's money and then sold to the soldiers by the victuallers at fixed prices sufficient to recoup the purchase cost.

Under the onslaught of complaints, Gardiner and Paulet agreed to lower the prices even if the King made a loss, although they would not extend the price reduction to beer brewed in England or to fresh goods.[246] The scarcity and cost of food did not, however, affect the King. After his arrival in France, venison was shipped to Boulogne from Hampton Court.[247] By the end of the campaign Paulet himself appears to have been seriously out of pocket. He details how he was charged with responsibility for the King's ships and the ordering of victuals for 1,500 men in Boulogne and 400 men of his own, for 'the keeping of his tables for all comers and goers' and the victualling of Montreuil by over 100 carts a day, all at an estimated cost of £3,000 more than the King's allowance.[248]

During June 1544, Paulet and Sir John Gage, the Comptroller of the Household, supervised the embarkation at Dover for Calais. On 2 July Charles Brandon, Duke of Suffolk, reported to the Council how the two men had been 'wonderfully diligent', that most of the horses and men had already been 'shipped' and he expected the two men to organise musters in France.[249] Paulet had arrived in Calais by 8 July and the King landed there on the 14th.[250] Henry was suffering poor health due to the ulcers on his leg and cancelled the proposed march to Paris, setting Suffolk and Norfolk to besiege Boulogne and Montreuil.

On 19 July Suffolk moved the camp from Calais to Boulogne and began the artillery bombardment against the town. In his own account of the siege, Paulet portrays himself as one of the commanders (an assertion borne out by a memorandum from the Council) with control of the trenches around Lower or Basse Boulogne, which was the area around the harbour, and of three mines.[251] The Duke of Suffolk, Lieutenant of the Army, and half a dozen 'expert' men had established that Boulogne was mineable. The mines were underground passages, excavated under the wall or gate of the town, in which gunpowder was placed to blow up the fortifications. The besieging force dug trenches in zigzag lines and established concealed batteries which were aimed at the point where the mines would finish. Preparations for an assault could take weeks. While the sappers were digging the mines, skirmishes were made against the enemy, and temporary fortifications were raised in the field to protect the army from the continual artillery assaults made daily from the town. Many men were killed or wounded and the soldiers' tents were 'shott through … till the King had raised a fence against the town which made a great staye'.[252] The two opposing armies were living very close to each other. The trenches were so near to the walls that the soldiers in them could speak to the men of the town and a letter from Paulet to the Lieutenant of Boulogne was thrown over the city wall.[253] Some English miners only narrowly escaped death when the French, hearing them tunnelling, had come to attack them and would have 'killed them in their mine had they not made the better shift'.[254]

On Monday, 21 July, Basse Boulogne fell and the French were driven into the high town. Two days later, the King asked for Paulet to travel to him. Suffolk replied asking him not to take Paulet away because 'he is here one of my hands and the man whose painful and hardy service all manner ways cannot be here well forborne ... If your Majesty knew what a lack I should have of him you would not take him hence.' However, he did agree that Paulet should travel to the King early next morning although Paulet was probably back with Suffolk by 26 July, when the King himself reached Boulogne.[255] Paulet was proving to be indispensable to Suffolk. The two men were on very good terms and when Brandon died the following year Paulet was one of the three executors of his will.

While the fighting for Boulogne continued all through August and into September, the two sides were holding diplomatic talks. On 19 August Paulet was instructed to hold one visiting French emissary, charge him with being a 'spy' and interrogate him about the state of the town and the men inside.[256] By Thursday, 11 September, three mines had reached the walls of the castle in the upper town and a 'train of powder being set to the castle' the King saw the castle fall, injuring many soldiers with flying stones. Next day a Privy Council memorandum suggested how the commanders Suffolk, Lord Admiral Lisle, Paulet and Mr 'Candyshe' should order their men for the assault at the several breaches which had been created.[257] The size of the army made communication between units difficult and it was decided that when an assault on the town began each commander should warn the others by the shooting of a gun so that each knew what was done.[258] The town was attacked and early in the morning of Saturday, 13 September, two French ambassadors left Boulogne and were escorted by Paulet and Sir Thomas Palmer to discuss terms for surrender with Suffolk and the Council. It was agreed that those people who would not swear allegiance to the King would be allowed to 'avoid' the town and next day the ambassadors made the 'rendition' to the King who later watched 4,000 men, women and children leave Boulogne.[259]

Montreuil, Henry's second target, was in a strong position and held out against the Duke of Norfolk's siege. Norfolk's force was not as well supplied as the army with the King at Boulogne and there were complaints of a scarcity of drink and bread. It also appears that he did not have enough men to secure Montreuil, leaving opportunities for the French to escape.[260] On hearing that Charles V had made peace with France and that the Dauphin was set to march against Norfolk, Henry ordered a retreat from Montreuil. Norfolk and Paulet set out with 5,000 men to raise the siege and, beginning during the night of 27 September, the siege was ended by 10am.[261] The King, satisfied with his success at Boulogne, returned to England on 30 September but before leaving France he knighted 27 men, one of whom was Paulet's son, John.[262]

Paulet was back in Dover by 9 October and was ordered to stay there until the army had returned from France. Henry, determined to keep Boulogne, had left Norfolk and Suffolk to protect the town but when it was known that the Dauphin was marching to besiege them the two commanders moved their troops to Calais leaving Boulogne victualled and garrisoned. Paulet was soon sending supplies to Calais by the 'next wind' and providing sufficient quantities of wheat, malt, beef, butter and cheese to victual the ships for fourteen days at a time.[263] Even so, by 20 October there were reports of a scarcity of food at Calais and Boulogne and Paulet sent commissioners to Kent to order that wheat should be threshed and brought to coastal ports, along with malt, for shipment to France. Despite a meeting between the ambassadors of England, France and Spain to conclude peace terms, the French fleet was harrying English ships between Calais, Dover and Sandwich. Supplies were laden in boats to steal across singly at night, and the army could only return to England by stealth when the weather allowed. Paulet had returned to the Court at Westminster by 23 November and spent Christmas with the King at Greenwich, but he continued to oversee the transport of supplies to France until the following summer.[264]

During the spring of 1545, in England plans were in hand for the defence of the realm. France and England still disputed control of Boulogne, and France had started to build up its navy to attack the English fleet. There were fears of a threat of invasion from both the French and the Scots. By June, as well as Hertford's army in the north, 'three great armies', each with at least 30,000 soldiers, had been positioned in Essex, Kent and the west of the country.[265] In May, Paulet had two commissions in Hampshire, one to protect part of the south coast of Hampshire and the Isle of Wight and the other to call up the military force in Hampshire and the surrounding counties in preparation for war.[266] On 28 May he was at Portsmouth organising the provision of ten ships and victuals, and two days later he joined the King at Greenwich where he stayed throughout June, apart from five days when he and Norfolk visited the north and west counties to put them 'in a state of defence'.[267]

Paulet returned to Portsmouth in July, rejoining the Privy Council when the King arrived there on the 15th to oversee preparations for the expected French invasion.[268] On Sunday, four days later, the Emperor's ambassador, Francis van der Delft, wrote to Charles V that whilst the King had been at dinner on his flagship, the *Great Henry*, in Portsmouth harbour 200 French ships had arrived in the Solent. The King had left the ship, and the English fleet sailed to encounter the French, shooting at five galleys that had entered the harbour. But the English were becalmed through lack of wind and could not leave port. When the wind rose the *Mary Rose*, ship of Vice-Admiral George Carew, heeled over as she turned and water entered by the lowest row of gun ports, which had been left open after firing. The ship foundered and only 25 or 30 of the 500 crewmen did not go down with her. There followed a week of skirmishes as the two fleets fired at each other and the English awaited the threatened invasion. On Tuesday, 21 July the French landed on the Isle of Wight and burnt a dozen small houses but were opposed by a force of 8,000; a week later the French fleet sailed away.

By 31 July the King and all the Privy Council, except Suffolk, Lisle and Paulet, had left Portsmouth for safety, taking a leisurely progress through Surrey on their way to Windsor. Lisle, Suffolk and Paulet remained to face any further attack and had some hope of recovering the *Mary Rose* which had been 'with such rashness and negligence cast away'.[269] On Saturday, 1 August Paget, the King's secretary, wrote that the raising would require 'two great hulks, four of greatest hoys, five of greatest cables that may be had … thirty venetian mariners and one venetian carpenter.'[270] The three councillors put plans into action and on 5 August they reported to Paget that three cables had been tied to the masts, 'other ingens to wey her upp', and on every side was a 'hulk to sett her upright'. She was to be raised up supported by the two ships on either side, emptied of water and ordnance and brought 'by littel and litle' to the shore. But four days later the cable broke the ship's foremast and more time was needed to drag her to shallow ground. It appears that the two ships were needed elsewhere because Lisle and Paulet argued that owing to the importance of the ship and the ordnance in her, the two hulks needed by the army should stay with the *Mary Rose*. However, the attempt to save the ship failed and the *Mary Rose* was lost when the Lord Admiral called away all the ships allowing her to sink again. It was not until 1982 that her remains were lifted from the seabed.[271]

Paulet had become closely involved in the salvage attempt because, on 8 August, he had replaced Suffolk as Governor of Portsmouth. The Duke, who had been ordered back to Court, had written to Paget that he thought the King wished Paulet to have charge of Portsmouth as, being in his own county, he was the 'meetest man' to organise the defence and victualling of the town and the Isle of Wight.[272] Paulet took control as governor at a very difficult time. At the beginning of August it was reported that a disease was spreading amongst the soldiers and mariners and they were suffering 'swelling in their heads and faces and in their legs, and divers of them with the bloody flux'.[273] This may have been the same contagious disease that had first been noted amongst soldiers returning from Calais the previous October and which killed many of Paulet's own horsemen.[274] However, Paulet believed the sickness was caused by provisions that had rotted in the heat in the ships. Many men were dying and he was ordered to dismiss all the ships which carried wheat and to buy 'fair hulks', clean vessels, thus removing infected wheat.[275] He also replaced the sick men and re-stocked the ships with two weeks supply of food, which was otherwise intended for the Isle of Wight and Portsmouth garrisons, but he warned that this would then leave no provisions for re-victualling the latter two weeks later. The Privy Council acknowledged this and sent large sums of money to him – £5,000 on 16 August and another £2,000 two days later. Paulet was proved correct. Lisle had been ordered to leave Portsmouth and take the navy to sea on 11 August, and on 20 August the Admiral reported that the ships were waiting for victuals to come out from Rye and that a shortage of beer might result in the sailors having to drink water. Water stored in barrels was likely to be insanitary. By the next day some men were already drinking water and Lisle delivered beer to other ships from his own vessel's supply.[276] To exacerbate matters there was talk of sending a force to France and Paulet was ordered to stockpile food and drink for September and October against the possibility of Admiral Lisle sailing to Calais with 5,000 men.[277]

Once again Paulet was trying to equip and feed a large number of men with limited resources. Lisle had 12,000 men on over 100 ships. The quantity and quality of the victuals was not the only issue affecting the military. Lisle sent a message to the King that the men in the army needed coats 'having not a rag to hang upon their backs' and also that they were fed up with being shut in the close confines of the ships. The King agreed that money should be provided to buy coats for all those travelling to France.[278] However, Lord Chancellor Wriothesley was not happy with this and on 14 September he wrote to Cecil on the need for more men and for money for coats, asking the Council to remember that 'this year and last year the King has spent about £1,300,000' and lamenting 'the danger of the time to come'. 'Lands are being consumed, plate of the realm molten and coined … You write to me still pay, pay, prepare for this and that.'[279] Wriothesley's concern over the lack of money was a matter which had to be addressed the following year.

By 11 September the flux was decimating the men on the ships and Paulet was facing the difficulty of providing fit men to send to Calais. Men could not be moved out of the ships for fear of spreading the disease and on 14 September he informed the Council that only about 700 men were both free of duties such as fishing and were fit for sailing.[280] Within days Paulet himself was seriously ill, having succumbed to the disease.

As Paulet tried to move his body rebelled. He lay back upon the bed within his chamber at Basing House and sighed as he thought of the news which had just been brought to him. His physician, Dr Augustyn, had died that morning of a painful disease which he had most probably caught from Paulet. By his profession the doctor was associated with such risk but Paulet was sad that he should have been the source of the good doctor's death. He had been at work on 16 September and now here he was, only days later, as weak as a baby. The first sign of illness had been pain and discomfort in his bowels and then a bodily chill followed by a fever. He had watched other men develop these symptoms so had known what would happen next. A day later the diarrhoea began, worse than any he had suffered before – the constant feeling of needing to empty his bowels when all he could pass was a little jelly-like mucus and blood, and the pain and burning sensation associated with his exertions. He had felt weak, so weak, unable to take himself to the close-stool without assistance. His mouth was dry and he was so thirsty that he could hardly move his tongue, yet water did little to ease the feeling. Dr Augustyn had told him that he had twice swooned on one afternoon, and Paulet had seen enough men with the bloody flux to know that his face must look haggard, his eyes sunken in his face. He had known that his chance of survival was small. So many men had died in Portsmouth that the privy councillors had stopped visiting him for fear of contracting the disease.

The doctor had given him his best care. Paulet had been put to bed in a dark, quiet chamber and fed silverweed tea with peppermint, which was especially good for bloody flux and camomile tea to treat inflammation and pain in his gut. He had not suffered the nausea and vomiting which he had witnessed in other men but perhaps the doctor's infusion of ginger root had prevented that. The treatments worked and Paulet remembered with relief how after four days he had felt some improvement.

Dr Augustyn had thought that Paulet would survive the illness and had made plans to move his patient to Basing House to recover. Paulet had known the journey would be exhausting but he was sure he would recover more quickly at home with Elizabeth to care for him than in Portsmouth. His servants had made him as comfortable as they could, on a bed made up on a cart, but the journey had been long and uncomfortable. The ground was very dry and the road surfaces were hard and rutted. On the first day he was brought to his house at Netley but by the time they arrived Dr Augustyn was showing signs of the disease. Paulet agreed that the doctor should remain at Netley and try to ride out the sickness but as he continued his journey, he knew that he might never see his friend again. Paulet reached Basing House after spending a night in Winchester on the way. He felt such relief on being driven through the gateway of his own house to be greeted by Elizabeth. He was an old man, already over 60 years of age, and he knew that he was lucky to have survived an illness to which thousands of younger men had succumbed. But he was still very ill and it would take a great deal of care and effort for him to recover fully.[281]

During Paulet's illness the King wrote him 'letters of comfort' and, after summoning him to Court before he was fully recovered, the King granted Paulet the rare honour of allowing him to sit beside him.[282] The reason for the summons appears to have been to reward Paulet for his efforts during the previous two years by appointing him to three new offices – Lord Great Master of the Household, Lord President of the King's Council and Warden and Chief Justice for all the King's forests and parks south of the River Trent.[283]

Paulet was fit enough to attend Privy Council meetings by 18 November 1545 and on 23 November, at the opening of Parliament, he assumed the title of Lord Great Master for the first time.[284] This post was the pinnacle of the Household hierarchy and gave Paulet complete control of the King's Household, both above and below stairs, ceremonial and domestic. His predecessor as Lord Great Master was the Duke of Suffolk, who had died at Guildford on 24 August and it is probable that Paulet had already been selected to fill the vacancy when he fell ill. It appears that John Dudley, Viscount Lisle, was hoping to receive the post himself. He wrote to Paget on 22 September referring to a conversation between them concerning the possibility of Lisle acquiring an office 'which was lately in a great man's hands and now is determined upon one that at our then communing was said to be sore sick'.[285]

In his re-organisation of the Household in 1540, Cromwell had replaced the position of Lord Steward with the new post of Lord Great Master in an attempt to increase control over spending and to improve efficiency. This brought all aspects of court life under the command of one officer who was to have overall control of the *Domus Providencie* and the *Domus Regie Magnificencie*, and thus over the Lord Chamberlain. The post existed for only thirteen years, being held by three people – Suffolk, William Paulet and Lord Lisle – before being abandoned by Queen Mary in favour of a return to the post of Lord Steward.

Paulet's appointment has to be seen as the reward for his competence and a recognition of the esteem in which he was held by Henry VIII. The position of Lord Great Master was highly prestigious and the holders were people of high rank. Brandon was a duke, a close friend of the King and was married to the King's youngest sister, Mary. Dudley was an earl (later a duke) and assumed the title of Lord Great Master while he was the most powerful man in Edward VI's Privy Council. Paulet had no comparable background or power. It was a splendid promotion but it is perhaps strange that, with the King's preoccupation with magnificence and grandeur, he did not elevate Paulet, the supreme head of his household, to a title higher than Lord St John, especially since the man who replaced Paulet as Lord Chamberlain was Henry Fitzalan, Earl of Arundel, over whom Paulet held seniority in court. Paulet was the only Lord Great Master or Lord Steward in the sixteenth century who was not at least of the rank of earl and while Henry VIII ruled he remained Lord St John.

As Lord Great Master, Paulet took on all the duties assigned in the Ordinances to the Lord Steward. He had responsibility for all the King's houses and the army of servants they required, controlling all the provision and service departments and the Counting House. He sat on the Board of the Greencloth as chief financial officer of the Household and adjudicated in disputes, maintaining control through the Cofferer who ran the Counting House in his absence. Because priority would have been given to attending on the King and to Privy Council meetings, Paulet's attendance at the Board of the Greencloth and as Master of the Court of Wards and Liveries would have been limited. The Lord Great Master assumed the Lord Steward's role of 'judge of lyfe and lymme' within the Court and of keeping the Court 'according to the law and ancient custome of the King's house'.[286] He upheld the law both within the Court and in the surrounding verge, an area extending to a distance of up to twelve miles. Controlling the movements and behaviour of people within the many buildings was not easy. Poor behaviour among the courtiers brought dishonour upon the Court and the Monarch. A court full of ambitious young men was a potential source of trouble because they were all keen to uphold their honour and, if allowed, would resolve their differences by participating in sword duels. Much attention was given to protecting the King's property from thieves and watch was kept for the illicit removal of valuables and illegal 'perquisites'. Attempts were made to exclude undesirable people, especially at times of plague and sweating sickness, and any member of the Court who wished for temporary leave of absence had to have a licence from either the King or one of the senior officers of the Court.[287]

Paulet benefited greatly from Suffolk's death. In addition to being Lord Great Master the Duke had also held the two other posts that Paulet received – those of Lord President of the Council and Warden and Justice of the King's forests south of the River Trent. Suffolk had become Lord President when Sir Thomas More replaced Wolsey as Chancellor in 1529, splitting the previous historical connection between those two titles. After his appointment as Lord Great Master in 1540, the Duke had held the two posts of Lord President and Lord Great Master concurrently, a situation which continued under his two successors. Now that the Council was not controlled by a single powerful man such as Wolsey or Cromwell there was the potential for the Lord President to use his position for his own ends, but neither Suffolk nor Paulet appear to have done this. The President's role was to chair the Council meetings when the two most senior councillors, the Lord Chancellor and the Lord Treasurer, were absent and he held the power to convene and disband the Council. Suffolk was a soldier rather than a politician and, at times of military activity, was often absent from Court but his rank and status did give him sufficient authority to elicit respect and obedience within the Court and at Council meetings. Paulet was very junior in rank by comparison, having held the title of Lord St John for only a few years, but his age and experience must have counted for much. Paulet was a conscientious councillor, attending meetings regularly. In Council discussions the Lord President was the final councillor to speak and so was well placed to influence other councillors' decisions. However, Paulet does not appear to have tried to usurp control while Henry VIII was alive, and during Edward VI's reign, when he retained the position of Lord President for a further three years, his authority to convene and dissolve the Council was assumed by Somerset, removing most of Paulet's potential power. The Earl of Warwick reassumed the full authority of the office to control Council business when he succeeded Paulet as Lord President in 1550.

The real prestige of the title of Lord President was the position it gave Paulet in the pecking order of the Court. He now ranked third behind Lord Chancellor Wriothesley and Lord Treasurer Norfolk and ahead of the Lord Privy Seal, the Great Chamberlain and the Lord Chamberlain, all of whom were earls. He also took precedence over those dukes and marquises who had higher aristocratic rank than him but who held no post at Court.

Why Henry chose Paulet to succeed Suffolk as Lord Great Master and Lord President is not obvious. There were certainly other candidates of higher rank who had great experience as members of the King's inner circle of advisers. But Paulet had more experience than any other courtier of the many departments in the Royal Household. Brandon had no real knowledge of how the Household functioned. Paulet's appointment suggests that the King wanted a tried and tested manager. As Lord President, Paulet may have been viewed by Henry as a safe pair of hands. The President of the Privy Council was in a strong position to acquire personal support, providing an opportunity to establish a faction against either the King or other privy councillors. As Paulet did not come from a powerful family he was no threat to the King. There are no indications that he sought power by formulating policy and influencing others, rather, he supported those whose views he shared. However, he was prepared to stand alone on issues he believed in strongly. On the subject of religion he seems to have taken a middle road – certainly not a reformer but neither an unbending Catholic. The King may have viewed him as a moderating influence within the Council, unlikely to become involved in personal politics but strong enough and honest enough to be an effective President.

On Christmas Eve 1545, Paulet listened as the King, on his final visit to Parliament, gave an impressive oration calling on the Prelates and Lords, and the Commons at the back of the hall, to display charity to, and unity with, each other. During the Parliament, Paulet heard three readings of a bill for the dissolution of chantries, colleges, hospitals and free chapels. The money raised from the sale of these properties went into the King's coffers but their sale, together with that of other capital assets such as Crown lands, reduced the King's long-term income making the need to improve his finances a priority.

The cost of the wars in 1544 and 1545 had been huge. As Wriothesley pointed out, the King had spent £1,300,000 on fighting in Scotland, the siege and garrison at Boulogne, the navy and the fortifications in England – and the expense continued. Throughout the winter many warrants were issued authorising the delivery of money to enable Paulet to pay for provisions for the navy. The Privy Council wanted an end to the drain on the country's finances. In spite of the cost of maintaining Boulogne, the King wanted to keep the port because it gave control over the Channel. But he couldn't afford to keep it. In April 1546 he decided on peace, although while negotiations were taking place in May, Paulet was commissioned to prepare the people of Kent in case the French 'attempt anything'.[288] In June, England and France signed a peace treaty with the condition that England retained Boulogne until 1554 when France would buy it back for two million crowns (£500,000), and an agreement that the French pension of £35,000 a year should be restored to Henry.

During the spring of 1546 moves were made to assess the state of the King's finances. Since 1540 such vast sums had been used for war that all the money collected from taxation, loans and the sale of religious houses was insufficient to balance the books. There had been benevolences, or forced gifts, in 1542 and 1544, forced loans and heavy subsidies in 1543 and 1545 and during the latter years about a third of a million pounds was received from the sale of ex-monastic lands. Henry had spent all the money accumulated both by his father and by Cromwell's attempts to restore the King's financial situation. He had also debased the coinage. This re-stamping of the coins with a higher face value, while not increasing the precious metal content, destroyed confidence in the currency and had long-term effects which Paulet wrestled with in later years.

During May and June, groups of five or six privy councillors were instructed to assess the value of the King's wealth and to raise further income. Because of his experience in dealing with finance courts, Paulet was assigned to several of the commissions. He was instructed to sell certain Crown lands and to assess 'a loving contribution' to be given by the King's subjects in Hampshire 'towards their defence' against the King of France. He was also on a commission to survey all the plate and jewels in the houses used by the King, Anne of Cleves and the royal children, and in the keeping of the Master of the Jewels and of Sir Edmund Peckham, who was Treasurer of the Mints and Cofferer of the Household. Another commission was to examine the state of the revenue courts and here the councillors were given wide powers to collect all they could. They could command treasurers, receivers and collectors to hand over money they held, collect debts and enforce payments, and even charge officers who had allowed debts to increase to an unreasonable level.[289]

By the end of Henry's reign Paulet had wider experience of handling the King's finances than any other courtier. At a local level he understood about collecting taxes from the people. He had overseen the expansion of the Office of the King's Wards into the Court of Wards and Liveries. He had been Treasurer of the Household, had responsibility for the vast sums involved in provisioning the army and navy during the wars and, finally, he had been on many of the commissions to investigate the King's finances.

But the commissioners were not entirely successful in restoring the royal finances. In April 1571, a year before his death, Paulet wrote a letter to Elizabeth I setting out the origins of Henry's lack of funds at the end of his reign:

> he had spent all the treasure his father left, and as much more taken of the subjects, of whom he could take no more. And then was it devised to take of the clergy, and so was it done. And so near was that wasted, when his grace came to the 32nd year of his reign, that he devised to consider his estate for maintenance of the same, which could not be found before the end of his life.[290]

There were signs that the King was reducing his workload and delegating tasks. In March 1544 the Duke of Norfolk and the Lord Privy Seal were permitted to use the King's stamp to authorise payments because 'the King is not in such good health that he may conveniently attend to the signing of so many warrants'. By 1545 more privy councillors, including Paulet, were authorised to make out warrants under the King's stamp for payments in the King's affairs. As his health declined, his inability to work was masked by the excuse that he was 'otherwise empeached with weighty affairs of the realm'.[291] But the King was still strong enough to go on progress and at the beginning of September 1546 he set off for Oatlands, Guildford and Chobham, reaching Windsor in early October. As often before, Paulet remained behind with Wriothesley and Gardiner as the 'Council in London', but on 4 September a letter to the 'Council with the King' suggests that they would prefer to be on the progress. There had been a 'great killing of stags' at Oatlands and the three men gave their 'humble thanks' for such venison as His Highness had sent them, and hinted at their regret at missing the sport by asking the councillors with the King to 'add a word for us, in our leisure to have licence to resort to some of the King's grounds hereabouts'. The King's finances were still uppermost in their minds though and they pointed out that 'Our daily travail is about the King's debts ... the mint is drawn dry'.[292]

Their letters to the 'Council with the King' kept Henry informed of their meetings and of matters they thought were of interest. Business was often carried out over dinner. On 8 September they dined with the French ambassador at the Lord Chancellor's house where, after spending a little time in 'ordinary conversation and viewing the gardens', they discussed disagreements over the supply of victuals to English towns and forts in France. The following day the three councillors dined together again, this time at Paulet's house at Austin Friars.[293] On Sunday, 18 September, Paulet joined Wriothesley and Gardiner for dinner with the Emperor's ambassador and also to meet the French ambassador's wife who had 'lately arryved to se their facion'. The courtiers, especially the women, would have been keen to hear of the appearance and dress of foreign ladies and the three men's report to the Council with the King gave their honest impressions of both ambassadors' wives. The French ambassador's wife was a 'right proper woman' whose 'apparrel was well trimmed' but they were not quite so complimentary in their description of the wife of the Emperor's ambassador. She was 'not soo fayre, nor so propre a woman as thother, but of the meanest sorte … she seameth also very honest, and that she lacketh in beauty, she helpeth with gaye geare'.[294] Similarly, the foreign ambassadors in England sent home descriptions of English men and women. The Venetian ambassador Soranzo described the English as 'of handsome stature and sound constitution with red or white complexions, their eyes also being white. According to their station they are as well clad as any other nation whatever.'[295]

By 5 October 1546, Paulet was at Windsor with the King and Council. The King's health was deteriorating. On occasions he was unable to walk and was carried around in a chair, similar to a sedan chair, covered in velvet with embroidered roses.[296] As the winter approached it was apparent that the King was nearing the end of his life. Prince Edward was only nine years old and the Court speculated over who would govern during the Prince's minority. Courtiers jockeyed for position as they lined up behind those they thought would be the new power behind the throne. The Privy Council was splitting along religious lines as the struggle developed between the Catholics and the Protestants. The conservatives in the Council were led by the Howard family and Bishop Gardiner. Aligned against them was the Prince's uncle, Edward Seymour, who was Lord Great Chamberlain and was high in Henry's favour and had the support of Lord Lisle.

On 25 October Paulet returned to London for a meeting with Wriothesley and Gardiner but he was back at Windsor by 1 November and moved to Westminster with the Court on the 11th. He also met with Gardiner, Wriothesley and Lord William Windsor at Westminster on 4

November when they had been the only members present in the Lords to witness Parliament open and be immediately adjourned to 14 January 1547.[297] Early in December a disagreement over land between the King and Gardiner gave the religious reformers the opportunity to have the Bishop excluded from Court. That same month they collected enough evidence to arrest Norfolk and his son, Henry, Earl of Surrey. Surrey was arrogant, despising those councillors of humble birth, and in his coat of arms he had used a heraldic quartering of Edward the Confessor from whom he claimed descent. Since this quartering belonged only to the heir apparent, Surrey was accused of asserting that he had a claim to the throne against Prince Edward. Surrey was found guilty of treason by a group of peers, which included Paulet, and he was beheaded at Tower Hill on 19 January 1547.[298] Norfolk was interviewed in the Tower by Paulet and William Paget concerning alleged conspiracy against the King. He denied wanting the return of Papal power to England claiming to be loyal to the Sovereign but, on 12 January 1547, Paulet was present when Norfolk signed a statement confessing to bearing arms which included those of the King and concealing the fact that his son also did.[299]

A Bill of Attainder was passed against Norfolk and Surrey, the latter having already been executed. On 27 January the royal assent to the Act was given in the Lords by four commissioners – Wriothesley, Paulet, Russell and Hertford. The King was too ill to attend 'but wished it passed without delay in order that certain offices held by Norfolk might be given to others against the approaching creation of the Prince.'[300] The reformers had achieved their aim – to remove the powerful leaders of the Catholic faction from Court – but they were cheated of the coup de grâce when Norfolk escaped execution because the King died before signing the death warrant.

As happened so often, Norfolk and Gardiner who had helped to bring about the downfall of Wolsey and Cromwell were themselves brought down by their enemies. Just a few years later the scenario would be repeated when those same enemies, Edward Seymour and John Dudley, suffered a similar fate at the hands of their opponents.

The King's health deteriorated during December and January and access to him was restricted to members of the Privy Chamber and the Privy Council. The Queen was at Greenwich and Christmas and New Year at Court were very subdued after the feasting and revelry of previous years. The King's isolation resulted in rumours about his health and on 8 January the French ambassador, de Selve, recorded that the King had been so ill that there were rumours he was dead. But Henry rallied yet again and on

17 January he was sufficiently well to receive both the French and Imperial ambassadors, possibly the only outsiders to witness the King's condition for themselves.[301]

The contents of Henry's will were probably already known to the Privy Council. On 26 December, Hertford, Lisle, the King's secretary, Sir William Paget and Sir Anthony Denny, a gentleman of the Privy Chamber, were with the King when he revised his will, leaving the Crown to Edward, followed by Mary and then Elizabeth. He named sixteen executors who were also to act as a Regency Council until Edward reached the age of eighteen, and a further twelve as assistant executors to give assistance when required. Paulet was listed as a member of the Council after the Archbishop of Canterbury and Lord Chancellor Wriothesley. His other co-executors were the Earl of Hertford, Lord Russell, Viscount Lisle, Bishop Tunstall, Sir Anthony Browne, Sir Edward Montagu, Justice Bromley, Sir Edward North, Sir William Paget, Sir Anthony Denny, Sir William Herbert, Sir Edward Wotton and Dr Wotton.

There is some uncertainty about the signing of the will. It is dated as having been signed by the King on 30 December 1546 but the clerk records it as the next to last document to be stamped in January.[302] The will was not in fact signed. It was stamped by dry stamp to leave an impression of the King's signature which the clerk could later ink in. Being stamped so late in the month it is possible the inking-in was not done until January and the order of recording documents may not have been of relevance.

The fall of the Howards and the exclusion of Bishop Gardiner from both the Court and the list of executors left Hertford in a powerful position and during December the Council met away from Court at his house at Ely Place in Holborn. Paulet was present there every day from 9 to 29 December and then in January they resumed their meetings at the Court at Westminster, where Paulet also attended all but one of the sessions of Parliament when it resumed on 14 January.

Henry VIII died early on the morning of Friday, 28 January 1547, but nobody outside the Privy Chamber was aware of this until the 31st when Wriothesley announced the fact to Parliament. For three days life at court had continued as if the King was still alive, while the Privy Councillors prepared for the future. Van der Delft wrote to the Emperor on 31 January that the King was dead 'although not the slightest sign of such a thing were to be seen at court, and even the usual ceremony of bearing in the royal dishes to the sound of trumpets was continued without interruption.'[303] This was not unusual. When Henry VII had died late on 21 April 1509 his death was not known outside the royal apartments until the evening of the 23rd and was not announced to the people until the following day.

Henry VIII's reign saw tremendous changes for Paulet. He rose from the gentry to be not only a lord but one of the most influential men at Court, ranking behind only the Lord Chancellor and the Lord High Treasurer. But the King's death signalled the beginning of the most exciting and turbulent period of Paulet's life – a time during which he rose even higher in the nobility and twice took actions which, if events had fallen differently, could have been construed as treasonable.

9

Lord Keeper of the Great Seal and the Fall of the Seymours

When Henry VIII died, the English crown passed to the nine-year-old Prince Edward but the country was to be governed by the sixteen executors who formed the Privy Council. This gave them the opportunity to wield enormous power and influence and they quickly set to work to establish their position.

The Earl of Hertford rode immediately to tell the new King Edward VI of his father's death and on the afternoon of 31 January 1547 he brought Edward to the Tower, where Paulet and other councillors had already gathered. It was the practice for a new monarch to stay at the Tower before his coronation and some of the Council lodged there with the King. Although Paulet's house was only about three-quarters of a mile from the Tower, it is likely that over the next three weeks he spent time living in the great fortress. An eerie experience perhaps – courtiers generally only lived in the Tower prior to a coronation or when they were incarcerated there as prisoners, often under sentence of death.

Keeping the King's death a secret for three days gave Hertford time not only to bring Edward into the city from the country but also to make arrangements for his own rise to power. The day after Henry died, Hertford had written to Paget that they should meet and agree matters so that there would be no controversy in the future. The letter is not specific but another letter by Paget written two years later asks Hertford to 'Remember what you promised me in the gallery at Westminster before the late King died, and immediately afterwards, planning with me for the place you now occupy – to follow my advice before all other.'[304] It is probable that Hertford and Paget were agreeing on how best Hertford could take control of the Privy Council.

The same day that the King arrived at the Tower, Paulet and twelve of the other executors met to hear Paget read part of the King's will. They agreed to abide by Henry's wishes but with one amendment. The will stipulated that, with regard to 'anything appointed by this Will', none of the councillors should do anything alone 'but only with the written consent of the majority'.[305] The Council decided that, for the dispatch of important matters and for the 'honour, surety and government' of the King and to deal with foreign kings, some 'special man' should be 'preferred in name and place before others' and be recognised as head of the councillors.[306] This special man was to be Hertford and he was to have the title of Lord Protector. The King had worded his will to prevent any one man holding ascendancy and usurping power. The councillors overturned his intentions and although they may have intended Hertford to be only a titular head, he had other ideas and soon took overall control. The councillors themselves created the very situation that Henry VIII had tried to prevent.

On 1 February, thirteen executors again heard the will read before they took their oaths to the new King and swore to observe the will as they had resolved the day before. Edward agreed to their proposal that Hertford should be Protector with the proviso that he acted only with the advice and consent of the other executors. At 3pm Paulet joined the Council to accompany Edward to the chair of state where they, with other nobles who were present in the Tower, made their 'obedience' to him by kneeling to kiss his hand. They returned to the council chamber during the evening to write letters to Charles V and Francis I, no doubt informing them not only of the King's death but also of Hertford's new situation. The next day Paulet joined the two committees that had the mammoth task of organising all the pomp and ceremony required at the funeral of the dead King and the coronation of the new one.[307]

On the afternoon of Sunday, 6 February Paulet was with the Council at the Tower to listen to a statement by Paget. The King's will included bequests to his councillors. Paulet, with Wriothesley, Russell, Hertford and Lisle each received £500, the largest of the bequests. The Archbishop of Canterbury received 500 marks (£333 6s 8d) and the remainder of the executors were left £300.[308] As Secretary, Paget had been in close contact with Henry and he affirmed that they had discussed plans to advance some councillors and courtiers to higher honours and to distribute lands which had belonged to Norfolk and Surrey amongst these men to support them in their new ranks. The King died before his wishes could be carried out but he had left orders that any unfilled promises he had made were to be performed.

Henry had initially intended that Hertford should become a duke, the Earl of Essex a marquis, Viscount Lisle and Paulet with Lords Russell and Wriothesley were to become earls and ten others were to be advanced to the title of baron. Paget had explained to Henry that some of the nominees were not satisfied with the proposals, thinking that the lands appointed to them were too little to support their new titles, while others endeavoured to remain as they were, perhaps also because of lack of funds. It may well be that Paulet was one of the latter and declined the advancement, regardless of any ambition he held, because when Henry had amended the list Paulet and Russell and four of the knights were no longer proposed for elevation. Paulet and Russell had been created barons together in 1539. Lord Russell was Lord Privy Seal but his three predecessors had all been earls so it was appropriate to consider him for elevation. Similarly, Paulet as Lord Great Master and Lord President was following the Duke of Suffolk and the Earls of Sussex and Shrewsbury who had both been Lord Steward. Paulet and Russell were finally elevated to earls, again at the same ceremony, in 1550 when Lisle took control from Hertford.

Henry had also adjusted the distribution of lands he had intended as rewards to some of his ministers and councillors. Paulet was initially to receive land worth £200 but this was reduced to £100.[309] The Council accepted these proposals and in due course Paulet received various parcels of land with manors, houses and a water mill.[310] The first Council meetings of Edward's reign were held in the Tower. Although it was the custom that such meetings should be held where the King was – at Court – on Thursday, 10 February Paulet and the other councillors met at Hertford's house on the Strand, a practice which was to become common during his term as Protector.

It was announced that the coronation was to be held at Westminster Abbey on Sunday, 20 February, but before that the Court had to bury the old King. The chief mourner was Henry Grey, Marquis of Dorset, and Paulet was the first of the twelve official mourners who accompanied him. The body lay in state at Westminster until Monday 14, February, when it was to be taken to Windsor. At 7am the coffin was laid on a chariot and the long procession began, with Paulet and the other mourners riding on horses draped in black velvet. The procession reached the church at Syon at 2pm on the first day and, after the coffin had been placed in the church, the mourners retired to lodgings for the night. Next morning they rose early and took their places in church to hear masses sung for Henry's soul, an event which had happened daily since his death. By 7am the procession was on the road again, riding to Windsor where the coffin was set on the floor of St George's chapel in preparation for the burial next day.[311]

On Wednesday the mourners attended mass at 6am before breakfast and then returned to the chapel for the funeral service. One of Paulet's sons, Chidiock, took part in the ceremony riding into the chapel on horseback as a 'man of arms' and his brother, Richard, assisted in carrying the palls presented as offerings at the service. During the service the household officers broke their white sticks, symbolising that their term of office had ended with the death of the King, and hurled them into the grave. Paulet as Lord Great Master led the way followed by the Lord Chamberlain, Treasurer, Comptroller, Sergeant Porter and four Gentlemen Ushers who all 'with heavy and dolorous lamentation brake their staves in shivers upon their heads, and cast them after the corpse within the pit'. The interment was finished by 6pm and the mourners retired to the castle for a meal.[312] The following day, having hastened back to the Tower, Paulet received a new stave of office from the new King and was re-installed as Lord Great Master. This was also the day on which the last elevations planned by Henry were fulfilled. Hertford was elevated to Duke of Somerset, the Earl of Essex to Marquis of Northampton, Viscount Lisle to Earl of Warwick, Lord Wriothesley to Earl of Southampton and the new Lords, Seymour, Rich, Willoughby and Sheffield, were created.

Paulet was riding in procession again on Saturday, 19 February, this time as Edward rode from the Tower through the City to Westminster for his coronation. The long cavalcade set off at about 1pm and made its way into Fenchurch Street and along Lombard Street and Cheapside, past St Paul's to Ludgate Hill and on into Fleet Street and the Strand and so to Westminster. The route had been well prepared. The streets were gravelled so the horses would not slip and railings were put up along part of the route to protect the onlookers. The windows and walls of the houses were hung with tapestries, some woven of cloth of gold, and with streamers and banners. The purpose of the procession was to let Edward see his people and also for them to see him. Ahead of him rode hundreds of courtiers, ambassadors, clergy and noblemen, amongst them Paulet, while behind Edward were hundreds of yeomen, soldiers and members of his household. All along the route Edward stopped to be regaled by singing choirs and pageants and to listen to verses recited by children and adults, all of them praising him and the kingly virtues, while everywhere wine flowed from the fountains. At one church he stopped to watch a man sliding downwards, head first with arms outstretched, on a rope attached from the top of the steeple to the ground.[313]

By 7am on Sunday Paulet was at Westminster Palace where the King had slept and where all the nobles were gathered in their best array to accompany Edward to his coronation. Edward landed at the privy stairs at Whitehall Palace with the noblemen in two barges at about 9am and was conducted through Whitehall to be dressed in his robes while the nobility put on their robes of estate.[314] They then processed into Westminster Hall where they joined the grand procession which was to escort the new king into Westminster Abbey. Among the members of the procession that formed up in Westminster Hall was Paulet's son, Giles. Giles was one of Edward's playmates and school fellows. He was one of eighteen young men and boys, all the sons of noblemen, who had been selected for these roles. They were a very select band and their fathers must have hoped that this early familiarity with the King would bring them later rewards.[315]

Paulet had a prominent role in the grand procession which led Edward to the throne in Westminster Abbey. The gentlemen, esquires, knights, choirs and bishops led the way. Then came three noblemen – Paulet, the Earl of Derby and Lord Russell – who each carried one of three unsheathed swords. Somerset with the crown and Suffolk and Dorset with the ball and sceptre preceded the King and following behind him were the gentlemen of the Privy Chamber, the nobles and guards. The King was crowned Edward VI with three crowns – the crown of King Edward the Confessor, the Imperial crown and one made specially for the occasion, a smaller one that fitted him. After the crowning, Paulet, with all the peers and bishops, swore allegiance and kissed the King on his left cheek before walking back to Westminster Hall to join Edward at his coronation banquet.[316]

Two weeks after the coronation Paulet found his status at court enhanced yet again when he became Lord Keeper of the Great Seal. This seal was generally in the keeping of the Lord Chancellor, the highest judicial official in England, and was used to authenticate the most important documents issued in the name of the King. On 6 March, less than three weeks after becoming Earl of Southampton, Wriothesley was ordered to deliver up the Great Seal and forfeit the office of Lord Chancellor. Paulet was amongst those who signed the charge against him asserting that he had used the seal without authority to commission officers of the Chancery Court to hear cases in his place while he attended to Privy Council matters. It was a tenuous reason for dismissal but Somerset needed to gain firm control of the Council. Wriothesley was opposed to him and might have been an obstacle to Somerset's attempt, later in the month, to increase his power. Wriothesley was temporarily placed under house arrest but was later released and returned to the Council. It was the next day, Monday, 7 March, that Paulet was appointed Lord Keeper of the Great Seal.

This ancient post had evolved into that of Lord Chancellor and was still used when the latter position was empty. The document of appointment stated that until the King appointed a new Chancellor, the Great Seal must be entrusted to the care of a 'special man of great trust'. No other person was thought 'so meet to be put in trust and credited in that behalf' as Paulet, who was required to accept the situation 'notwithstanding his manifold occupations in service to His Highness otherways'.[317] The King delivered the Great Seal to Paulet, granting him custody for fourteen days with further grants to be made as needed to extend the time until a new Chancellor was appointed. Although there were rumours that Paulet was resigning as Lord Great Master, this was not the case.[318] The appointment was only intended to be for a limited time and to be held alongside his other posts.

Paulet now held two of the most powerful positions at Court but he was never to be Lord Chancellor. It is reasonable to expect that he would have acceded to this post as did Sir Thomas Audley and Bishop Goodrich, both Lord Keepers. It is possible that, regardless of his legal training, he was not fully competent as a lawyer although an assertion that during his tenure as Lord Keeper he was incompetent in the Court of Chancery and begged to be allowed to resign is not supported by any evidence.[319] Probably Somerset just wanted to keep the Great Seal in the care of one of his supporters while he established himself and he had no desire for Paulet to become Lord Chancellor and thus resign as Lord Great Master. Paulet held the title for only six months before being relieved of the position when Lord Richard Rich was appointed as Lord Chancellor in October 1547. As Keeper of the Great Seal, Paulet was entitled to certain allowances and the commission which authorised these illustrates how emoluments were paid from various sources. From the Hanaper (part of the Chancery in the Lord Chancellor's domain) he received the diets and livery for himself and the Masters of Chancery at £542 15s for the year, and £15 for each term's attendance in Star Chamber with a further £300 a year over and above that. From the

Butler he was paid twelve tuns of wine worth £64 and from the Wardrobe 16lb of 'wax' (candles) yearly.[320]

Paulet was soon required to exercise his new authority. The executors wanted confirmation that they had the power to use the Great Seal and to make decisions for the King. On Sunday 13 March at Westminster, where the Court had resided since the coronation, Somerset, Paulet, Russell, Northampton, Cheyney, Browne and Paget asked the King for a commission to give them full authority while he was a minor so that their signatures, without his, were sufficient warranty for Paulet to pass documents under the Great Seal.[321] On 21 March Paulet used the Great Seal to authorise a royal commission, which confirmed the executors' powers and Somerset's authority as Governor of the King's Person and Lord Protector of the Realm. This allowed Somerset to act in all matters of government, with the advice and help of the Privy Council, and to nominate members of the Council at will. He could select whom he wanted from the 26 men Henry VIII had named, or any others, until the King came of age at eighteen. This was a powerful tool, which could have allowed Somerset to pack the Privy Council with his supporters, although he appears not to have used it constructively; rather, he began to operate outside the Privy Council. If Wriothesley had remained as Lord Keeper he might have refused to use the Seal on the objection that the commission gave Somerset too much freedom and that may have been the reason for his removal from the Council.

The relationship between Edward VI and his Privy Council was different from that between Henry VIII and his. Henry's will stipulated that Edward was to be ruled regarding 'all affairs' by his councillors, but Edward never chose them. Initially they were his father's choice and later those of Somerset and Warwick. Under Henry, the Privy Council was controlled by a powerful monarch who had experience, strong opinions and well-formed ideas, who took decisions and could impose his will on the council members. He could punish them, even execute them, and they were in fear and awe of him. Henry was big and impressive, both in bulk and in character. Having a minor as monarch made a huge difference. Unlike his father, Edward had no physical 'presence'; he was only a child with no experience or power of his own. During the early years of his reign he did not often attend Privy Council meetings and his knowledge of the affairs of the realm and of the actions of his councillors was based on the reports of the few men who were close to him, men such as Somerset, and what they told him influenced his decisions. He was not a direct threat to the councillors, not likely to punish or banish them. He did not propose the arrest of traitors, the Privy Council did. He did not instil fear in his councillors, as his father had done, but conversely he could not offer them the protection that Henry had given to men such as Wolsey and Cromwell when factional interests worked against them, as evidenced when Edward agreed to Privy Council decisions to send both his Seymour uncles to the scaffold. A councillor under threat needed strong supporters within the Council, something Wriothesley lacked. Any threat to a councillor came from another and especially from whoever had influence over the King. Factions within the Privy Council could remove a member, where previously the King had been the final arbiter. But the councillors did respect Edward's position as monarch, and their actions were constrained by the assumption that he would eventually take the reins of power from them, with the ability to punish past mistakes and misdeeds.

Having a boy king presented a small group of men with the opportunity to wield enormous control over England. Such a thing would have been impossible for them under Henry VIII but now they were more able to work for themselves. None of the executors came from ancient noble houses or from powerful families. They were generally self-made men, members of the gentry and sons of knights, who were raised to their present position by Henry because of their ability or their friendship with him. Edward VI's reign presented a rare opportunity to grasp wealth from the Crown and, by the end of the reign, many titles and much land and property had been distributed among the councillors.

Henry had created this Privy Council with the intent of removing religious disagreement amongst the members. Of the Catholic faction, Gardiner had been excluded, Norfolk was in the Tower and Surrey had been executed. Tunstall and Wriothesley, the remaining ardent Catholics, were outnumbered by those who supported religious reform. In March 1547, Paulet was described alongside Wriothesley as being 'not unduly attached to the "sects"' but of having always supported Gardiner.[322] Wriothesley was open about his Catholic beliefs but Paulet does not seem to have aired firm religious views and his support for Somerset does suggest that he did not strongly oppose the Protector's plans for religious change.

Edward spent his time primarily at Whitehall and Greenwich so that was where the Privy Councillors lived their lives. Paulet was as conscientious as ever, attending nearly all the meetings. One of the main preoccupations of the Council was its relations with France and Spain and meetings between councillors and ambassadors took place regularly. The Emperor's ambassador, Van der Delft, did not always find Paulet easy to

GVIL. MARCHIO. WINTON. THES. ANGL ::

William Paulet, 1st Marquis of Winchester, wearing his Garter collar and holding the staff of office of Lord Treasurer. Unknown artist c.1600. (By permission of Winchester City Council Museums Service. Photograph by John Crook)

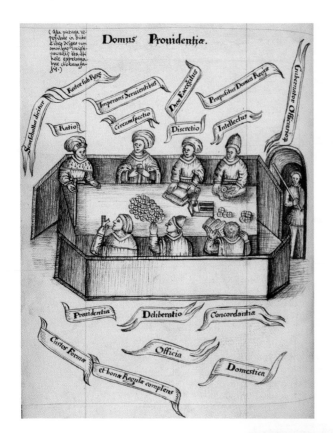

A meeting of the Board of the Greencloth. Two of the 'white sticks', holding their staves of office, sit on settles in the Counting House with the clerks. Counters lie upon the board and the clerks hold parchment rolls. The scrolls display the qualities the men are expected to observe in their work. (© The British Library Board, Harley 642)

William Paulet, an engraving of a late sixteenth-century portrait. (Hampshire Record Office, Portrait/P/5)

The Wriothesley Garter Book: Henry VIII in Parliament, *c*.1530, Sir Thomas Wriothesley. The lords sit on the benches on the right and the bishops on the left. The floor tiles are painted in the Tudor colours of green and white. (The Royal Collection © 2010 Her Majesty Queen Elizabeth II)

King Henry VIII, after Hans Holbein the Younger. Henry valued Paulet's work and was generous with his rewards, creating him a baron and a Garter Knight and appointing him Lord Great Master. (National Portrait Gallery, London)

Henry VIII dining in his privy chamber by Hans Holbein. The cloth of state and cupboard displaying
items of gold and silver were a reminder to the courtiers of the King's royal status. (© The Trustees of
the British Museum)

The Siege of Boulogne by Henry VIII in 1544 where the English set up camp outside the walls of the town. Trenches were dug to give the soldiers protection and to allow miners to tunnel under the walls and lay explosives. James Basire (1730–1802) 1788 (detail). (The Royal Collection © 2010 Her Majesty Queen Elizabeth II)

The Family of Henry VIII, c.1545. A dynastic portrait of Henry VIII with Prince Edward and Jane Seymour (who died 12 days after Edward's birth) and the Princesses Elizabeth and Mary. This chamber at Whitehall Palace illustrates the magnificence of the rooms used by the King. British School, Tudor.(The Royal Collection © 2010 Her Majesty Queen Elizabeth II)

'Encampment of the English Forces near Portsmouth 19 July 1545', James Basire (1730–1802) 1788 (detail). The two masts above the water identify the site of the sinking of the *Mary Rose*. (The Royal Collection © 2010 Her Majesty Queen Elizabeth II)

An allegory of Edward VI's reign. Henry VIII confirms the succession from his death bed and the boy is enthroned. Protestant councillors, Cranmer amongst them, look on impassively as Catholic clergy flee (bottom left) and the more conservative councillors look a little uncomfortable with developments (bottom right). (National Portrait Gallery, London)

King Edward VI by an unknown artist after William Scrots. Edward's reign was an opportunity for ambitious courtiers to wield power. (National Portrait Gallery, London)

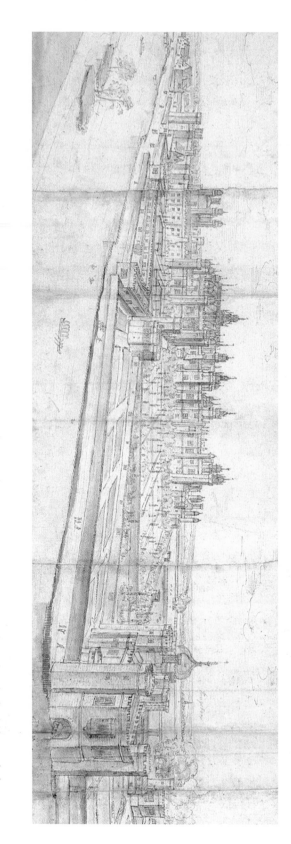

Hampton Court Palace as Paulet knew it, with the gatehouse towering up on the left, the skyline covered in a myriad of cupolas and at the back the roof of the Great Hall. 'View of Hampton Court Palace from the South, with the River in the Foreground', *c*.1558–62, Wyngaerde, WA.C.I.G.IV.9B (detail). (Ashmolean Museum, University of Oxford)

Westminster and Whitehall, a later interpretation of the Agas map of 1578 (though not in fact originally created by Ralph Agas). The Thames connects London, Westminster, Lambeth and Greenwich.

'The Siege of Basing House', c.1644, by Wenceslaus Hollar. Although drawn in the seventeenth century, after Basing House was destroyed during the Civil War, this engraving gives an impression of the grandeur of the house that Paulet built. (© The Trustees of the British Museum)

Philip II and Mary I, by a follower of Antonio Mor. Mary's marriage to Philip of Spain lasted for only four years before her death in 1558. (Reproduced by kind permission of His Grace the Duke of Bedford and the Trustees of the Bedford Estates)

Sir Thomas Wyatt, instigator of the 1554 rebellion that bears his name. The prime motivation for the uprising was considered by most commentators of the time to be the Queen's marriage to Philip of Spain, As the famous chronicler of London John Stow put it in his *Summarie* (1565) it was 'so grievously taken of divers noble men and a great number of gentlemen and commoners, that for this, and religion, they in such sort conspired against the Queen.'

The burning of Latimer and Ridley at Oxford, 16 October 1555, from John Fox's *Book of Martyrs*, 1563. The preacher Dr Richard Smyth rejoices, having been forced to recant part of his Catholic beliefs on almost exactly the same spot eight years earlier. He would be fleeing for his life in 1559.

Queen Elizabeth I, by an unknown artist. After a visit to Basing House Elizabeth is reputed to have said that, if only he were younger, she would marry Paulet. (National Portrait Gallery, London)

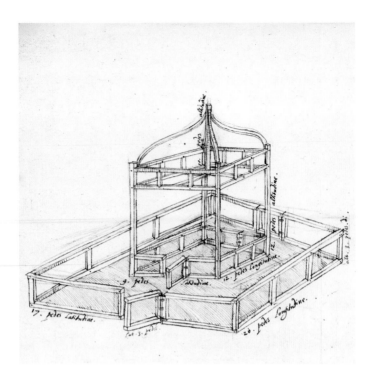

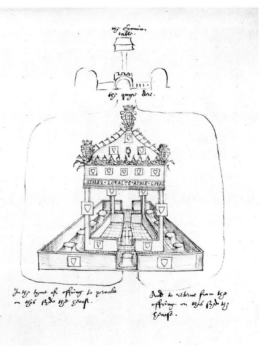

The wooden frame of the hearse for Paulet's funeral was covered in black velvet and taffeta with shields displaying his arms. The coffin sat within the structure and inside the low wall were covered stools for the chief mourners. Ashmole MS 836, f. 212. (The Bodleian Libraries, University of Oxford)

work with and, indeed, preferred working with Paget. There was much trade between the Low Countries and England and in June 1547 Van der Delft complained that Spanish merchant ships were stopped by English sailors at sea. He hoped to resolve this matter better with Paget than he had so far with Paulet on another matter. Paulet had been negotiating with him regarding a claim against a man called Renegat whom Van der Delft accused of piracy. After two meetings they were no further forward and the Privy Council instructed Paulet to confer again with Van der Delft and if no agreement could be reached Paget was to take over. After that Paulet 'agreed amicably to settle the matter to everyone's satisfaction'.[323] Later that year Paulet, Paget and Petre dined with Van der Delft to discuss complaints about the burden on the Emperor's subjects of customs and tallies on imported goods. During the talks, after dinner at the ambassador's house, 'great disputes ensued' and some were 'growing quite heated in their arguments'. Since the ambassador was later to single out Paget as easy to deal with, it appears that he considered either Paulet or Petre, or both, to be intransigent.[324]

There were further complaints about Paulet's stubbornness in August 1550 when Van der Delft's successor, Jean Scheyfve, tried to deal with him regarding assaults on Dutch seamen in England. Paulet countered with the claim that English sailors were likewise ill-treated and assaulted at Antwerp. The Privy Council wrote to the Admiralty to resolve the matter but there was no change. A further approach by Scheyfve to Paulet was met with the reply that members of the Council should not be applied to for such trifling matters and that the Lords were not to be molested. Scheyfve could get nothing more out of Paulet and reported to the Regent of the Netherlands that he intended to bring this to the notice of the Council.[325] There is no record of their response.

To survive and rise at the Tudor court it was sometimes necessary for men to trim their sails to the wind, shaping their conduct to suit the prevailing view of others. Because of his remarkable longevity at court and the lack of censure against him, history has mistakenly marked Paulet down as one of these timeservers – 'a willow, not an oak' who bent with the times and shaped his policy to best serve his own interests. In reality Paulet may be better described as 'an oak, not a willow', unbending and holding fast to his beliefs and principles. Like many men he adapted and accepted change to survive but he was also prepared to stand up for what he believed in and he would propose change when he thought it was in the best interests of the monarchy and England. When necessary he was prepared to jeopardise his own position by following the course which he believed was right for the country. For him the future of crown and government were paramount and this conviction led to him being one of the instigators of the downfall of the Duke of Somerset.

The Privy Council's expectation that the Lord Protector would only act with their advice and consent was soon proved false. Somerset developed the practice of determining much council business at home, assisted by a group of his own supporters, none of whom were original executors of Henry VIII's will. The Privy Council was increasingly excluded from the process of policy-making as Somerset followed his own agenda. Eventually, his foreign policy, his support for Protestantism and his sympathy for the plight of the common man led to his downfall.

Somerset's policy in Scotland aggravated an already tense relationship with France. He wanted to see England and Scotland united and the marriage contract of Edward and Mary reinstated. He believed this could be achieved by force and, in August 1547, took a large army over the border and defeated the Scots at Pinkie on 10 September, killing nearly half their number, and then established fortifications before returning to England. The following summer the French went to Scotland's aid, landing troops to besiege the English forts and removing Mary Stuart to France on her betrothal to the Dauphin. Skirmishing went on until the English retreated home in the autumn of 1549 and in the meantime, many English soldiers had been tied up costing large sums of money. Somerset's plans for Scotland were in ruins.

Meanwhile, action was taken to defend the south coast of England against possible invasion by France with watches being kept and fortifications improved. The fortifications were often under the control of a local noble or councillor and in July 1547 Paulet was made Keeper and Captain of the Castle of St Andrew on the coast at Hamble in Hampshire. He was paid an annual fee of £19 3s 4d with a further 8d a day each to pay a porter and master gunner and 6d per day for each of six soldiers.[326] A further grant in September of that year laid out his responsibilities with regard to another fortress at Netley, close to Hamble. Paulet had been given Netley Abbey by Henry VIII in 1536 and the grant also included a pardon because he had constructed a stone fortress and barbicans at Netley at Henry's behest but without written permission. He was given licence to maintain, enlarge and crenellate the fort and to provide guns, powder and other armament for the defence of the coast. He was to appoint nine men to defend the fortress and had permission to assemble the local inhabitants on holy days or holidays and train them for war. To pay for the cost of all this he was granted three manors and parks and houses including the 'capital house' in Chelsea, which had belonged to Sir Thomas More.[327]

With the heavy expense of maintaining an army and improving defences, there was of course concern about the King's finances. In September 1547 Paulet was appointed to two commissions, the first to inventory the contents of all the palaces and royal houses listing everything – 'money, plate, jewels, apparel, silks, household stuff, stable stuff, munition, artillery, tents, revels and other implements'. The second was to examine the state of all the finance courts and to ascertain the annual revenue and outstanding debts.[328] As the reign proceeded, the matter of the King's finances took on growing importance.

Although Somerset's plans for religious reform had the support of the King, there was opposition from both the Privy Council and the people. In the summer of 1547, religious behaviour that could be regarded as in any way 'superstitious' was banned. Many relics and images were ordered to be destroyed, kissing of, or kneeling to, images was forbidden and candles were no longer to be placed before images or pictures. In an attempt to make services more accessible, each church was to provide a Bible in English. The Church Paulet knew was changing and, as a councillor, he was a signatory to those changes. Physical expressions of worship, such as kneeling before statues, and visual points of focus, like the statues themselves, were vanishing and leaving a void in the people's pattern of worship.

Paulet witnessed further attacks on the old Church from Parliament. During the autumn of 1547, an Act of Parliament was issued for the dissolution of the chantries, confirming the action proposed by Henry VIII. The assets of many chantries went to swell the King's coffers although some which had served educational or charitable purposes were allowed to continue these functions. Early in 1549 Parliament ordained that the order of worship, now to be conducted in English, should be as written in the Book of Common Prayer. It was hoped that this defined service would stem the swelling discontent concerning the changes in religious practices. For many people, the most important aspect of their Catholic faith was that it offered them salvation and a place in heaven when they died. The new religion still offered this and some of the populace were content to obey the King's orders and accept the changes. But the Book of Common Prayer was a compromise, particularly in its ambiguity regarding the doctrine of transubstantiation, and did not completely satisfy the leading exponents of the Catholic faith or the Reformers. Princess Mary, for one, refused to accept the new prayer book and Somerset allowed her to continue to celebrate mass privately in her own chamber.

Whilst these changes were taking place, Somerset's brother, Thomas, Lord Seymour, was charged with high treason. Seymour resented the fact that his brother held so much power, and he so little. His arrest, after inadvertently shooting Edward's pet dog in a suspected attempt to abduct the King from his bedchamber, gave his enemies the opportunity to bring no fewer than 33 charges against him, the most serious being that he had conspired against Somerset, had sought to gain power through control of the King and had attempted to marry Princess Elizabeth. On 23 February 1549 Paulet was with the other councillors at the Tower to hear Seymour's denial of the articles of high treason but he received no trial. A Bill of Attainder was passed against him on 5 March and on 20 March he was beheaded at Tower Hill.

The members of the Privy Council became increasingly frustrated by Somerset's actions. By the spring of 1549 the people too were becoming unsettled. The web holding society together was weakening. As Paget pointed out to Somerset, to operate effectively for the benefit of all, society had to abide by religion and laws.[329] People needed limits to their behaviour and these were set by the word of God and the laws of the King. Somerset had relaxed state control over people by repealing the treason and heresy laws, thus giving them more freedom. The Church was in a state of flux where the old religion was forbidden but the new one was still developing and not yet fully accepted. When the laws and guidance were not sufficiently rigid, people no longer respected them.

The people's lives were particularly affected by the economy, which was in a poor state. Money to pay for the wars had been raised by debasing the currency, which increased inflation. A poor harvest in 1549 pushed up prices, and population growth further increased the demand for food. Agricultural methods were not capable of increasing yield sufficiently. In the countryside, people were unhappy because the increasing use of enclosures for landowners to run large flocks of sheep was depriving them of land and forcing them into the towns. There were calls for common land to be unfenced and for land to be returned to the plough.

Somerset had some sympathy for their plight and he knew that the commoners were likely to rise up in rebellion if dissatisfied. Poverty and hunger could lead to riots. He made moves to act against enclosure and large-scale sheep farming and to remedy the lack of care for tenants. In June 1548 an inquiry was set up to collect evidence of illegal enclosing and the following winter Parliament introduced a tax on sheep of 3*d* for each ewe kept on private land and 1½d for each sheep on common land.[330] Both these actions were unpopular with the Privy Councillors because, as landowners, they were themselves affected. By mid-April 1549, unrest was starting among the people as they failed to see any improvements in their situation. Somerset was reluctant to use harsh means to quieten them but by July the situation was getting serious and riots broke out in Yorkshire and southwards through all the midland counties and throughout the east, south and south-west of England. People were assembling in large numbers, trespassing, causing damage and pulling down fences around enclosed land. Any large mob of people was viewed as a threat by the authorities, and the justices, knights and gentlemen were ordered to return home to their counties so they would be ready to put down any local riots. Most of these risings were confined and suppressed but in the extreme east and west the rioters were more organised and moved across the county boundaries raising more supporters.

The Western Rebellion began in Cornwall. Here, although men were concerned about enclosure, the sheep tax and inflation, they also had serious concerns over the changes to their religion and a dislike of the new prayer book. Their demands included the restoration of the Six Articles, the Roman Catholic Mass to be said in Latin and the return of traditional forms of worship with the ancient ceremonies. In early June Cornish rioters marched into Devon where they met with more rebels and together moved on to besiege Exeter. Somerset sent Lord Russell with a small force to restore order but Russell was not a military man and did not have sufficient troops; it was not until mid-August, supported by Lord Grey and Sir William Herbert, that he took Exeter and defeated the rebels.

The rising in the east had different demands. Norfolk was a more Protestant area and much of the unrest there was due to social and economic factors. There were complaints against enclosures and demands to improve the rights of tenants and to restrict the rights of landowners over common land. The people also called for better administration of local justice. They had a distrust of the governing class and were dissatisfied with the way the eastern counties were governed. A small rising – which began in June with the breaking down of hedges around common land in Norfolk – attracted the support of a landowner, Robert Kett. Under his leadership this grew to a force of several thousand men within a few weeks. Kett led the men to besiege Norwich and on 23 July they took the city and held it for nearly four weeks until Warwick defeated them with a force of 12,000 men.

What these risings demonstrated was a lack of leadership and support for the commoners from the gentry. The rebel leaders were generally yeomen and tradesmen, together with some clerics in Cornwall. The strength of feeling the rioters exhibited and the animosity they displayed towards the ruling class frightened the Privy Council. The fact that many of the riots were contained in their own counties prevented the country erupting into civil war but the riots in Norfolk and the south-west were able to grow to a significant size because of slowness on the part of Somerset to control them. His attempts to resolve the situation by treating the commoners gently delayed the recourse to using troops, so that he not only lost the support of the people but also the landowners.

By the end of the summer Paulet was one of a group of Privy Councillors who wished to see Somerset's power curtailed. They had never imagined that giving him the title of Protector would result in him taking control from them and making decisions without consultation. They did not support all his ideas for change and many of his policies were disastrous – all hope of joining with Scotland was lost, inflation was rising, there was still no consensus on religion, his policy of tolerance with regard to the commoners had nearly resulted in civil war and, in the midst of all this turmoil, France attacked Boulogne.

Somerset was arrogant and had alienated many councillors. He had no powerful supporters and had failed to fill the Council with his own men. By making decisions at meetings in his own house, away from the Privy Council and advised by his own supporters and friends, he had usurped Paulet's role as President of the Council. The councillors were not always aware of the subject of these meetings, and Somerset sent out letters in his name, rather than that of the Privy Council. Paget warned Somerset that some men in the Council were frightened of his temper and advised that he should not be so overbearing and should sometimes follow the advice of the other councillors.[331] Under an adult King the Privy Council would have been advisers. Under Edward they should have made policy – they increasingly did neither while Somerset was in control.

In October, events resulted in the Privy Councillors removing Somerset from his position as Lord Protector. After putting down the Norfolk rising, Warwick had returned to London in September and began to plot Somerset's downfall. He plotted with Paulet and with Southampton and Arundel, two strong supporters of Catholicism and natural opponents of Somerset, to take control from the Protector. Warwick may have elicited Southampton and Arundel's support by proposing to restore Catholicism to England. A letter from Van der Delft at the end of the month in which he refers to Southampton's illness, continues, 'If he fails us now matters might never be righted.'This may have been hinting at the Catholics' intention to return England to their faith.[332] Their hope that Princess Mary would support an attack on Somerset was dashed when she refused to be involved in government matters.[333]

By the beginning of October, Somerset was aware that several of the councillors had been dining together and he may have suspected that there were plans to move against him. Paulet arrived at Hampton Court to join the King and a small council of Somerset, Cranmer, William Cecil, Petre and Paget on Wednesday, 2 October. However, on 4 or 5 October he made the decision to return to London and join the rest of the Privy Council. As he left the palace, Paulet must have been aware that there was soon to be a move against the Protector and he may have been keen to distance himself from Somerset.

On Saturday, 5 October, Somerset issued a proclamation calling people to the aid of the King and himself and he sent letters in the King's name ordering all the Council to Court the following day. That evening the councillors' belongings arrived at the palace in carriages but they themselves did not follow the next day. Reports that night of 2,000 horsemen riding from London to take Somerset galvanised him into fortifying the palace. Logs were piled up against the back gate to limit entry to the front gate, where stones dug from the courtyard were stockpiled to be thrown onto assailants' heads. The horsemen never arrived.[334]

On the Sunday, Petre was dispatched from Hampton Court to discover the reason for the councillors' meetings and to warn them that if they arrived at Hampton Court in a confrontational mood they would be arrested. The nine councillors abandoned their plan to ride to meet Somerset and remained in London, meeting at Warwick's house, Ely Place in Holborn. Paulet was with Warwick and they were accompanied by the Earls of Arundel and Southampton, Sir Edward North, Sir Richard Southwell, Sir Edmund Peckham, Sir Edward Wotton and Doctor Wotton and were joined by Petre. Although the group numbered ten influential councillors, Somerset with fewer supporters had the ear of the King. The group was opposing the most powerful man in England and, if Somerset survived their opposition, they could well face charges of treason.

The councillors were soon busy outlining their grievances to the Lord Mayor and aldermen in London. Letters were sent to noblemen and gentlemen countermanding any orders from Somerset and instructing that no arms should be sent to him. During the day, Paulet left the meeting and rode across the city to take control of the Tower, preventing Somerset from taking control of the armoury or exploiting the safety of the fortress.[335] By Sunday night Somerset's position was looking very weak and late that evening he took the young King and rode with him to Windsor Castle, which could be more easily defended than Hampton Court.

During the next few days, a series of letters passed between the Protector and the 'Council in London'. On Monday, 7 October the number of councillors meeting in the Mercers Hall had risen to sixteen with the addition of Lord Chancellor Rich, Sir Thomas Cheyney, Sir John Gage, Sir Edward Montagu, Sir Ralph Sadler and Sir John Baker. On being informed that Somerset had taken the King to Windsor, they sent provisions and items that Edward might need, together with a letter assuring him of their allegiance and good intentions. They pointed out that Somerset had refused to heed their advice and that their intention was to ensure the King's safety and that of the country. They also sent a letter to Cranmer and Paget at Windsor, asking for Somerset to leave the King and for his troops to be disbanded.[336]

The following morning the councillors met at the Guildhall where the Mayor and aldermen promised to give aid.[337] The King wrote to the councillors in London pointing out the danger in which he felt himself to be and asking them to be moderate in their actions and to end the quarrel. Cranmer, Paget and Secretary Sir Thomas Smith also wrote to the councillors, assuring them of their loyalty to the King and announcing that Somerset would yield his office on honourable terms if his life were spared.[338] On this day, the balance of military power also turned in favour of the councillors. Somerset had previously ordered Herbert and Russell – who were on their way back to London after the Western Rising – to march to his aid. But on the 8th they declared their support for the councillors in London and dashed any possibility of Somerset maintaining control by force.

On Wednesday, 9 October the Council – its ranks swelled to 22 – met at the house of Mr York, the Sheriff of London. They sent a letter to the King reaffirming their allegiance, declaring their complaints against Somerset and asking that he should submit. An additional letter to the councillors with the King said that it was strange that, in the King's own household, he was surrounded by armed strangers, while his own servants were kept away. They reiterated that Somerset had severed the Council from the King and had broken the terms of Henry VIII's will by ignoring their advice.[339] The following afternoon the councillors gathered at Paulet's house to discuss events and share supper. When news arrived that Somerset was removed from the King's presence and that Edward's servants were again in attendance, the Council dispatched Sir Anthony Wingfield, Sir Anthony St Leger and Sir John Williams to Windsor to guard the King and to prevent Somerset escaping. Wingfield arrested Somerset the next morning and on Saturday 12 October Paulet travelled to Windsor with the other councillors where, on their knees, they explained their conduct to the King.[340]

Edward rode back to Hampton Court on Monday but before they left, the councillors interviewed Somerset and ordered him to be taken to the Tower. Once they arrived at the palace one of their first actions as a Privy Council, unfettered by the Protector, was to decree that in future at least two members from a group comprising the Marquis of Northampton, the Earls of Arundel and Warwick and Lords Wentworth, Russell and Paulet were always to be in attendance on Edward in his Privy Chamber 'to give order for the good government of and education of the King'.[341] By this means they would ensure that he was constantly under their influence.

The deposed Protector still had supporters amongst the people and, although wanting to be rid of him, Warwick was not keen to execute him and face the risk of an uprising. Wriothesley, though, was determined to see Somerset dead. During early December, four or five councillors visited Somerset at the Tower every day to interview him concerning the charges against him.[342] The main examiners were Wriothesley, who had been deprived of the Chancellorship by Somerset, Paulet, whose position of Lord President had been weakened under Somerset, and Arundel. When Somerset argued that he had acted with the advice of Warwick, Wriothesley decided to use this to implicate Warwick and so remove both men. Arundel agreed with this plan but Paulet was more guarded in his response. His next action destroyed their scheme. During the night Paulet went to Warwick's house at Holborn and divulged the plan, warning him that by working for Somerset's death he could bring about his own.[343] Warwick realised that the only solution was to save Somerset's life. In February, Somerset was released under house arrest after accepting 31 articles of accusation against him.

The removal of Somerset and Warwick would have presented the opportunity for Wriothesley and Arundel to take control of the Council. If their intention was to try to return England to the Catholic faith, Paulet's visit to Warwick thwarted those plans. Warwick was aware of their enmity and needed to remove them from the Council. He had ousted Somerset and could now follow his ambition. To have power he had to be supported by the King. Edward was Protestant and many people shared his beliefs. Warwick, too, had to follow the King. He turned away from the Catholic lords and sought support from Protestant councillors, bringing the Marquis of Dorset and Bishop Goodrich into the Privy Council to strengthen his position. Paulet continued to side with Warwick, though the Spanish ambassador considered that he 'still held to the good faith', and that in his support for a man who supported Protestantism Paulet illustrated how 'each pursued his own particular advantage and all parties were nourished by envy and ambition.'[344] Paulet does appear to have put his allegiance to King and self before religion. In mid-January Arundel was ordered home and Wriothesley withdrew from Court. Arundel appeared before Paulet, Northampton, Wentworth and Wotton on charges of maladministration as Lord Chamberlain.[345] The charges were most probably concocted but as had been demonstrated against Wriothesley in March 1547 accusations of mal-practice were an effective way of removing opposition from Court without resorting to either imprisonment in the Tower or execution.

10

Lord High Treasurer and Marquis of Winchester

Paulet was well rewarded for supporting Warwick. On 19 January 1550 he was created Earl of Wiltshire for services to the King and to Henry VIII, with a grant of £20 a year in support of the dignity.[346] In reality his creation was a 'thank you' from Warwick and to encourage future support. At the same time, Russell was elevated to Earl of Bedford. Parliament had been sitting since November and when the two men resumed their seats in the Lords on the following day, they joined the elite group of thirteen other Earls and the two Marquises of Dorset and Northampton who were the only nobles above the rank of baron. The Dukes of Somerset and Norfolk, both prisoners in the Tower, could not attend Parliament.

Further honours came to Paulet in February when he was appointed Lord High Treasurer in place of Somerset, relinquishing his titles of Lord Great Master and Lord President to Warwick.[347] He held this post for 22 years until his death in 1572, after being re-appointed by both Queen Mary and Queen Elizabeth. The prestigious position brought with it certain dignities such as holding the basin of water while the monarch washed his hands when dining in state.[348]

As Lord Treasurer he had charge of the Exchequer. The position had evolved because a King's wealth consisted not of paper money but of real treasure – gold and silver plate and jewels as well as coins. This treasure was stored in chests and store rooms and the Treasurer and his two deputy chamberlains were responsible for its safety. As treasure moved in and out of their control, receipts were issued to charge and discharge them of responsibility. By Edward VI's reign, much of the King's income was raised by the finance courts but the Exchequer still handled income from ancient sources. This was the money collected as rent and fees from tenants, customs and subsidies, fines from royal justice such as the Courts of Chancery, Star Chamber and the King's Bench, and fines from local justice such as the assizes and hearings before magistrates.

The Exchequer was the largest department after the Household and was divided into two parts – the Upper Exchequer or Exchequer of Account and the Lower Exchequer or Exchequer of Receipt. The former was where accounts were drawn up, legal disputes settled and the payment of overdue debts enforced. The latter was the treasury and pay office, responsible for the receipt, safe-keeping and issue of all money in the Exchequer. Like the Board of Greencloth, the Exchequer took its name from the great exchequer table. This measured about ten feet by five feet and was covered in a black cloth marked out with white lines that formed squares to resemble a chequerboard. A shallow ledge around the edge gave it the appearance of a gaming table and counters placed on the cloth represented a value from 1*d* to £1,000 determined by the square on which they were placed.

In the fifteenth century the accounting methods used by the Exchequer were cumbersome but relatively accurate. Sheriffs bringing money collected in the counties into the Receipt were given a tally stick. This was a wooden stick carved on one side with notches to represent the amount of the payment. The rod was split lengthways across the notches and one half given to the sheriff as a receipt. The other half was kept in the Exchequer and the transactions were recorded in documents known as pells for income and counterpells for expenditure. However, by the time of Paulet's appointment, methods had changed and four tellers were personally responsible for recording and storing much of the money, a system which led to misuse of funds and less reliable records. Paulet came to the post with enormous financial and administrative experience and was more active in the role than his predecessors. His expertise was in the routine operation of the Exchequer rather than in determining fiscal policy. During his time as Treasurer the revenue courts were reorganised and as the Exchequer handled increasing amounts of money, the Treasurer's influence increased, although not to the extent that Paulet always got his way. He was unsuccessful during Queen Mary's reign in his bid to return to the old methods of accounting.

Fuller, in his *Worthies of England*, describes the importance of a treasurer: 'Kings without treasure will not be suitably obeyed, and treasure without a

treasurer will not be safely preserved.' The position was one of great responsibility and trust, but also one of possible personal profit. Fuller suggests
that it was not uncommon for people in Paulet's position to use the King's
money for their own benefit, not by stealing but by 'borrowing' to invest
and then repaying. 'He that is a bad husband for himself, will never be a
good one for his Sovereign, and therefore no wonder if they have advanced
fair estates to themselves, whose office was so advantageous, and they so
judicious and prudent persons, without any prejudice to their master, and
injury to his subjects.'[349] Paulet had already proved to be a 'good husband'.
By 1546 his landed estate was worth over £1,000 per year.[350]

Paulet and the other councillors did, however, nibble away at the King's
wealth by awarding themselves honours and money to support their new
positions. Edward's minority offered a limited period in which they could
propose their own rewards, before he reached the age of 18 and took the
reins of power from them. Somerset and Warwick knew that the Lords were
fickle in their loyalty and rewarded them in the hope of ensuring their
continued support. Paulet's title of Earl of Wiltshire and his position as Lord
Treasurer brought him an annual income and he received further rewards
of land and manors, some of which had belonged to Thomas Seymour.[351]
These latter grants were for eleven manors with their associated land and
for a further 2,000 acres. During 1550 he also acquired land from the Earl
of Westmorland – two manors, 160 cottages and sites for further houses, and
over 3,000 acres of land.[352] He was becoming a very wealthy landowner.

On 30 June 1550 some arrests were made of people who were practising magic and the 'art of invocation'. To Paulet's great concern his wife,
Elizabeth, was questioned and confessed that she had asked to be told the
fortune of her husband and of Bedford, Warwick and some others. Her confession that she did it only out of curiosity, to see what 'good or evil might
befall her husband', probably saved her from imprisonment. Two years later
the Countess of Sussex was less lucky when she was jailed in the Tower for
five months to teach her 'a lesson to beware of sorcery'.[353]

The anxiety over his wife occurred at a busy time for Paulet as steps
were taken to resolve the finance crisis. In May he began to renegotiate the
extension of foreign loans amounting to £54,800 and at the same time he
was to investigate with Rich, Paget, Sadler and North how to resolve the
King's debts, beginning with an examination of finance statements from the
revenue courts. During August it was decided to melt down all gold crosses,
images and church plate that remained in the Tower and to use it as thought
best.[354] It was probably used for new coins.

Edward went on progress that summer and Paulet accompanied him as he travelled to Guildford, Woking, Nonsuch, Oatlands and Richmond before returning to Westminster on 16 October. However, Paulet's journey was interrupted when he was sent to London on 28 September to 'give order for the preservation of the city with the help of the Mayor'.[355] The city and the country were short of food. The usual problems of inflation and the growing demand for food, combined with the poor harvests of 1549 and 1550, led to a serious food shortage exacerbated by some people storing food in the hope of selling at a higher price in the future. Earlier in 1550 there had been two proclamations prohibiting the export of meats, butter, cheese, grains, ale, leather, wool, wood and tallow, except to Calais. On 24 September a further proclamation banned the export of these goods when their prices rose above prescribed government limits. The limit for wheat was 6s 8d per quarter and for beans and peas 4 shillings. In an attempt to prevent hoarding, the people were only allowed to buy flour and grain for their personal family use unless they were bakers or brewers. There were also orders to the justices to search out surplus grain and place it for sale on the open market.[356]

The Privy Council must have been fearful of another revolt. Paulet was sent to London to ensure the citizens abided by the proclamation, and to oversee the searches for stored grain. But still insufficient food was available for sale and in October the Privy Council set maximum prices in the hope that people would release food onto the market. Best wheat was set at a top price of 13s 4d a quarter, best malt at 10 shillings and beans and peas at 5 shillings.[357] Even this did not have the desired effect and grain was still not released. Ultimately, in December, the Privy Council removed the maximum price limits, grain prices rose and food did at last appear for sale.[358]

Under Warwick's control, the Privy Council returned to more acceptable methods of operation. Meetings were held at Court and on a more regular basis, and documents and records were signed. Paget made a list, possibly early in 1550, of proposals for how the Council meetings should be organised. There is no indication of whether they were all instigated but they do give a good illustration of acceptable working practices in the mid-sixteenth century. First, Paget exhorted the councillors to love one another as brethren or dear friends. He proposed that at least six of them were to be continuously at Court including at least two of the group comprising the Lord Chancellor, Lord Treasurer, Lord Great Master, Lord Privy Seal, Lord Great Chamberlain and Lord Chamberlain. The six men were to be able to conduct affairs which the others would ratify at a later date. The Council was to meet to attend to the King's affairs on at least three days – Tuesday, Thursday and Saturday – each week. These meetings were to be held in the council chamber from 8am until dinner and then from 2–4pm, and private suits were to be heard on Sundays after dinner from 2–4pm.[359]

During the spring of 1550, Somerset was freed and rejoined the Privy Council. He was still ambitious and his desire for power clashed with Warwick's. Ultimately only one of them could survive and Warwick was to be supreme. In seniority among the lay members of the Privy Council, Paulet was now second only to the Lord Chancellor but Warwick wielded more power. As Great Master and Lord President, but with no strong King or Protector to rule him, Warwick was in a position to do what Paulet had never been able to do – use his position to exert control in the Council. He presided at council meetings and appointed over a dozen of his own supporters as members. His authority spread. He was responsible for the royal household and he controlled access to the King by appointing Sir Thomas Darcy, Sir Andrew Dudley and Sir John Gates as Gentlemen of the Privy Chamber. Warwick knew he needed the King's support and Gates was able to influence Edward with Warwick's ideas while depriving others of the same opportunity.

To preserve his position and stay in power, Warwick had to solve the problems which had contributed to Somerset's downfall. He needed to bring the country to believe in one religion, to solve the financial crisis and to adopt a practical foreign policy that the country could afford. Wars and the expense of maintaining ports in France were draining the King's wealth. The latter problem was resolved in the spring of 1550 when Boulogne was surrendered to France for a payment of 400,000 crowns (£100,000). Under Somerset, England and France had been fighting on foreign soil for two years without a formal declaration of war. On 8 August 1549 the French ambassador had arrived at Court and on behalf of Henry II declared war with the intention of taking Boulogne. France wanted both Calais and Boulogne but knew that the Emperor had an agreement to come to England's aid if the French attacked Calais. However, this protection did not extend to Boulogne and although the town was due to be returned to France in 1554, the French King was not prepared to wait. A surprise assault on Boulogne failed and skirmishing only achieved the taking of outposts. Because of the fear of uprisings in England, the country could spare neither money nor troops to fight the French or maintain the town. Both Warwick and Henry II welcomed the proposed treaty, bringing peace between the two countries and leaving Calais as England's only foothold in France. In July 1551, a marriage treaty was agreed between Edward and Princess Elizabeth of France. An initial request by England that France should recognise the betrothal between Mary Queen of Scots and Edward, and thus union between England and Scotland, was rejected by France who maintained that Mary was betrothed to the Dauphin, thus bringing Scotland under their control. However, they were agreed that their own Princess should wed the English King and England was forced to accept that there was no likelihood of taking control of Scotland in the near future.

One of the Privy Council's actions against Catholicism was to remove the Catholic bishops from their positions of influence. Stephen Gardiner, Edmund Bonner, Nicholas Heath, George Day and Cuthbert Tunstall were all deprived because of their refusal to conform to the new religion. Gardiner, particularly, became an irritation after preaching at St Paul's Cross in the churchyard of St Paul's Cathedral. This was a wooden pulpit, set upon stone steps and surmounted by a cross, from where speakers were invited to speak on topics approved by the Council. Paulet attended some of these sermons, joining citizens, Privy Councillors and occasionally the King himself. In 1548 Paulet was present when Bishop Gardiner declared his belief in the presence of Christ in consecrated bread and refused to acknowledge the Council's authority to decide on matters of religion.[360] Shortly afterwards, at the end of June, Gardiner was sent to the Tower on a warrant signed by Somerset, Paulet, Cranmer, Russell and Cheyney. However, Paulet may not have actually signed this until much later in 1550 when Gardiner was brought to trial. Paulet and Russell entered their signatures as Wiltshire and Bedford, two earldoms which they did not receive until January 1550. These signatures were later erased and St John and Russell entered in their place.[361]

Gardiner spent two years in the Tower before the Council considered releasing him. On 9 June 1550, Paulet with Somerset, Parr, Russell and Petre visited him in the Tower with an offer of freedom and a pardon on condition that he accepted the Book of Common Prayer, an offer to which he agreed. However, some of the councillors did not want his release and on 9 July Paulet made a further visit, this time with Warwick, Herbert and Petre, at which Gardiner was asked to subscribe to certain articles of faith and to a confession of guilt in opposing the Council.[362] The Bishop agreed to the articles: that the King was Supreme Head of the Church in England and could dictate Holy Days and fasting days and had the power to reform rites and ceremonies, and that he accepted the Prayer Book, agreed to obey all the King's laws and statutes and acknowledged that the Statute of Six Articles was repealed. But he would not confess to having been in error by opposing the Council's plans for reformation, maintaining that his beliefs were a matter of conscience. His refusal to sign any further articles of faith or confessions of guilt resulted in a trial which began the following December. Paulet was one of the witnesses called. His deposition stated that at Gardiner's sermon at St Paul's Cross, the King, all the Privy Councillors present and all others of the audience that he could talk to 'were much offended with his said sermon'.[363] Gardiner was found guilty of opposing the reformation of religion and was returned to the Tower. He remained there until Princess Mary came to the throne.

The Princess's views on religion were another vexation to the Council and Paulet was involved in negotiations with her about her refusal to give up the Catholic faith. Mary believed that no changes should have been made to the religion of the country until the King was old enough to decide for himself. For two years, from 1547 until May 1549, Somerset had allowed Mary to continue to worship as a Catholic but in May 1549 the Act of Uniformity became law and banned the mass. Mary still refused to give up her religion and the Protector told Van der Delft that she could continue to worship in private within her household. However, the Emperor was not satisfied with this verbal assurance and asked for confirmation in writing. During May 1549 Somerset's response was that he could not grant written permission for Mary to act in contradiction of an Act of Parliament. But he still agreed to her hearing mass in private, saying that he would not inquire into her religious practice if she had not yet come to their way of thinking and she should 'do as she thinks best until the King comes of age'.[364]

In early September 1549 Paulet and Paget met with the ambassador and reiterated that the Council wished the Princess to conform to the laws but, since she would not and because they desired to please her as the 'second person in the realm' after the King, they promised that she could continue to celebrate mass in her house with her priests and household members. Again, Van der Delft asked for written confirmation, arguing that in the future this promise could be broken or that the councillors with knowledge of it might no longer be present. The two men did not disagree with this and returned to the Council to examine the issue. Once more the request was rejected, with Somerset replying that the ambassador 'had cast a reflection on his honour by rejecting his word'.[365] It was a month later that Somerset was removed from power but Van der Delft's continued efforts to gain written permission for Mary to hear mass still resulted in failure. When the ambassador met with Paulet in January 1550 the latter avoided any discussion on matters concerning the Princess.[366]

By the end of 1550 the King was becoming insistent that Mary should cease to practise Catholicism. When she attended Court around Christmas time Edward told her there was a rumour that she regularly heard mass. At this, Mary invited Paulet to join their discussion since he understood the situation, and he in turn asked several other councillors to come and witness their talk. Mary reminded the King of the assurance she had received through the ambassador from Paulet and Paget that she might hear mass in private and Paulet confirmed this. But on 17 January 1551 the Council wrote a letter to Mary in which they claimed that Paulet and other councillors had no recollection of this promise. Mary was greatly upset at this and wrote a long letter setting out her understanding of the situation. Edward joined in the exchange of letters, writing to maintain that she was breaking the law and that she had wrongly interpreted the promise made to her. His toleration of her religious practice was not permission to break the law but done in the hope that she would be encouraged to obey it. He warned her 'I will see my laws strictly obeyed.'[367]

In February Paulet, Paget, Petre and Sir Philip Hoby again confirmed to the Emperor's ambassador that the promise made by Paulet and Paget had only been for the Princess to follow her religion as long as the King permitted, not indefinitely. Again the ambassador disagreed with this interpretation claiming a promise was made to the Emperor that Mary could follow the Catholic faith until the King was 'of more years'.[368] Mary was called to Court and, on 15 March 1551, she rode through London with an entourage of 130 gentlemen and ladies, all wearing rosaries, which were now banned.[369] On 17 March, Paulet witnessed Mary's arrival at Court. She was met at Westminster with very few formalities and led before the King and the entire Council to be told that the promise made to her was for only a limited time and was now to end. They said that grave trouble would arise if she, as the King's sister and heir to the Crown, was known to be practising the Catholic faith.[370]

The Emperor was enraged, not only because of the refusal of the Council to give written assurance that Mary be allowed to hear mass, but by the demands of Sir Richard Morrison, the King's ambassador to the Emperor. Morrison had been arguing in favour of the Protestant religion and asking that the English ambassador in Brussels should be allowed to use this form of worship since the new Imperial ambassador, Jean Scheyfve, was permitted Catholic worship in England. The day after Mary's meeting with Edward, Scheyfve arrived at Court with a warning that the Emperor would declare war if the Princess was not allowed to continue hearing mass. The threat of war frightened the Privy Council. Morrison later described how the King was brought to the council chamber where Paulet went down on his knees, followed by the other councillors, to plead with Edward to allow Mary to hear mass and so protect the country from the Emperor. The writer did not think highly of Paulet's oratorical skills believing him capable of neither 'learned talk or plain simplicity' but Paulet spoke persuasively enough and the King and Council decided not to deny Mary her religion.[371]

However, in August 1551, the Council finally decided that Mary's stubbornness was not to be suffered any longer and a letter was written ordering her staff and chaplains to permit only the Anglican service within her household. Throughout the month Paulet saw how the repeated orders to her household officers not to allow mass to be said resulted in Mary becoming ever more resolved not to give in. Still she refused to conform, only agreeing that 'When the King's majesty comes to such years that he may be able to judge these things, his majesty shall find me ready to obey his orders in religion.'[372] In the end events on the continent meant that the problem solved itself. War broke out between France and Spain and the Emperor ceased to demand written agreement for Mary to hear mass. For the Privy Council, it was easier to allow her to continue to hear mass privately in her own chamber than to continue the battle, which they must have realised they might never win.

Edward VI was considered to be intellectually precocious and on one occasion Paulet was unable to satisfy the young King's curiosity. Every year, on St George's Day, Paulet joined the other Garter Knights and the King at a church service followed by a feast. On 23 April 1551, they assembled at Greenwich and, after hearing a sermon in praise of the saint, they retired to the Presence Chamber where Edward addressed them with the question: 'What saint is St George that we have so honoured him?' The lords did not know what to answer and Paulet replied 'If it please your majesty, I did never read in any history of St George but only in the *Golden Legends*, where it is thus set down, that St George, mounted on his charger, out with his sword and ran the dragon through with his spear.' The King burst into laughter at the thought of the knight on a steed wielding a spear in one hand and a sword in the other and asked what he did with his reins meanwhile. That question Paulet was unable to answer.[373]

That spring England was unsettled again. The military situation was worrying with the threat of war from the Emperor, and the Privy Council was still frightened by the uprisings of 1549 and concerned at the possibility that the same could happen again. Lack of confidence in the currency continued and there was insufficient food. One way of eking out the dwindling meat supply was by enforcing abstinence days. While the Church used these days to encourage men to 'subdue their bodies unto soul and spirit' the government supported abstinence for economic reasons and as a way to preserve stocks.[374] In fact it was such a generally accepted principle that people were exhorted:

> With sometime fish, and sometime fast,
> that household store may longer last.
> The land doth will, the sea doth wish,
> spare sometime flesh, and feed of fish.[375]

On 9 March 1551, a proclamation was issued enforcing the Statutes for Abstinence due to a 'great scarcity of victuals and especially of flesh'. It asserted that Lent was the best time for 'breeding of flesh' and that by eating fish at times of abstinence much meat could be bred. More fishing meant that the fishermen benefited from extra income and they were better trained to serve in the navy. The eating of flesh was prohibited on Fridays, Saturdays and in Lent with a threat of punishment of a 10-shilling fine and ten days' imprisonment. Everyone was banned from eating flesh in those times unless they had a licence, and the owners of taverns and hostelries were ordered not to serve flesh. Even the butchers were ordered not to kill or sell meat to be eaten upon those days unless by licence and secretly. However, those in authority could get round the ban. In 1553 a licence was granted for Paulet and his wife, with two friends at their table, to eat flesh and milk foods in Lent.[376]

As Lord Treasurer, Paulet bore some responsibility for a decision to devalue the currency which unintentionally damaged the already struggling economy. During the previous seven years a series of debasements had reduced the silver content, or fineness, of the coinage. For the King, this meant that a larger number of coins could be minted using the same quantity of silver. However, the people equated the value of a coin with its silver content and thus prices rose. This problem was compounded by a proclamation issued on 30 April 1551 announcing that on the following 31 August the teston, or shilling, would be devalued from 12d to 9d and the groat from 4d to 3d, bringing their market valuation closer to the value of their silver content. This caused panic and prices rose to such an extent that the devaluation date had to be brought forward and the currency was devalued even further, pushing the teston down to 6d and the groat to 2d. By mid-August the value of the coinage had halved. In an attempt to remedy excessive overcharging, the price scales set for victuals the previous year were re-introduced and the Privy Council set maximum prices for the sale of animals. The greatest fat ox was to cost no more than 53s 4d, while the greatest lean ox no more than 40 shillings. A great fat sheep was to be no more than 5 shillings and a great lean sheep 3s 4d.[377]

As the people struggled to feed themselves they were about to be beset by another and more deadly ordeal. On 4 July 1551 the King enjoyed a day of entertainment when he rode to Blackheath, with all his retinue, and in the evening he joined the Council to dine on board a ship at Deptford.[378] One week later he was on his way to Hampton Court with just a few courtiers, withdrawing to the country to escape the sweating sickness. The first sign of this killer disease in London appeared on 7 July and it ravaged the city until the end of the month. One source estimated that 960 people died of the sweat during the first few days. It had started at Shrewsbury in mid-April and did not finally finish in the north of England until the end of September.[379] As shops and businesses closed and people waited to see if they would survive, the King and Privy Council instructed the bishops to encourage people to amend their sinful lives and to pray for deliverance from the illness.[380]

Sweating, or 'hot sickness', like the plague, carried a high risk of mortality.[381] It was passed from person to person and the crowded living conditions of the city were perfect for the disease to spread. The symptoms were varied – chills and shivering followed by high fever and sweating, weakness, severe headache often with heart pains, vomiting and stupor. Death followed quickly, often within a few hours. In 1552 Warwick, suspecting that his daughter-in-law had died of sweat, wrote that 'The night before she died she was as merry as any child ... She sickened about three in the morning in a sweat and was in continual pangs and fits until she died at six in the evening.'[382] Escape to the country did not necessarily guarantee safety. The young Duke of Suffolk, Henry Brandon, and his brother Charles both died within a few hours of each other, extinguishing the Suffolk title. For Paulet, this was the third outbreak of the sweating sickness in his lifetime and it was a period of great uncertainty. It was, however, to be the last major outbreak of the disease in England. Stow wrote of the events of 1551 that 'This was a terrible time in London, for many one lost suddenly his friends by the sweat, and their money by the proclamation.'[383]

While the risk of infection was high, access to Edward was restricted. On 14 August Paulet was one of only ten councillors with him at Hampton

Court but a few days earlier, when 24 councillors discussed the measures to be taken against Princess Mary, they met away from the Court at Richmond. By 22 August it was felt safe for the King to travel again and he set off on progress around houses close to London. During mid-September Paulet left the King and was back in London with Warwick and Herbert to consider the re-minting of coins and the payment of debts.[384] Although the three men joined those lords who had remained in the city as the Council in London during the King's progress, they did not stay long. On 16 September Paulet rode down to Farnham to report to the councillors accompanying the King and was back in London two days later. On 22 September he, Warwick and Herbert met at Warwick's house in Chelsea and the following day they all left Chelsea to return to the Court which had now moved on to Oatlands.[385] Before the King returned to Hampton Court, the councillors granted a passport for Mary of Guise, the Dowager Queen of Scotland, to travel across England. Foreigners were not allowed to land on English soil without permission and Mary of Guise was planning to return to Scotland after visiting her daughter, Mary Stuart, in France. Journeys by sea were quite perilous and she hoped to travel part of the way across land. On her journey to France a year earlier her ship had been blown into Rye by a storm and she had requested a passport allowing her to land. On that occasion Scheyfve reported that Somerset, Paulet, Northampton and Russell were not pleased at this news and only granted the licence after much deliberation. In the event, the lady only landed for two or three hours before resuming her journey.[386]

On Sunday, 11 October, shortly after the Court had settled back into Hampton Court, Paulet was raised into the very highest echelons of the aristocracy when he was elevated by the King to Marquis of Winchester. At about 9am, after morning service, he was in the King's apartments with Warwick, the Marquis of Dorset and Sir William Herbert. Warwick was to become Duke of Northumberland, Dorset to be Duke of Suffolk and Herbert to be Earl of Pembroke. The men donned their robes, Paulet in a gown of black damask with squirrel and marten fur and velvet trimming, and waited to be individually escorted to the King.[387] When Paulet's time came, after Warwick and Dorset, he was led by the Marquis of Northampton on his right hand side and the Earl of Bedford on his left, with the Earl of Rutland bearing his coronet, Lord Cobham his sword and Garter Knight with his patent. They passed along the gallery strewn with green rushes, through the Great Watching Chamber and into the Presence Chamber where the King stood under the cloth of state attended by the other nobles. After bowing three times, Paulet knelt before the King and the patent was passed to Edward who handed it to the Secretary, Sir William Cecil, to be read. During the reading the King put a sword 'baldrick wise' (hung from a leather belt worn slung from one shoulder across the breast) onto Paulet and placed the coronet on his head before finally handing him the patent. Paulet gave him thanks and stood on the King's left hand side while Herbert was invested. When all was finished Paulet and the others were led into dinner in a grand procession with the trumpets blowing and, after the second course of the banquet, the trumpets blew again as the herald announced the men's new titles to the accompaniment of fanfares.[388] Paulet's climb through the ranks of the nobility had reached its zenith. As a marquis, along with Northampton, he came second in precedence only to dukes, of whom there were then only three – Somerset, Northumberland and Suffolk – since Norfolk was still in the Tower under an act of attainder. With his new title came the necessity of living in a manner appropriate to his rank, a costly matter. Although the allowance in support of his new dignity was only 50 marks or £33 6s 8d, a new land grant further increased his income.[389]

It is worth noting that Paulet's sudden rise from baron to marquis in less than two years was not due to royal favour and patronage but to the exceptional political circumstances of Edward VI's reign. The young King's chief political advisers distributed titles amongst themselves with the King's agreement. The marquisate was an acknowledgement of Paulet's support for Northumberland. It is unlikely that either Queen Mary or Queen Elizabeth would have elevated him to such an exalted position. Both Queens were somewhat restrained in giving patronage and although Paulet's talents as an administrator and councillor were recognised, and rewarded by Henry VIII with the title of Lord St John, they did not in themselves warrant elevation to marquis. Northumberland was hoping that both the marquisate and the earlier honour of Earl of Wiltshire would help to ensure Paulet's future co-operation. Paulet benefited from supporting the right man at the right time.

Somerset attended the ceremony as an attendant to Dorset but only five days later he was imprisoned in the Tower again. There were various rumours about his plotting – that he hoped for his daughter to marry the King, that he planned to raise support from the people in the north and that he would take Northumberland and other lords as prisoners at a banquet and assassinate them. The rumours were probably largely untrue but the Privy Council were so afraid of any threat of Somerset returning to power that they agreed to move against him and charge him with treason.

Paulet was appointed High Steward of England to preside at the trial and on 1 December he took his place in Westminster Hall, sitting under a cloth of state set three steps above the floor, while one step lower sat 27 peers of the realm.[390] The charges against Somerset were that he planned to seize the King and to govern himself, to imprison Northumberland, Northampton and Pembroke, and to raise a force in London and take the Tower. He denied all the charges. Somerset objected that Northumberland, Northampton and Pembroke sat with the peers as his judges since many of the charges were for actions against them but Paulet decreed that it was presumed that a peer would always give an honest verdict. Northumberland would not agree that an action against himself could be construed as treason and so Paulet decided that it should be a charge of felony.[391] The Lords acquitted Somerset of the charge of high treason but found him guilty of felony and Paulet sentenced him to be executed. It was the custom for prisoners found guilty of treason to leave the Hall preceded by a Sergeant-at-Arms carrying an axe with the blade turned towards the accused. Somerset left with the axe turned away from him signifying that he was innocent of treason and the crowds erupted shouting and throwing up their caps in their belief that he was to be released. But they were wrong – he was still to be executed. It was this support for Somerset from the people that Northumberland and the Council feared. Somerset was brought down because he had few supporters amongst those in power who had more or less fabricated the charges. In a letter to Admiral Clinton after the trial, Paulet set down how Somerset had been found guilty of asking Lord Strange to persuade the King to marry Somerset's daughter, an act which showed the Duke to be presumptuous with 'little consideration of the King's majesties honour'. But he made no mention of the other charges.[392]

Somerset returned to the Tower to await his death. The King and Court moved to Greenwich to celebrate Christmas, a season which this year was particularly full of entertainments and feasting. Northumberland was worried that the young King might pardon his uncle and so arranged for him to be constantly occupied to divert his attention from the forthcoming execution. Somerset was a threat to the peace and security of the country and to his enemies on the Council who feared that the people could rise to support him if he should attempt to take control. Although he had not succeeded in improving conditions for the people he had given them hope and was still more popular than Northumberland. The execution took place on 22 January 1552. However it affected Paulet and the other councillors, Edward was unmoved by his uncle's death and in his diary he recorded only that: 'The Duke of Somerset had his head cut off upon Tower Hill between 8 and 9 o'clock in the morning.'[393] The Spanish ambassador believed that Somerset was innocent and that with his removal Northumberland now had no strong opposition. This left him in a position to remove any councillors he considered might become a threat. There were rumours that Paulet and Lord Rich might be arrested and imprisoned in the Tower but nothing came of it.[394]

Paulet, the man who declared Somerset's fate in Westminster Hall, became responsible for the upbringing of the Duke's three sons as, after their father's death, they were made wards of the King and brought up in Paulet's house. Thomas Norton, who had been appointed by Somerset to instruct the children, continued in his position and was asked by John Calvin about the children's situation. Calvin's doubts, as a staunch Protestant, were that Paulet still held to the Catholic faith and might be a bad influence on the boys. Norton replied on 13 November 1552 in a letter that gives first-hand information on Paulet's own religious practice. He said that the children were 'liberally educated' and that Calvin should have no concerns about them residing in the house of the Marquis, even though reports about his religion may have led Calvin 'to entertain a doubt'. He continued, 'he is a worthy and religious man, nor do I see in what respect he differs from us; so that, even supposing he were to think differently, which I do not believe to be the case, yet as he does not draw us aside, but even goes before us in religion, by his own example, there is no danger.'[395]

Paulet's exact religious beliefs are not known because he has left no definitive statement but most contemporary commentators seem to have viewed him as being a tolerant Catholic, taking the middle way. Although Norton's comments appear to contradict these views he admits that Paulet might possibly 'think differently' from himself. As an isolated comment perhaps it should not be given too much weight, although Norton did live in Paulet's house and as a tutor saw how the household lived at close quarters. He did not see any overt signs of Catholicism and even suggests that Paulet openly practised the new reformed faith and did not secretly hold other beliefs. Paulet was certainly sufficiently tolerant of Protestantism to allow Somerset's children to worship as the King directed. All the other indications are that he was a Catholic although not such a firm believer that he surrounded himself with religious icons or attended mass openly.

One man who did berate Paulet as being a Catholic was the Scottish preacher John Knox. It was probably during the autumn of 1552 that he gave his last sermon before the King in which he made a vituperative attack on Paulet and Northumberland, comparing Paulet to Sobna who was Comptroller, Secretary and Treasurer to King Ezechias in the Bible and Northumberland to Achitophel, a secret councillor, who deserted King David to support his son Absalom. Knox suggested that Paulet would never have been promoted to such high office by such a worthy monarch as Edward 'if the treason and malice which he bare against the King, and against God's true religion, had been manifestly known'. He described Paulet as: 'a crafty fox, and could show such a fair countenance to the King, that neither he nor his council could espy his malicious treason.' But he does draw a picture of a competent and reliable councillor. He believed Paulet 'to be the soul and life to the council in every matter of weighty importance' and acknowledged his capabilities when he asked: 'Who could best dispatch business that the rest of the Council might hawk and hunt, and take their pleasure?' Knox believed that Paulet was devious and underhand, and in asking: 'Who was most frank and ready to destroy Somerset and set up Northumberland?' he questioned Paulet's loyalty to his fellow councillors. But any credence his attack might have had was undermined when he continued: 'Who cried "Bastard, bastard, incestuous bastard Mary shall never reign over us", and who said "Agree to his grace's last will and perfect testament, and let never that obstinate woman come to authority"?' Knox wrote this down from memory after Mary had come to the throne and the latter part is referring to events which supposedly happened *after* he gave the sermon. Paulet was in fact a strong supporter of Mary and held reservations about Edward's plan for the succession.[396]

Knox's tirade and Norton's letter, both probably delivered within weeks of each other, give two opposing views of Paulet's faith. It is probable that Knox was closest to the truth since Paulet was generally believed to be Catholic. Whatever his real beliefs, they were not so strong that he was prepared to stand up and be counted against the official line. Like so many others, it may have been that Paulet was content to do as the King ordered. His first loyalty was to the monarchy and what it represented, and that included the King's position as Head of the Church in England.

On 22 October, only six days after Somerset had been arrested, the councillors were diverted from the business of gathering evidence against him by the arrival of the Dowager Queen of Scotland. On her return journey to Scotland Mary of Guise had once again been driven ashore in England, this time into Portsmouth. She decided to avail herself of the passport which the Council had given her for safe passage across the country and to continue her journey overland, visiting Edward on the way. Some of the gentlemen of Hampshire, amongst them one of Paulet's brothers, were ordered to ride to her at the coast and offer their services. Paulet's eldest son, Lord St John, was amongst the gentlemen who escorted her on the final two miles of her journey to Hampton Court on 31 October.[397]

Paulet and his wife also played their part in greeting the Dowager Queen. The Lady Marquis was called to attend upon her at Southwark Palace on 3 November and to accompany her on her visit to Court the following day. Paulet was with the King when he received Mary for dinner at the palace and later he, with Northumberland, Bedford and Northampton, visited her to deliver a diamond ring as a gift from the King. On 6 November Mary of Guise left on her journey to Scotland. An escort had been organised to accompany her to the border and she received a grand farewell from London. Northumberland, Pembroke, Lord St John and other nobles, each with their own mounted escort, rode through London with her until they met the gentlemen of Middlesex who were to escort her on the next stage of her journey.[398]

One month later, on 7 December, Paulet's men were on parade when the King reviewed a muster held in St James Park. Although the date for this had been set earlier in the year, with Somerset awaiting execution this was a timely display of force. Paulet's escort of 100 men of arms on great horses, all with pikes, wore coats of red and white and on his white standard was a gold falcon.[399] Several of the other lords present had 100 men each and these were the foundation of the new fighting force, the first army, which Northumberland created. The previous February, it was declared that the King should have a standing army of 900 men for his own safety and to quell uprisings. However, the cost of maintaining this number of men and horses readily available for the King's use proved to be too expensive. Edward reviewed another muster in May 1552 but in September the force was disbanded. Northumberland may have intended the army to protect him in the event of a coup but, with Somerset gone, that threat was reduced.

Northumberland was feeling more secure in his position and his increasingly confident actions resulted in the resignation of Lord Rich as Chancellor. Rich was concerned at the way Northumberland was starting to sideline the Privy Council, passing documents without the counter-signatures of sufficient of the councillors. Northumberland argued that Edward had now assumed full responsibility and that the royal signet was sufficient to authorise a document. In November, Rich had been ordered to draw up the commission for Somerset's trial, which now needed only Edward's signature. Rich, who was suffering from a serious illness, resigned on 21 December 1551 and Paulet was present to witness him hand over the Great Seal, which was later given to Bishop Goodrich as Keeper of the Seal. Goodrich was confirmed as Lord Chancellor towards the end of 1552 amidst a certain amount of speculation. The Spanish ambassador reported rumours that Northumberland might become Lord High Treasurer, Northampton would become Duke of Buckingham and that Paulet could be elevated to Duke of Somerset and made Lord Chancellor.[400] These were only rumours and Paulet was never to attain those dizzy heights. Perhaps if Edward had lived longer there would have been time for these three protagonists to award themselves further honours.

On the day following Somerset's execution, Paulet took his seat when Parliament met for the first time in nearly two years. He achieved a near perfect attendance record, missing only four of the 55 days on which the Lords sat and he witnessed, and voted for, changes which finally removed all Catholic ceremony from church services. Many acts of a social and economic nature were passed, ranging from relief for the poor to orders concerning the manufacture and sale of cloth and the fillings to be used in beds and mattresses. However the most important measure was the Second Act of Uniformity, which ordered everyone to attend church on Sundays and enforced the use of a new, revised Book of Common Prayer. This book was more Protestant in its terminology and in the simplification of services by the removal of many ceremonies. The mass was to be known as the Lord's Supper or Holy Communion and the altar was to be the communion table. There was to be no blessing of the water at baptism, no sign of the cross at confirmation, and prayers for the dead were prohibited. Most vestments were banned and only necessary items of plate were to be used.

The Protestants accepted the new book although John Knox objected that kneeling to receive communion implied veneration of the bread and wine as if transubstantiation had occurred. The position was clarified in October with a declaration that the bread and wine remained in their natural substances and thus could not be adored and that the natural body and blood of Christ were in heaven. Parliament was dissolved on 15 April 1552 although not in the presence of the King. Edward was recovering from what he described in his Chronicle as an attack of measles and smallpox. By 12 May he was completely recovered and riding in Greenwich Park once more.

11

The Death of Edward and
the Disputed Succession

During the spring of 1552 the Council was again exercised by the threat of an uprising. Information came to them of a possible conspiracy in Hampshire and on 16 May, when Lords Lieutenant with military powers were appointed to nineteen counties, Paulet was given responsibility for Hampshire and the Isle of Wight.[401] A senior resident noble or privy councillor was usually chosen as Lord Lieutenant for a county. His primary responsibility was to ensure the defence of the county against both internal and external threats by training and arming suitable men and by raising a force to serve abroad when necessary. However, because many of the lieutenants were councillors in London, much of the work was carried out by deputy-lieutenants usually chosen from the ranks of the justices of the peace.

Although the availability of food had improved since the previous summer and prices had fallen around the country, those in London remained high. The Lord Mayor and aldermen were ordered to control the prices of merchandise, especially of food, and in September the prices at which London butchers could sell meat were fixed at 1¼ pence a pound for best beef, mutton and veal.[402] The Council knew that to help ensure stability of the economy the coinage needed to be restored to a purer gold and silver content. While Paulet remained in London during the King's progress in 1551 he had examined the quality of experimental coins containing varying amounts of silver – but new coinage alone would have been insufficient to resolve the King's financial problems. Henry VIII had spent over £2 million on defence during the 1540s and Somerset had similarly spent over £1 million in just three years, much of this being financed by the sale of capital assets such as land. The sale of this land to courtiers and others of course decreased the King's income from rents. There were debts at home and abroad and the royal annual income could not accommodate anything other than routine expenses. The re-minting of coins even increased the cash flow problem by using large quantities of the King's store of gold and silver.

Paulet and Sir William Cecil oversaw a review of the administration of the Crown's finances that eventually restored them to a sound basis. A commission in March 1552 to examine the state of the revenue courts proposed combining the five courts and improving accounting and auditing to remove the opportunity for malpractice. Overseeing the King's money would be much simpler if it was under the control of a single finance department and this would also reduce staff numbers and therefore salary costs. The following year the first steps towards implementing some of these proposals were taken in Parliament but the movement for change was halted when the King became ill. It was not until Queen Mary's reign that Paulet saw the Courts of Augmentations and First Fruits absorbed into the Exchequer, although Wards and Liveries and the Duchy of Lancaster were left unchanged. Paulet's own position as Treasurer must have been enhanced by the improved status of the Treasury and the increased revenue it handled.

The government's finances were in a parlous state and throughout 1552 Sir Thomas Gresham was working to reduce the country's overseas debts. By manipulation of the currency market he was able to make sufficient payments to prevent defaulting on debts in Flanders and then to begin repaying those debts. The Treasury experienced difficulties paying even small bills at home with the result that some payments were halted. In a bid to reduce costs, workmen were dismissed and a letter to Anne of Cleves explained that the pensions to her servants were to be delayed. The authorities in Calais were ordered to 'create no unnecessary charges' and a decision was made to sell gunpowder and redeem bullion 'with the money growing thereof'.[403] On 20 January 1553 Scheyfve reported that the King was still deferring paying officers and servants and that the last remnants of Church property were being sold. Paulet was one of the commissioners for Hampshire ordered to inventory all the jewels, plate, vestments, bells and other goods the churches held and to remove any items surplus to the Church's requirements.[404]

By the spring of 1552 the King was attending some Privy Council meetings and presenting agendas together with proposals for both improving the Council's methods of operation and concerning topics of special interest to him. The latter covered many aspects from defence of the realm to depletion of timber supplies and the means of improving the financial state of the Treasury. An attempt was made to improve the efficiency of the Council by creating committees of just a few councillors to attend to particular issues, thus creating a 'partition of labours'. Paulet was to attend the committee for matters of state which Edward himself attended on Tuesday afternoons.[405] In January 1553 the King drew up a detailed set of rules for the working of the Privy Council, based upon the proposals Paget had made in 1549. On Sundays, after church, the councillors were to answer letters and finish all items begun the week before. On Monday mornings, suits and petitions were to be heard and debates held that afternoon and on the other four weekdays. The King was to be given a written summary of the week's matters each Saturday. When a matter was unfinished, notes of the progress of the debate were to be made to save time at the next meeting and, for long and tedious matters, a committee was initially to discuss the subject, again to save time in the council meetings. Edward also proposed that decisions could be made by four councillors and then ratified at the next meeting when at least six of them met, and no councillor was to leave Court for longer than two days unless eight others remained.

On 7 July the King left Hampton Court to begin his first major progress, during which he visited several of his courtiers' houses. The entourage that set off was enormous. Fifteen Privy Councillors accompanied him bringing with them an armed escort of 345 men, of whom Paulet provided 30. With the usual complement of courtiers and household staff, the country through which they passed was unable to provide sufficient food and forage and, after two weeks, the number of councillors was reduced. Paulet was one of the nine councillors who accompanied the King for the whole progress, although with a reduced band of 20 men-at-arms. The Court travelled to Oatlands and Guildford, through Sussex and so to Bishops Waltham in Hampshire, 'a fair great old house' which then belonged to Paulet and where Edward enjoyed 'good hunting and good cheer'.[406] The manor of Waltham had previously belonged to the Bishop of Winchester but when Bishop John Ponet was nominated to the See in August 1551 he was forced to surrender the property to the Crown, which then granted it to Paulet for his lifetime.[407] As Catholic bishops were being replaced by Protestants the King acquired more wealth by forcing the new bishops to accept a lower income. Unfortunately for Paulet he did not keep Waltham house for long. He spent £1,000 repairing the house but only two years later the Catholic Bishop Gardiner recovered the manor when he was restored as Bishop of Winchester by Mary.

The party left Waltham on 8 August after spending four nights with Paulet, by which time his purse was probably feeling very light. For the following month the King perambulated around Hampshire and Wiltshire, spending between two and five days at each of the nine houses he visited, before he arrived at Basing House on 7 September and Paulet had to dig deep in his pocket to host Edward and his entourage for another three nights. On 15 September they returned to Windsor – one imagines much to Paulet's relief. It must have been a long, tiring and very expensive ten weeks for him.

Paulet had ordered his servant to prepare a 'stew', a large tub with hot water. He felt tired and dirty after riding in the King's party all day. He was very particular about his cleanliness. He took a bath every few days and insisted on wearing a clean linen shirt each day to absorb perspiration and protect his doublet from becoming sweaty. His hose and doublets and gowns could not be washed but each week they were brushed and shaken. As he walked into his large bedroom a scented fragrance filled the air, herbs mixed with roses. The fire was banked high and before it stood a large wooden tub with sheets laid round about on the floor. More sheets hung from the ceiling around the tub, giving privacy and protecting it from draughts. Paulet greeted the servant who was busy arranging sponges in the bottom of the bath – a large one to sit upon and six more spread across the floor of the tub to place his feet upon. The servant took a large sheet and draped it over the sponges and around the sides of the bath so that his master's body would not touch the wood when he sat in it. His servant helped him to undress and then he stepped into the bath and sat down. On a table beside the tub was a large basin of hot water and on the surface floated herb leaves.

Paulet sat upright as the servant took a soft sponge, dipped it into the water and washed his master's body. When he had finished, he dipped the sponge into a second basin of water, this one with rose petals floating on the surface, and rinsed Paulet's body with this sweeter smelling water. Paulet raised himself up and took his servant's hand as he stepped out of the tub to stand on the foot-sheet. He stood still as the servant, taking a large clean cloth, gently dried him and helped him to don a linen shirt before placing a cloak around his shoulders. Paulet sat upon the chair before the fire and watched as the servant removed the basins and took down the sheets. Carrying these away, he soon returned with another servant to carry out the tub. At last all was finished and after his servant had removed the cloak and placed a night-cap upon his head, Paulet climbed onto the great four-poster bed to be lulled to sleep by the faint smell of rose petals.[408]

Edward spent his final Christmas at Greenwich. During January 1553 his health began to deteriorate. He had difficulty breathing and it was not until the end of February that he began to recover from what was probably an attack of pulmonary tuberculosis.[409] Paulet appears to have been ill at the same time. He was absent from the Privy Council during most of December and all of January, not returning to Court until 2 February; after one week he was again absent, this time for three weeks. A letter from him to Cecil on Monday, 27 February expresses his pleasure at hearing of the King's recovery and his hope of being ready to attend the start of the next parliament. In referring to his own illness, Paulet asks the King to allow him a further ten days absence for his recovery.[410] However, he returned for the opening of Parliament on 1 March and from 6 March he was back to his normal routine, attending every Council meeting. Paulet was by now nearly 70 years old; given his previously near perfect record for attending the Privy Council, such a long absence from Court suggests that whatever ailment he had was serious.

When Parliament opened Edward was still not fully fit so the initial session took place in the Palace of Whitehall, the peers joining the King in the Great Chamber. It was a short parliament and Paulet missed only one sitting before the King dissolved it on the evening of Friday, 31 March. Royal assent was given to fourteen acts, several of which were to do with finance. The merging of the finance courts was enacted, improvements were proposed for the collection of royal revenue and a subsidy bill was passed to allow the collection of taxes to raise funds.

Princess Mary visited Edward during his recovery; her reception at Court was very different to two years earlier. It was apparent that the King's illness was serious and, if he should die with no heir, Mary would be next in line to the throne. Courtiers who had slighted her in the past were keen to regain her favour and she was received with great ceremony. Paulet's wife, the 'Lady Marquis' of Winchester, was amongst the ladies who attended Mary as she rode through London and at the gate of Whitehall Paulet was one of those who met her and escorted her to Edward in the Presence Chamber.[411]

On 11 April Edward made his last earthly journey when he moved to Greenwich from where, a month later, he watched as three boats sailed past on a voyage to attempt to find a north-east passage, a new trade route to the East. What they actually found was Muscovy, or Russia. The venture was seen as an investment opportunity and Paulet joined other Privy Councillors and London merchants in investing £25 each to finance the charter and outfitting of the vessels. The expedition was a disaster for two of the ships, which were forced to land on the North Cape in August after running into bad weather. With no hope of rescue, the crews eventually perished. The third ship, the *Edward Bonaventura*, sailed into the White Sea and landed at Archangel. From there the captain, Richard Chancellor, travelled to Moscow where he was received by Tsar Ivan IV, later to be known as Ivan the Terrible. Trade links were set up between the two countries and the venture was successful enough for Paulet to continue investing in future explorations. On 26 February 1555 the Merchant Adventurers of England were established by charter for the discovery of lands and territories. This gave official backing to voyages of exploration, not only for the discovery of new lands but also to open up new trade routes to the northwest and north-east. The grant also allowed the explorers to plant the royal standard on newly found land and to subdue the people as subjects of the English monarch. Paulet, perhaps with an eye to a profit, supported this company and headed the long list of 190 investors who, at their own cost, fitted out the ships.[412]

By the middle of June, Edward's condition was serious again and the Court was awash with rumours about his successor. Scheyfve feared that Northumberland might take control to keep power and that he had already 'formed some mighty plot' against the Princess Mary.[413] On 11 June Edward suffered a violent fever for 24 hours and was left weak, with swollen legs and unable to keep down his food. By 15 June it was rumoured that Lady Jane Grey, the eldest daughter of the Duke of Suffolk, was to be queen and not Princess Mary. On 21 May, Lady Jane had married Guildford Dudley, one of Northumberland's sons. If Jane became queen, Northumberland would be able to wield power through his new daughter-in-law.

In his will Henry VIII had left the succession to his three children, Edward, Mary and Elizabeth, followed by the sons of the three sisters Jane, Catherine and Mary Grey and their cousin Margaret Clifford, all grand-daughters of Henry's sister Mary. Edward did not want his own sister Mary to become queen as he knew she would attempt to return the country to Catholicism. Edward believed he could change the succession even though, as a minor, he could not make a legal will. He ignored the fact that his father used an Act of Parliament to overcome the problem of having previously declared Mary and Elizabeth to be bastards and to extend the succession to include the four cousins. Edward drafted his 'Devise for the Succession' in which he denied the Crown to his sisters and also to the young Mary, Queen of Scotland. Leaving the Crown to Queen Mary would not only have put a Catholic on the throne but, because of her betrothal to the Dauphin, could have put England under the control of France. Edward had no male relatives in England and his next closest relatives were the Grey sisters and Margaret Clifford. The succession confirmed by Henry had been to the 'Lady Jane's heirs male'. The addition of two small words, to 'Lady Jane *and her* heirs male', changed the succession and provided a living heir to succeed Edward.

Edward needed the 'Devise' to be drawn up in a will. On 12 June the King ordered Sir Edward Montagu, Lord Chief Justice and a Privy Council executor, with several senior lawyers, to his bedside where Paulet and other councillors were waiting. Edward instructed the lawyers to draw up his will based on the 'Devise' but they refused, arguing that this would be treason since it was against the Act of Succession, which could not be swept aside. On 15 June the judges were again called before the King and again commanded to write the will. Eventually Montagu and the others agreed.

By 18 June there were rumours that Paulet, Arundel, Russell, Shrewsbury and Sir Thomas Cheyney were among councillors who did not agree with Northumberland over the proposed succession.[414] The 'Devise' was contrary to Paulet's loyalty to the Crown and to the legal succession. Even if the whole Council signed, it could still be treason to agree to the document. The Council discussed the matter for several days until eventually the objectors, including Paulet, agreed to endorse the 'Devise'. On 21 June Paulet signed the letters patent which set out Edward's plan for the succession. It may well be that the councillors who were wavering signed out of fear or were bribed, rather than because they supported Edward's intentions. Scheyfve reported that the King had left legacies of income in land for the Lords of the Council and that Northumberland had obtained more money and was doing his best to make friends by means of gifts and promises.[415] One hundred other signatures accompanied Paulet's, those of Montagu and the judges, the great officers of state, peers including Paulet's son, Lord St John of Basing, privy councillors, household officers, the Lord Mayor and aldermen and sheriffs, although some of the latter may have been added at a later date.[416] Paulet's prominence on the list, third after Cranmer as Archbishop of Canterbury and Thomas Goodrich, Bishop of Ely and Lord Chancellor, was dictated by his status at Court and not necessarily by his enthusiasm for the matter. He also signed the 'Engagement', a document in which the Privy Council agreed to observe the will fully and to maintain the succession as defined by the King. Again, his signature followed those of Cranmer and Goodrich.[417]

It became apparent that the King could die any day. 'His body no longer performs its functions, his nails and hair are dropping off, and all his person is scabby.'[418] The Council were concerned at how the people might react to the prospect of Jane as queen. The night watch around the city and at the Tower was increased and ten ships were stationed in the Thames, with others at Harwich and Portsmouth, to guard the Channel against any Spanish ships which might try to support Mary. Mary, who had been so feted on her visit to Court in February, now moved farther from London, riding to Kenninghall in Norfolk.

Northumberland had few supporters on the Privy Council apart from those adherents who needed his support to maintain their own positions. It appeared to those about him that he must be a prime instigator of the 'Devise' since it would make his daughter-in-law queen but it is unlikely that this had been a long-standing plan. Until January 1553 there was no real reason to believe the King would not survive to maturity and have children. Edward was soon to be sixteen and Northumberland must have realised he would have to start handing over power to the King; indeed, he may well have been encouraging Edward to take a greater role in governing. Perhaps through his son's marriage he saw a last and unexpected chance to maintain some control over the affairs of the country.

Edward VI died on 6 July. His death was kept secret for two days while Northumberland took control. On 7 July Paulet and Shrewsbury secured the Tower, discharged Sir James Croft, the Constable, and installed Lord Admiral Clinton in his place. The following day, the Lord Mayor and aldermen of London were told of Edward's death and Paulet was one of the signatories on letters to justices telling them to support Edward's succession plans and to maintain order in their counties.[419]

Lady Jane arrived at the Tower by boat on 10 July and was proclaimed queen through the streets of the city. That night Paulet took the crown to her to see if it needed alteration. She was reluctant to try it on, saying that it would do as it was, and became indignant when Paulet told her that her husband was also to be crowned.[420] Meanwhile Mary had reached

Kenninghall and proclaimed herself queen; she then sent a messenger to the Council demanding that they give her their allegiance and proclaim her as such. By 12 July the Council realised that support for Mary was so strong that they would have to send an armed force to oppose her. Families in East Anglia had risen to support her and, around the country, nobles and gentry were declaring her to be the rightful monarch. It was not only Catholic families who supported her – many Protestants loyal to the Crown had also gone over to her side. The Council agreed that Northumberland was the best man to lead troops against Mary even though he was reluctant to leave the city and the other councillors. He already suspected that some of them, including Paulet, might not be loyal to him and was worried that more might follow. That night, weapons and men were moved into the Tower and two days later Northumberland set out with fewer than 2,000 men to face Mary's supporters, having been assured by the councillors that they were loyal to him. Even so, he left his only real supporter, the Duke of Suffolk, who was the new Queen's father, to control the Privy Councillors and keep them under close surveillance within the Tower.

Once Northumberland had left for Suffolk, the councillors were able to make their own plans. Paulet was one of the leaders of the coup against Northumberland and William Cecil described how he had schemed with Paulet to win over Lord Russell and take Windsor Castle for Mary, while Paulet and Russell were to raise forces in the west. Paulet wrote to his son, Lord St John, instructing him to follow Cecil's directions and to keep him safe if he failed to take the castle. It appears that blank passports, already signed by the Council, were ready in case of the need to make a quick escape from England. Cecil was planning to use the alias of Hardinge.[421] Pembroke and Cheney tried without success to leave the Tower but during the evening of Sunday, 16 July Paulet left the fortress to visit his London house at Austin Friars. At about 7pm the gates of the Tower were shut and the keys carried to Jane but she, fearing some 'packing' or conspiring in Paulet, ordered his return and at midnight he was brought from his house back to the Tower.[422] The guards who surrounded the Tower, ostensibly to protect Jane from 'popular tumult', could also be used to prevent the councillors fomenting trouble outside.

Mary moved to Framlingham Castle in Suffolk as ever more supporters rallied to her, and six warships Northumberland had stationed off Yarmouth to prevent her leaving the country also declared for her. Northumberland reached Cambridge on 16 July but with so many of his troops deserting to Mary he was forced to give up. On 19 July it was obvious that Jane's reign had come to an end. Paulet, Arundel, Shrewsbury, Bedford, Cheyney, Paget, Petre and Sir John Mason left the Tower to go to Baynards Castle and join Pembroke who had escaped earlier.[423] Once ensconced in Pembroke's house, the Council took control. The Lord Mayor and aldermen were called to Baynards Castle to be told the new state of affairs. A force was dispatched to take the Tower from Suffolk. Between 5 and 6pm Paulet went with Arundel, Shrewsbury, Pembroke and other councillors to Cheapside where the trumpeters blew and the heralds proclaimed Mary as Queen, after which they all went to St Paul's and heard anthems sung to celebrate the new monarch. All through London there were bonfires, the bells were ringing and people toasted the new Queen. The people were by and large content with Mary and were not concerned that she was a Catholic because she was the legitimate heir, the daughter of Henry VIII.

Late that night the Council sent a letter to Northumberland ordering him to disband his forces and not to return to London without the permission of the Queen. Arundel and Paget were sent to Mary to declare the Privy Council's allegiance and to ask for her pardon and, on 28 July, all those Lords of the Council who were not needed to carry on business in London rode to meet her. Northumberland was arrested within a few days by the earl of Arundel and delivered to the Tower. Suffolk appealed to Paulet, as an old friend, to work to obtain the Queen's pardon for him and his family. At that point Paulet was unsure where he stood in the new Queen's favour and replied to Suffolk that he was no surer of his own safety but that he would certainly help if he could.[424]

Lady Jane's reign lasted nine days. Even though forces were gathered there was no real fighting and both her accession to the throne and her fall were peaceful. Northumberland did not understand that the people believed more in the Divine Right of Kings than they did in the new religion. Many of the Privy Council had followed Northumberland in endorsing the 'Devise' voluntarily, possibly to protect their own skins. Others, including Paulet, may have been coerced into signing and he was one of the first to desert Northumberland when he realised which way the wind was blowing. His change of allegiance may have been self-preservation, but it may have happily coincided with his own beliefs. Writing of the coup against Somerset, Sir Richard Morrison described Paulet as willing 'to help to betray his master so he might thereby please his fellow councillor', and ready to serve 'as many masters as can happen in his days'.[425] Paulet may well have been one of the instigators of the downfall of both Somerset and

Northumberland but he was not alone, being well supported by most of the Privy Council. In both instances it seems reasonable to assume that Paulet acted to uphold the rights of the Crown.

Princess Elizabeth rode into London on 29 July to await her sister's arrival on 3 August. Five days later Paulet was the chief mourner at Edward's funeral at Westminster Abbey. His youngest son, Giles, was one of the four young lords still living at Court who had been amongst Edward's friends and schoolmates and they too attended the funeral, an Anglican service at which Cranmer preached.

12

Matters of Finance and the Return of Catholicism

The late King's councillors must have been apprehensive about what action Mary might take against those who had supported Lady Jane. On 2 August Paulet, with the Earls of Pembroke and Shrewsbury, rode out to meet Mary as she approached London. Their purpose was to beg her pardon in person, in the hope of being allowed to remain at Court and of being appointed to the new council. Mary did not immediately pardon them. She did, however, allow the three men to kiss her hand and the next day they were present as she rode into the city.[426] Although Paulet had proved his loyalty to the Crown under previous monarchs and had not been a prime mover in the attempt to put Jane Grey on the throne, it appears that he and Pembroke were confined to their houses for a while where they still remained on 11 August.[427] Shrewsbury was appointed to Mary's Privy Council on 10 August but Paulet and Pembroke had to wait until 13 August before they were sworn in as members.[428] The two men were at Richmond at the time, although the Queen was at the Tower accompanied by the councillors she had already appointed. These numbered over 30 and included household officers and friends on whom she had relied for advice during her flight and subsequent stand in Norfolk, and those who had sheltered and supported her. Now safe in London, it was time for her to appoint men with experience and knowledge of government, men such as Edward's own councillors, 'so as to learn from them the secrets of state, to sweep away evil influences and win them over to her side as good vassals and subjects'.[429] Paulet, together with the Earls of Bedford, Pembroke and Shrewsbury, Lord Rich, Sir John Baker, Sir Thomas Cheney, Sir John Gage, Sir John Mason and Sir William Petre were all re-appointed. The Duke of Norfolk and the Catholic bishops Gardiner, Tunstall, Thirlby and Heath were also sworn to the Council in readiness for Mary's intention to restore Catholicism to the country.

Four days after his swearing-in, Paulet travelled to London to join the council. Sixteen councillors were listed as present but by 21 August, when the Queen had moved to Richmond and Paulet was again present, this had risen to 27.[430] Not all the councillors attended every meeting, some being present only when required for special business. The attendance figures until the end of October were high, being generally between ten and twenty for most meetings and occasionally more. By this time the full list of Mary's councillors numbered over 40. Such a large group made decision-making very difficult and soon a smaller group developed to handle much of the business. Letters from Simon Renard, the Emperor's ambassador, refer to a small group of men who were governing the country. He named Lord Chancellor Gardiner, Lord Steward Arundel, Secretary Petre, Lord Privy Seal Paget, the Comptroller Sir Robert Rochester and Bishop Thirlby. Occasionally Paulet is mentioned as one of this small group but he was not a regular member.[431] For the first four weeks of the reign Paulet attended almost every meeting and then his presence became spasmodic. Indeed, as 1553 progressed his presence at the Privy Council became quite infrequent. Throughout December 1554 to February 1555 the record shows he only attended seven meetings. For much of that time the Court was at Westminster and, while it is possible that he may have been active on the Queen's business, age may have been taking its toll and forcing his absence through illness.

In February 1554, eleven committees involving a total of 24 councillors were set up, each to consider specific matters. This was an attempt to organise the unwieldy council into groups that operated more effectively and gave continuity. Paulet was on three committees whose remits were to ensure supplies for the garrisons on the borders, in France and on the south coast, to consider the laws to be established in the present parliament and to investigate patents and annuities.[432]

Life within the Court and the Privy Council was changed by having a woman on the throne. The Privy Chamber was staffed by women with only a handful of men in attendance. Some of these ladies and gentlewomen were the wives of courtiers and were in a position to try to influence the Queen on behalf of their husbands. However, there was much less political intriguing than there had been in the time of Henry VIII and Edward VI. Within the Privy Council, Paulet found himself adapting to a new situation. Under Henry VIII, decisions were made by the King with the council's advice. During Edward's reign the King was advised of decisions taken by the council. Mary's relationship with the council was different yet again. She was 37 years old when she came to the throne and had received no training to equip her for her new position. After the treatment she had received previously from the Privy Council there were few councillors she trusted, and the friends and household officers who had been faithful to her did not hold positions of influence. Mary trusted her Spanish friends – the Emperor and his ambassador and, later, her husband, King Philip. She felt close to the Spanish people and knew that they would support her in restoring Catholicism to England.

Mary rarely attended Privy Council meetings and was probably advised by the small group of councillors to which Renard had referred. But it is likely that she was also listening to advice which Renard himself offered based on the policies favoured by the Emperor. On occasions she may well have made her decisions before even talking to the council. Her early and most important decisions – her marriage to Philip of Spain and England's return to Catholicism – would appear to have been taken without seeking the advice of many of her councillors. They were no longer policy-makers, as during Edward's reign, and their role as advisers to Mary was diminished as the Queen accepted advice from Spain. They were not under the control of a single powerful councillor, as in Somerset and Northumberland's days, but rather were answerable to the Queen and their individual importance and influence at Court was more dependent on holding her favour than on the support of their peers.

Another change during Mary's reign was in the altered expectation of the councillors with regard to honours. During Edward's reign Northumberland in particular had been very generous in rewarding his supporters with titles but now Paulet's steady rise through the ranks of the nobility was halted. Mary elevated only six men to the nobility and restored four to titles lost by attainder, including Thomas Howard who regained his Dukedom of Norfolk.

Paulet was nearly 70 when Mary came to the throne, the same age as Bishop Gardiner, but they were not the oldest members of the council; they were younger than Sir John Gage, Bishop Tunstall, Lord de la Warr and the Duke of Norfolk. The latter three were not especially active as councillors, possibly partly because of their age but also due to the practice of using a relatively small group of working councillors. Paulet's advanced years do not appear to have been a hindrance and Mary reappointed him to be Lord High Treasurer and, as in previous reigns, he was appointed to various commissions. One of the first of these was to try Northumberland and his associates.

On 18 August 1553 Paulet was in Westminster Hall when Northumberland with his son, the Earl of Warwick, and the Marquis of Northampton were pronounced guilty of treason by the Duke of Norfolk. The following day Paulet presided at Westminster when sentences of treason were passed against Sir Andrew Dudley, Sir John Gates, Sir Henry Gates and Sir Thomas Palmer.[433] Although all seven men were sentenced to death only Northumberland, Palmer and John Gates were executed. Lady Jane Grey and her husband, Guildford Dudley, were imprisoned but not executed until the following year.

Meanwhile, Mary was preparing for her coronation. As was the custom, the streets were hung with arras (richly embroidered tapestry) and the citizens prepared speeches and pageants to be performed as the Queen rode through London on the day before her coronation. On 30 September Mary left the Tower in a chariot covered with cloth of gold beneath a canopy of state and drawn by six horses. The procession passed along Fenchurch and Gracechurch Streets into Cornhill and Cheapside to St Paul's and then along Fleet Street and the Strand to Westminster Palace. Before her rode the gentlemen of the Court with the bishops, lords and councillors. The Great Seal and the mace were carried before Bishop Gardiner and Paulet, and following behind them were Norfolk and the Earl of Oxford. Then came the Queen's chariot with another carrying Princess Elizabeth and Anne of Cleves. Riding beside the Queen were the Duchess of Norfolk, the Marchionesses of Winchester and Exeter and the Countess of Arundel. The following day, at the coronation service in Westminster Abbey, Paulet carried the orb, Arundel the sceptre and Norfolk the crown. Mary was crowned with three crowns for England, Ireland and France. The Bishop of Winchester then gave her a kiss of obeisance on behalf of the bishops and was followed by the Duke of Norfolk, Paulet as Marquis of Winchester and the Earl of Arundel, who all kissed her on her left cheek on behalf of the dukes, the marquises and the earls.[434]

Four main problems beset Mary: the impact of her decision to return the country to the Roman Catholic faith; the geopolitical implications of her marriage; establishing the succession; and the need to improve the country's finances. The latter topic was the one which most exercised Paulet. Mary reappointed him as Lord Treasurer, not because she particularly favoured him, but because he brought a wealth of experience and continuity to the position. Although there are references to him as Lord Treasurer in a letter dated 8 August and at the Privy Council on 17 August, he was not formally sworn in at the Tower until 30 September, shortly before the Queen set out to ride to Westminster for her coronation.[435] The post was a prestigious one, which other councillors coveted. In November, when the Spanish ambassador believed that Paulet might be under house arrest, there was talk that the position might be given to Sir Edward Waldegrave and in November 1554 rumours suggested that the Earl of Arundel wanted the post and that 'feeling ran high between the two parties.'[436] However, Paulet maintained his position. He did surrender his post as Master of the Court of Wards and Liveries in May 1554, probably not by choice since this was one of the most lucrative offices in the gift of the Crown. Mary gave the Mastership to Sir Francis Englefield, one of her supporters before she took the throne. This did not prevent Paulet continuing to enjoy the benefits of the Court and in September 1554 he was granted custody of the lands and manors of Joan Lyngen and the rights to arrange her marriage. Even in 1570 he was endeavouring to continue as guardian of several children.[437] In 1553 Renard described Paulet as the richest man in England who had made his fortune 'out of Church property and by devouring the substance of wards and minors'.[438] Renard viewed Paulet as rapacious but it was accepted that men working in the finance courts would always use their position to enhance their own wealth. It is difficult to be sure when these transactions were legal and when they were not.

Prior to 1550, when Paulet became Lord Treasurer, the holder of the title did not have complete control of the monarch's treasure. He was head of the Exchequer but much of the Crown revenue was handled by the various finance courts. In 1554 reform of the courts put the Exchequer back at the centre of finance as nearly all the money was now handled by its officers. Mary decided to implement the finance reforms that had been proposed during Edward's reign and, in January 1554, the Courts of Augmentations and First Fruits and Tenths were absorbed into the Exchequer while Wards and Liveries and the Duchy of Lancaster were left as independent courts. This meant that all Crown income except from the latter two courts was collected into the Exchequer of Receipt. Most of the Queen's income was now administered centrally and the Exchequer could more easily control both income and expenditure. During Edward VI's reign the Exchequer handled about £80,000 a year, less than one-third of the King's income. The reorganisation meant the tellers were now handling about £265,000 a year or over three-quarters of all Crown income.[439]

The Exchequer gained in importance as a result of the amalgamation and the officers found the status of their own positions improved. Their responsibility increased as they handled larger sums of money and further opportunities arose for collecting fees for transactions. Previously, duplicate officers had been doing similar work in different courts and the new centralised system was intended to allow for easier auditing and better control of expenditure. Historically, the Treasurer was the most important member of the Exchequer and hence the most powerful, but over the years his position had been eroded. By 1550 much of his work was in the hands of other officers and he no longer stood apart as the principal officer. Putting the Exchequer back at the centre of finance increased Paulet's status.

Paulet was conservative in his attitude to financial management and believed that a return to the 'ancient course' of old methods would have further enhanced his authority. This may have been the reason behind his support for Edmund Cockerell who was appointed as Clerk of the Pells in 1555. The operation of the Receipt had changed over the years and Cockerell was keen to return his position to the higher profile it had formerly enjoyed. Henry VII had taken the responsibility for the care of the money away from the Treasurer and the Chamberlains and transferred the charge and custody of the money to four Tellers. The post of the Treasurer's Clerk, or Clerk of the Pells, who had written the 'pells' or receipts each time money entered or left the Treasurer's control, declined in importance and was superseded by an Under-Treasurer. This new appointee was effectively in control of the Receipt but actually relied on the Writer of the Tallies who ensured that all the money paid into the Receipt was allocated to one of the four Tellers and then instructed them when payments were to be made. The money was not passing into a deposit but was constantly flowing in and out of the Exchequer. The Tellers recorded the movement of the money in and out of their charge and were responsible for its safe storage.

Cockerell wanted a return to the old style of organisation with a transfer of power from the writer of the tallies to himself as Clerk of the Pells. Paulet was aware that abolishing the position of Under-Treasurer would increase the control which he, as Treasurer, held in the Receipt. There had been scandals of misappropriation of money by Tellers and even Paulet came under suspicion of taking money out of the Exchequer. He was cleared and the charge set aside when he produced a warrant dated March 1553 showing that all the missing money, a sum of £1,435 9s 9d, had been delivered out of the Tower, where it had been stored, to the King's Privy Chamber.[440] Such charges, and an instance when a coffer was nearly stolen from a Teller's house, gave Paulet sufficient reason to demand a return to the earlier more secure system of accounting by the traditional officers. The fight was on to gain more power but the Under-Treasurer and the Writer of the Tallies were not prepared to give up their authority. During the autumn of 1557 Paulet presented his case in court but Sir John Baker, the Under-Treasurer, appealed to the Queen who ordered that there should be no change in the Receipt organisation.

For the whole of Mary's reign, Paulet and the other finance officers searched for ways to increase the Crown's income. The Queen was never free of financial problems. At the start of her reign in August 1553 the Crown debts were approaching £200,000.[441] Part of this inherited debt was owed to overseas bankers, particularly in Antwerp. This money was often borrowed for only a year or two, but at interest rates as high as 15 per cent. Repayments were often covered by further loans at a preferable rate or were paid by the merchant adventurers and staplers who were later reimbursed by the government.

In April 1556 Paulet was named on a commission to examine ways of making faster payments to both foreign merchants and the merchant adventurers and merchant staplers.[442] The usual methods of raising the Queen's income were by reducing costs, increasing the ordinary revenue or by collecting taxes from the people. The Privy Council set about reviewing where savings could be made. Paulet was commissioned to examine the costs incurred in Ireland, and the cost of English coastal forts and blockhouses to assess which were necessary and which could be destroyed.[443] Committees set up in February 1554 considered the provision of money and calling-in of debts, ways of reducing household costs and pensions and annuities, and the identification of lands that could be sold.[444] A month later Paulet was instructed 'to bargain and sell for ready money' manors and land belonging to the Queen, although he may not have been completely in agreement with this policy.[445] He disliked the sale of Crown land and endeavoured to stop the Queen giving away land without his agreement. Mary took note of his concerns, on one occasion writing to him that: 'at your departure from me I made you a promise not to determine the gift of any land without your consent', but the fact that further orders to sell land followed demonstrates that he was not entirely successful in preventing sales. However, he may well have had mixed views about the matter since he himself received land to the value of £400.[446]

The results of these reviews and committees did not resolve the lack of money and in October 1555 the government resorted to taxation not, as was usual, to pay for unusual costs such as war but to alleviate the Queen's debts. Parliament granted a subsidy based on the value of land and movable property. Landowners were to pay a tax of two shillings in the pound on land valued at over 20 shillings per annum and movable property was to be taxed at a variable scale of 8*d* in the pound for goods worth £5 to £10, 12*d* for goods valued at £10 to £20 and 16*d* on goods worth over £20. This tax was actually to be paid twice, in 1556 and 1557. The clergy were also to be taxed based on the value of their stipend. During the two years which followed Michaelmas 1555, subsidies accounted for over 40 per cent of the Exchequer income of £430,000.[447]

However, further measures were needed and one of the most successful was the review of the Book of Rates, the list of customs duties. The new book, which had first been proposed in 1552, was not introduced until the end of the reign so it was Elizabeth who benefited most. Earlier introduction might have eased Mary's financial straits. Customs duties were charged on the import and export of goods but the last major assessment of charges had been in 1507. Since then the type and quantity of trade had changed. The duties favoured the export of raw wool rather than cloth although by Mary's reign trade in the former had fallen. Many items were not subject to duty and others were undervalued. To increase income it was necessary to raise the valuations and to increase the number of goods on which duty was charged. To this end, Paulet with Paget, Thirlby, Petre, Francis Hastings Earl of Huntingdon and Sir John Baker talked to customs officers and examined their books in a review of the system.[448] The new rates came into force in May 1558. The number of imported goods to be taxed rose from 790 to 1,170 and the average increase in valuation was over 100 per cent. Customs revenue increased substantially from £29,315 in 1556–7 to £82,797 in 1558–9 and, to improve the collection of the duty, Paulet established the office of Surveyor General of Customs, initially for the port of London but with the intention of extending the control across the whole country.[449]

The amount of involvement Paulet had in planning finance policy may well have been limited. Certainly he was a reliable pair of hands to run the administration of the Exchequer but when a finance council was set up in 1558 he was not included among its members, being instead named on the Council of War. Earlier, under Edward VI, Northumberland had relied on Cecil, Sir Thomas Gresham and Sir Walter Mildmay for financial advice. Decisions regarding expenditure were taken by the Privy Council and as a member Paulet was closely involved in those discussions, but his primary role was to implement the decisions.

The state of the country's finances was a problem with which the Privy Council contended throughout Mary's reign but during the first year other matters demanded their more immediate attention. Mary's intention to marry Philip of Spain and her determination to restore England to the Catholic faith caused consternation not only amongst the councillors but also the people. Many councillors were prepared to accept the return of the mass but not a return to Papal authority. On 18 August 1553 a proclamation was issued announcing that the Queen intended to remain in the Catholic faith and, although offering freedom of conscience to her subjects, she hoped that they would 'quietly and charitably' embrace that faith willingly rather than by compulsion.[450] She did not intend to compel men in religion but believed that everyone would welcome the return of Catholicism and would follow her lead. Some people were not to be easily persuaded. Only days before the proclamation, Gilbert Bourne, Bishop of Bath and Wells, while preaching a sermon at Paul's Cross had narrowly escaped a dagger thrown at him when the crowd rioted after he had called for the release of the Catholic bishop, Edmund Bonner.[451] A week later, on 20 August, Paulet with the Earls of Bedford and Pembroke, and Lords Wentworth and Rich attended a sermon at Paul's Cross, sitting where the Lord Mayor and aldermen usually sat. On that occasion the audience were 'without any tumult', not surprisingly since 200 guards surrounded the preacher and the sermon and crowd behaviour were being witnessed by the councillors. Later that week Paulet was one of a group of councillors ordered by the Queen to restore Bonner to his position as bishop.[452]

The councillors had no choice but to work to further Mary's plans even if they did not necessarily agree with them. Henry VIII had used Parliament to change England's religion and so Mary had to use the same to undo his actions. Yet doing so acknowledged that the country's religion was defined by the monarch through Parliament and not by the Church. Paulet, and many of the other councillors, were to vote in Parliament to undo legislation they had enacted during the previous two reigns.

During Mary's five years on the throne Parliament met six times. The first sitting, from 5 October to 6 December 1553, saw the repeal of Northumberland's treason bill and of the Act of Uniformity. As a result of the latter repeal, the form of worship returned to that in practice during the last year of Henry VIII. Communion in two kinds (bread and wine) and clerical marriage were banned and religious images were allowed again.

Many churches were quick to restore altars and replace images, chalices and Latin service books, some even before it became official policy. Once again Paulet was able to celebrate mass. On 4 March 1554 the Privy Council issued a proclamation giving orders for the bishops and clergy to watch out for heretics and married clergy. They were instructed that church services were to be in Latin. Holy days and fasting days were to be kept and ceremonies such as christenings and confirmations were to be held as in the time of Henry VIII. Other proclamations were intended to prevent religious controversy. There were controls on the printing and distribution of documents and many Protestant printers were closed. Plays, ballads and rhymes concerning religious doctrine were banned and no one was to preach without permission.

Many people welcomed a return to the Church they knew and, while some clerics and congregations did not readily accept Catholicism, most Protestants outwardly conformed. A few worshipped in private, as Catholics had done during Edward's reign, and some moved overseas. This movement of people did have repercussions for Paulet. By mid-September 1553 John a Lasco (Jan Łaski) the Polish evangelical reformer and other foreign Protestants had returned to Europe and by the following summer Austin Friars Church in London was empty. In August the Privy Council reported this and instructed Paulet to organise the church so that it might be used for Divine Service – Catholic of course.[453] The Queen's intention was eventually to make England a truly Catholic country by restoring the supremacy of the Pope and in this she was supported by Bishop Gardiner and her close associates. However, this was to take many months and two parliaments to achieve. Some of her councillors were unhappy about the idea, knowing that there was a significant minority of the people who would not support Mary's plans. They were also concerned that it could result in many of them, as former recipients of church lands and property, being forced to return their gains. Mary, however, appeared to pay little attention to their concerns.

She also showed little concern at the popular dismay at her choice of Philip of Spain as her husband. Her marriage to Philip was a disaster, both personally and politically. Mary felt tied to Spain by birth, religion and her kinship with the Emperor, and she knew that Philip would support her plan to return England to Catholicism. However, people believed that, with Philip as monarch, England might be subject to Spanish rule. Most Englishmen wanted Mary to marry one of their own, but the only serious English candidate for her hand was Edward Courtenay, Earl of Devon.

He had royal ancestry but was unreliable and ambitious. However, he was the favoured choice of the Lord Chancellor, Bishop Gardiner, and of most of the Privy Council and the country. Gardiner was close to the Queen through their shared religious zeal and this gave him a favoured position resented by Lord Paget. Paget gave his support to Philip in the belief that, with the Spaniard as King, he would be able to act as his adviser and thus oust Gardiner.

Mary ignored the views of the councillors and the people and on 8 November told the Privy Council of her intention to marry Philip. They had no option but to accept her decision although the following week a parliamentary delegation asked her to consider taking an English husband, a request she ignored. By making her decision alone without the full involvement of the Privy Council, Mary created uncertainty among the members and intensified the rivalry between Gardiner and Paget and their respective adherents. Those who supported Courtenay, of whom Paulet was probably one, realised that they needed to change their allegiance quickly if they were to be favoured by the future consort. However, they were still fearful of the possible consequences of the Spanish match, particularly that England could come under Spanish rule. With this in mind the councillors set to work to finalise the terms of a marriage treaty that ensured the sovereignty of England. On 7 December the Privy Council met to discuss the terms of the treaty and Paulet joined Gardiner, Arundel, Thirlby, Rochester, Paget and Petre to report matters to the Imperial ambassador, Simon Renard. The terms of the document were agreed and signed on 12 January 1554.[454] It was necessary to reassure the English so the terms were very favourable to England even though Philip was not happy with them. The eldest son of the marriage was to inherit England and the Low Countries but would have no claim to Spain, Italy or the Indies as long as Philip's son, Don Carlos, or his descendants lived. There was a similar agreement if Mary and Philip left a daughter as heir, except that Don Carlos had to give agreement to her marriage. Philip was to be King and share sovereign power with Mary but he would have no claim to England if Mary should die first. He was to uphold the laws of England, could not appoint foreigners to posts within the Court and was not to involve England in war with France; indeed, he was to encourage peace between the two countries.

In spite of the controls in the treaty, many Englishmen were still unhappy at the prospect of the marriage and there was talk of Princess Elizabeth marrying Courtenay and taking the throne. During December 1553 plans were made for protests to be held the following spring against the prospect of a Spanish king. These were to take place in Devon, Herefordshire, Leicestershire and Kent but when news of the planned risings leaked out in January, Kent was the only county able to muster sufficient support immediately. There, Sir Thomas Wyatt raised over 2,000 men. The Duke of Norfolk rode out to meet them at Rochester but when many of his own men defected to Wyatt he was forced to return to Court. Reports reached the Privy Council that Wyatt was marching towards London and, at the end of January, Paulet was in London organising the Guilds and Lord Mayor and aldermen to raise men to defend the city. On 31 January, even though he was ill, Paulet reported to the councillors at Westminster that watches would be provided at the city gates day and night, and he appointed a further 500 men and 100 horsemen to join the defenders in London.[455] Wyatt was proclaimed a traitor and, on 1 February, the Queen rode from Westminster to the Guildhall to appeal to the townspeople to support her in her choice of husband and against Wyatt. She asserted that she would only marry 'out of her realm' with the advice and consent of the Privy Council and that she would only marry if her subjects were content with her choice, and to that end she announced that a Parliament would soon be called.

Wyatt reached Southwark on 3 February and marched to Kingston where he crossed the Thames and then turned back towards London. The Londoners rose in support of Mary, although not necessarily because they were endorsing her choice of husband but rather because they were not prepared to support Wyatt. On 7 February he marched with his men through Temple Bar and Fleet Street towards Ludgate. Many London citizens stood and watched, some possibly in sympathy with the marchers. In Fleet Street, 300 of Paulet's men commanded by his son, Lord Chidiock, passed by Wyatt's men on the other side of the road, all without saying anything. When he came to Ludgate, Wyatt was refused entry and realised that the support he had expected from the Londoners was not forthcoming. The rising was over and he was forced to surrender. Proceedings against the rebels were started quickly. On Tuesday 13 February Paulet headed a commission which sat at Westminster to try Wyatt and other leaders of the rising. Wyatt was found guilty and beheaded in April. Rebels were still appearing before Paulet in August and about 90 were executed although many who were sentenced to death were later pardoned. Even in January 1555 Paulet was offering pardons to men who pledged a sum of money as surety of good behaviour.[456]

Being then almost 70 Paulet was noticeably aged. One prisoner named Cuthbert Vaughan, who appeared before him in mid-February 1554, obviously believed that Paulet did not have long to live. After being sentenced to death by the Lord Treasurer Vaughan responded: 'It forceth not, my lord, since we shall go before and you shall not be long after us.' In fact Paulet lived on for another eighteen years.[457]

The uprising had consequences for Mary's relatives. Although Lady Jane Grey was not directly connected with the rebels, it was considered that she could be the focus of any future attempt to replace Mary on the throne. Jane was executed, along with her husband and her father, the Duke of Suffolk, who was one of the conspirators with the rebels. Elizabeth was also under suspicion because of the, albeit limited, support for her to take the throne and marry Courtenay. Disagreement over her future caused a further split in the Privy Council. Paget was in favour of Elizabeth remaining as heir but Gardiner wanted her excluded. There was disagreement about whether to place her in the Tower but, when none of the councillors would agree to take responsibility for her custody, imprisonment was the only option.[458]

On 16 March Paulet was with the Court at Westminster when the Privy Council visited Elizabeth and accused her of involvement in the Wyatt conspiracy. She denied any such complicity but they agreed that Paulet and the Earl of Sussex should move Elizabeth to the Tower. The following day the two men told Elizabeth that the three of them were to sail without delay while the tides 'which tarrieth for nobody' were favourable. 'Shooting', or passing below, London Bridge was dangerous because of the piers on which it was built and the speed of the water and was best undertaken at low tide. Elizabeth was horrified at the thought of imprisonment in the Tower and asked to be allowed to wait for a later tide but Paulet replied that: 'Neither time nor tide was to be delayed.' Her request to be permitted to write to Mary met a similarly negative response from him: that he was not allowed to permit it and that it might even harm Elizabeth's cause. For a man who always seems to have erred on the side of caution in his dealings, he was in a difficult position. He neither wanted to do anything to displease Mary or to upset the woman who might one day be queen. Sussex was more lenient, or perhaps more concerned that Elizabeth might rule, and he agreed to let her write the letter and promised to deliver it himself.

They missed the tide and next morning, Palm Sunday, the two men returned to the Princess at 9am with the news that the letter had not persuaded Mary to change her mind. They sailed down the Thames and arrived at Traitors' Gate. Elizabeth asked to be allowed to land elsewhere but they refused and she stepped ashore in the rain, declaring herself to be 'as true a subject' as had ever landed at those stairs.[459] Paulet was with Elizabeth again when several councillors visited her on 12 April and just a month later he returned, this time to oversee the loading of her belongings into carts when she was discharged from the Tower to travel to Woodstock in the custody of Sir Henry Bedingfield. Later in the year Elizabeth asked Paulet to do what he could to gain her release from house arrest but she remained at Woodstock for nearly twelve months.[460]

With the rising under control, Mary called a Parliament to ratify her marriage agreement. Paulet attended only half the sittings even though the session was short, opening on 2 April and ending on 5 May 1554, but he would have witnessed the increasing rivalry between Gardiner and Paget. In his determination to move the country towards full Catholicism, Gardiner planned to revive the heresy laws. Paget and his supporters were opposed to this because they feared it could be used to give the Church power to reclaim church land distributed to the nobility and gentry by Henry VIII and Edward VI. Gardiner's bill to enable him to punish heretics and a measure to extend the protection of the treason law to Philip were both defeated by Paget and his followers. The Queen was furious and dissolved Parliament and temporarily banned Paget. Soon afterwards Renard reported that there were also suspicions against Arundel and Pembroke and that Mary was using Gardiner, Paulet and Rochester as advisers.[461] The pace of the change of religion was slowed as the landowners argued to keep the church lands in their possession. Gardiner could not achieve a return to the Papacy until they reached an agreement on land ownership.

In the meantime the Queen's mind turned to the more immediate matter of her marriage to Philip. On 31 May she had travelled to Richmond for greater safety because of discord around the country, presumably as a result of the impending wedding. Paulet had been with the Court throughout May but, apart from brief visits on 3 and 20 June, he did not rejoin the Queen until 13 July at his old house at Bishops Waltham. He appears to have travelled to Hampshire in expectation of the wedding. He was at Southampton on 11 June, Winchester on 14 and 15 June and may have been at home at Basing House on 19 June when Lord Dudley and the Marquis de las Navas, who had arrived in England ahead of Philip, stayed there.[462]

The Queen remained at Bishops Waltham for ten days until Philip landed in England. Paulet had again left the Court in readiness to meet the new King when he landed at Southampton on Saturday 21 July and to accompany him to Winchester.[463] The Queen was already at Winchester when Philip arrived on Monday and the couple met that night and again on the following day, before their wedding on the Wednesday. At 10am Philip went to Winchester Cathedral with his nobles. The building was splendidly hung with arras and cloth of gold and a walkway was constructed from the West Door to the choir where a dais had been built so that the people could more easily witness the marriage. Half an hour later Mary, with her train carried by the Marchioness of Winchester, was preceded to the church door by the Privy Council and nobility. She joined Philip on the dais where the marriage ceremony was performed by Bishop Gardiner. When it was asked who gave the Queen to be a wife, Paulet, with the Earls of Derby, Bedford and Pembroke, gave her in the name of the whole realm while all the people gave a great shout.[464] The marriage treaty was sealed with the seal of Spain and delivered to Paulet to be kept in the Treasury and later, Paulet, Pembroke, Arundel and Gardiner joined the two monarchs as they dined in public at Winchester Palace.[465]

Two days later the royal couple set out on the journey to London, spending the first two nights at Basing House. Paulet paid all the expenses of what must have been a very expensive visit as he endeavoured to impress.[466] One observer wrote of Basing 'where was such noble cheer provided for them, and both their nobilities, as I have not seen the like for the time of my days'. Paulet may have almost overdone the hospitality. In early September there was a rumour that Paulet had given Basing House to the Queen. This was untrue but the tale does have echoes of Wolsey presenting Hampton Court Palace to Henry VIII. Paulet travelled with the royal party to Windsor and remained there with the Queen until she moved to Richmond on 12 August when he rode to Westminster where the Queen arrived six days later.[467] Renard noted that after Mary returned to London her councillors and the lords took their leave of the Queen 'in the accustomed manner after a progress and went home to rest'. Unfortunately for some of them, the Queen always needed a few councillors to continue working and Paulet was one of a group of nine, including Arundel, Bedford and Gardiner, who remained with her.[468] Since Paulet was not listed as attending Privy Council meetings, although letters were being addressed to him, it appears that when Mary and Philip moved on to Hampton Court on 24 August he remained at Westminster.

Paulet was spending far less time with the Court than he had during Edward's reign although while absent he was probably carrying out Privy Council business. He was often away from the Council during the summers when the Queen visited Hampton Court and Richmond or was on progress, and his attendance was highest when the Court was in residence at Westminster and St James's Palace. As Mary moved away from London he remained in the city attending to matters which arose there or which were directed to him by the Council with Mary. For matters of urgency he could be immediately recalled to the Court.

That August, Renard reported that there was discord between two groups of councillors – those who supported Gardiner and those who followed Paget.[469] Paulet was in the Chancellor's camp and Arundel and Pembroke with Paget. The ambassadors were always on the lookout for any friction within the Privy Council which they could report back to their masters and Renard may have exaggerated whatever tension there was. However, the number of councillors was still excessive and any attempt to create a Council of State with just five or six members met with the displeasure of those who were to be excluded. Paulet objected to one proposal in November 1554 which, surprisingly considering his wealth of experience, did not name him as a member of the inner council.[470]

The unrest that Renard reported was not confined to the Privy Council. There was also tension between Englishmen and King Philip's Spanish courtiers and violent altercations broke out between the two groups. Some Englishmen even began to take harquebuses (an early type of portable gun) with them when they went on a journey.[471] People were still concerned that the country would be taken over by Spain, that Spanish law could be introduced and that they could be drawn into war. They did not like the Spanish and the Spanish believed the English were heretics and that Philip had been insulted by the terms of the marriage treaty.

Philip's own popularity deteriorated and he spent most of his time out of the country. He could never be accorded the same respect as Mary while he was uncrowned. The birth of an heir would have strengthened his position enormously and given him an incentive to become more involved in the country's politics. The English would have welcomed an heir even though the baby would have been more Spanish than Mary herself. Although Philip may have tried to be friendly it was difficult for him to develop a relationship with the councillors, some of whom had reservations about him. He did not have a good grasp of English and probably conversed in French or Latin. He tried to elicit some support by the payment of pensions to those whose aid he most needed. Prior to Philip's arrival Renard had paid varying pensions of up to 2,000 crowns to certain members of Parliament, arguably as bribes, to 'render his Highness's coming secure'.[472] Paulet received an award when Philip arrived in England but the payments were often late. He was paid 1,000 crowns a year but at the end of both 1557 and 1558 he was still owed 500 crowns for the previous six months.[473] The money probably did encourage the pensioners to be supportive of Philip. One pension list, probably written by Count Feria, carries a short description of each recipient, and one of the most laudatory comments is for Paulet: 'He is a good servant of your majesty, and always has been.'[474]

The King was not deeply involved in policy and government but during Mary's third Parliament, which followed his arrival, he and the Queen unusually attended part-way through the proceedings. This Parliament was the longest of the reign, running from 12 November 1554 to 16 January 1555, and usually the monarch was present only on the opening and closing days. On this occasion, at 2pm on 22 November, Mary and Philip rode to Parliament to give their assent to a bill to repeal the Act of Attainder against Cardinal Reginald Pole. He had been attainted for treason in 1537 and had fled abroad but Mary was bringing him home from the Low Countries to oversee the restoration of the Catholic Church and the return of Papal authority in England. The repeal bill was pushed through and Pole returned to the country on 24 November. On 28 November he addressed both houses in the presence of Mary and Philip and announced that if the country repealed all the ecclesiastical legislation introduced since 1537, then England could receive absolution and return to Rome. Parliament agreed and at Westminster Palace on 30 November Paulet watched as Pole granted absolution to the whole country, and Catholicism – with the Pope as head of the Church – once again became the accepted religion of England.

During this Parliament the Lords sat on 44 days, though not on Christmas Day, 1st January or on Sundays, and Paulet attended 38 sessions. His title and position as Lord Treasurer gave him enormous status and, of the temporal lords, he ranked only below Lord Chancellor Gardiner. The two men had ridden side by side in the grand procession at the opening of Parliament on 12 November when Mary and Philip, with the lords, bishops and judges, had first ridden to Westminster Abbey for mass and then on to Parliament. On that day, for the first time, Paulet's son John was also present as he took his seat as Lord St John. By the end of the Parliament an act was passed to repeal all previous statutes against Rome although with the proviso that those with former Church lands could continue to enjoy the use of those lands, thus overcoming the revolt of the previous Parliament. Members of Parliament had wanted to ensure that their own interests were protected but once the problem of ownership of Church property was resolved they were content to make the religious changes. Other acts were passed against seditious words and rumours, for certain offences to be treated as treason and to revive statutes for the punishment of heresy.

Thus was Papal authority restored to England and the way opened for the trial of heretics. Between February 1555 and November 1558, 287 Protestants were burned in England. By the standards of the rest of Europe this was not a remarkable number but most took place in London and the south-east. The victims came primarily from the lower classes, since those with money could leave the country, but they did include some influential members of the clergy such as Cranmer, Ridley and Latimer. The government was concerned that the crowds at burnings often supported the heretics. Instructions were issued for order to be kept and Paulet and the other councillors may have witnessed some of the executions. Some people were pardoned at the stake if they submitted to Catholicism, while others were not burnt in expectation that they would receive a pardon. In August 1558 Sir Richard Pexsall – a sheriff in Hampshire and the husband of Paulet's youngest daughter, Lady Eleanor – was ordered to execute a heretic. He decided not to carry out the sentence when the culprit repented, but Pexsall was then ordered by the Privy Council to carry out the execution and was summoned to explain why he had delayed.[475]

In his capacity as the Pope's legate, or representative, and later as Archbishop of Canterbury, Reginald Pole worked to improve the state of the Church. He believed that discipline and order were important within the Church and he was keen to improve the standard of the clergy, both their capability and their commitment. Meanwhile, the Queen wanted Church property to be returned to the original possessors. Paulet was named on a commission with Gardiner, Rochester and Petre to consider the best use of monasteries and Church property in the possession of the Crown.[476] Several religious houses were restored. A Benedictine community returned to Westminster and further settlements followed. In November 1556 Paulet was accompanied by the Venetian ambassador during a visit to the monastery at Sheen which was being placed in the hands of the Carthusian order.[477] Some people resented the presence of the religious orders, and monks at Greenwich and Smithfield were subjected to demonstrations. Paulet was ordered to find out who had thrown stones at the monks and to seek speedy punishment of people who had caused disorder at Greyfriars.[478]

In spite of the determination of Mary, Gardiner and Pole to make England a truly Catholic country, they failed, and all three were to die by the end of 1558. Mary forged ahead with her plans even though some members of the Privy Council and Parliament did not agree with them, yet those same men still supported her and provided the legislation necessary to bring back Catholicism. Fear of execution made many Protestants 'reform' to Catholicism but it did not destroy Protestantism which indeed gained strength from the persecution. The martyrs become a rallying point, a symbol of a belief that many thought was worth dying for. England had been presented with a Catholicism that was rigid and brutal, and although the English were not unused to the spectacle of public burnings, the violence during Mary's reign was reminiscent of the Spanish Inquisition. Although many may have welcomed the return of the familiar religion, five years was too short a time for Mary to undo all the changes made by her father and brother.

13

The King of Spain and War with France

Early in 1555 one of Paulet's contemporaries, John Russell, Earl of Bedford, died. His career within the Court had followed a parallel course to Paulet's. He was born just a few years after Paulet and came from a similar family background. He too had been a member of the Privy Council since Henry VIII's time and had also received the Garter from him. In 1539 Paulet and Russell were ennobled together and they were then raised to the title of earl at the same ceremony in 1550. Russell had succeeded Paulet as Comptroller and had followed this with an appointment as Lord Admiral before becoming Lord Privy Seal. They had known each other well and Paulet left Court for a few days to attend his funeral and to act as an executor of his will.

Funerals of important people were grand, expensive affairs designed to impress. Russell died on 14 March and on 20 March his body was carried in a great procession from London to his country house, Chenies, in Buckinghamshire. Three hundred horses draped in black carried the mourners and three priests led the way bearing crosses. Then came Russell's standard carried before the gentlemen and head officers of his household who were followed by the heralds carrying his garter helmet, mantle and crest, banner of arms, shield, coat of armour and sword. Paulet, like the other mourners, rode behind dressed in black. As they passed through the countryside, the villagers came out to see the great procession and in every parish priests carrying crosses came out to pay their respects. Some of the watchers waited in anticipation since it was usual that, before dying, a wealthy person would often make provision in their will for alms to be distributed to the poor in each village through which their coffin passed. When the funeral took place the following day Russell's household officers all broke their staves and threw them into the grave, as was the custom, after which the mourners repaired to his house for a 'great dinner and great plenty to all the country about that would come thither'. There are no details for this particular feast but, only a few months earlier, at the funeral of the Duke of Norfolk, guests were reported to have been offered 40 great oxen, 100 sheep, 60 calves, venison, swans, cranes, capons, rabbits, pigeons, pikes, wine, bread and beer.[479]

Sometimes Paulet attended funerals in an official capacity on behalf of the Queen. When a foreign monarch died, mass was said for them in St Paul's and Paulet attended services for both the Queen of Spain in 1555 and for the King of Portugal in 1557. Paulet's wife, the Marchioness of Winchester, also carried out official duties and on 4 August 1557 she attended as chief mourner at the funeral of Anne of Cleves.[480] When the Emperor Charles V died in 1558 Paulet, with regard to his responsibility for preserving the Queen's wealth, proposed that a 'great saving of expense' would be made if Westminster rather than St Paul's was used for the obsequies.[481]

Most of Paulet's friends and acquaintances died of old age. During Mary's reign half a dozen councillors died, all from natural causes, but one friend, Charles Lord Stourton, was hanged on the gallows in the market place at Salisbury. On 12 January 1557 he and four servants murdered William Hartgill and his son over a long-standing feud concerning property which belonged to Stourton. He was taken to the Tower on 28 January and on 26 February, when he was charged in Westminster Hall, Paulet was among the lords who found him guilty. The following day Stourton left the Tower to enjoy a dinner with Paulet in his private chamber in the Exchequer of Receipt. Stourton came from a respected family with good connections and was obviously deemed to be sufficiently trustworthy not to abscond. Perhaps Paulet had to assume responsibility for his safe return to the Tower. The two men must have been on very good terms before the murder and Paulet was obviously not influenced by the guilty verdict. Indeed, it is likely that being a landowner himself and knowing the problems associated with land ownership he may have sympathised with the unlucky prisoner.[482] Because disputes over property could become so serious and have such violent consequences, the Privy Council sometimes took an interest in long-standing quarrels. In an effort to diffuse tension, Paulet was part of a committee in November 1558 instructed to 'travail and take some pains to bring Sir George Harbert and Sir Rice Manxwell to some good agreement and final end of all controversy between them'.[483]

One controversy which the Privy Council could not or would not resolve was the question of Philip's coronation. His image and status within the country would have been greatly improved if he had been crowned but Parliament would not agree to this. He was, however, granted the guardianship of the realm during a minority. This had become a pressing issue because Mary was pregnant and as a woman in her late thirties there was a risk that she might not survive the delivery. However, in the spring of 1555 her life was all she had hoped for – she was Queen with Philip as her husband, her country had been restored to Catholicism and she was expecting a child.

On 4 April the Court moved to Hampton Court for Easter and for the Queen to take to her chamber and await the birth. Paulet visited the Court occasionally but, yet again, it appears that he spent most of his time in London. He was at Hampton Court on 23 April, St George's Day, with Philip and the other Garter Knights to process around the courtyards while the Queen watched from her chamber. On 28 May Paulet was asked to have ready money to pay the messengers who were to take news of the birth to foreign monarchs.[484] However, the days passed and no baby arrived. Rumours circulated that there was to be no royal birth and that another infant was to be substituted. By July it was accepted at Court that, although Mary had convinced herself that she was pregnant, there was to be no child and life returned to normal, except that Philip prepared to leave for the Netherlands.

His father, Charles V, was planning to abdicate and during the next few months Philip assumed the crown of Spain and control of the Netherlands and Sicily. England became less important to him. Mary continued to ask him for advice and the Privy Council kept in touch with him, telling him their business rather than asking for advice. Before he left on 4 September 1555, Philip had established a Council of State which was to have responsibility for much of the decision making. This time Paulet's name was put forward together with Pole, Gardiner, Arundel, Pembroke, Thirlby, Paget and Petre.[485] At last, action had been taken to decrease the size of the working council.

After Philip's departure Mary's fourth Parliament was called, during which a reassessment of people's wealth was ordered in preparation for the payment of a graduated subsidy. Paulet attended every sitting from 21

October to 9 December. This may have been because Gardiner, who as Lord Chancellor was 'Father of the House', had died following an illness. In his absence, Paulet presided and on 9 December it fell to him, in the Queen's presence, to dissolve Parliament. Throughout the Parliament the Court was at St James's Palace and Paulet also attended nearly every Privy Council meeting. This too was probably on account of the absence of the Lord Chancellor since Paulet was now the senior councillor. During the rest of 1555 his attendance at the Privy Council appears to have followed the same routine as previously and he probably spent less than half his time actually with the Council accompanying the Queen. While the Court was resident in London he was generally at Privy Council meetings but when it moved into the country his name is absent from the attendance list. Letters addressed to him suggest that he remained in London.

When Philip assumed the Crown of Spain he also inherited that nation's ongoing conflict with France. Early in 1556 the two countries agreed a five-year truce but it held for only a few months. In September Philip's troops invaded the Papal States and, after Henry II of France broke the truce by going to the Pope's aid, war broke out in Flanders between France and Spain in January 1557. During March, Philip arrived back in England after an eighteen-month absence to ask the Queen and Privy Council to declare war on France. Mary was not bound by the marriage treaty to aid Spain in this war and she and the councillors were aware that there was insufficient money to support such an endeavour. They knew, too, that the people would be against war and that participation could result in a loss of support for both Mary and Philip. However, one incident helped to change the situation. On 23 April 1557 Thomas Stafford – a Protestant who had been in exile at the French Court – sailed from France with his supporters in two French ships. He landed at Scarborough where he took the castle and proclaimed himself protector of the realm, saying that Mary would be handing England to Philip if she crowned him. Stafford was defeated just days later but the Council, while not necessarily believing that the French were complicit in the plot, used the incident as a reason to give Philip military support.

War was declared against France on 7 June. Two weeks earlier Paulet's son, Lord St John, and his cousin, Sir Hugh Paulet, were given instructions to strengthen the garrisons at Poole, Weymouth and Portland. In Portsmouth another of Paulet's sons, Chidiock, was Captain of the town and responsible for the defence of the port.[486] Coastal defences were regularly under review and in June 1556 Paulet had yet again been ordered to survey and repair the

fortifications in Hampshire and the Isle of Wight. He had also been working with the Admiralty officers to plan the repair of the navy.[487]

England's navy was in a poor state by 1556. Six years earlier, because of
the severe lack of funds for defence, Edward VI had ordered that the fleet
be laid up apart from one squadron to be retained at Portsmouth. Although
this may have been intended as a short-term plan, by the end of his reign
the ships were starting to rot and the country had no effective sea defence.
Philip encouraged the overhaul and restoration of the navy and by the outbreak of war England had a fighting force that was to become, in an ironic
twist of fate, the basis of the fleet which defeated the Spanish in 1588. In
January 1556 Paulet took responsibility for signing naval warrants to ensure
that new ships were built and that old vessels were repaired, refurbished,
fitted-out and victualled and that the seamen's wages were paid. On the
advice of the Lord Admiral, Lord William Howard, Paulet was able to take
decisions to ensure that the navy was ready for war, and regular payments
of £7,000 to the Admiralty Treasurer every six months ensured that funds
were always available.[488]

On 5 July 1557 Paulet remained in London while the Queen and the
Court saw Philip sail from Dover, leaving England for the last time. Philip
took with him a force of over 7,000 men and travelled to St Quentin where
he defeated the French forces in August. When the bad weather of winter
came, Philip halted his army and sent many men home. The French, on the
other hand, took the initiative and marched towards Calais. By Christmas
alarm was beginning in the town and in England. On 3 January 1558 a letter
was sent to Paulet asking him to send victuals to Calais with all speed.[489] It
was already too late. The town was not prepared or supplied for an attack
and the French took Calais on 1 January. England had lost its last foothold
in France in a war which was not its own and which it could not afford. The
navy operated effectively, keeping the Channel clear for Philip's ships to sail
to the Netherlands and helping to repulse an attack on Gravelines during
the summer. Paulet had taken charge of 'thole marine affairs' to prepare
ships and mariners for action and in June Count Feria reported to Philip
that Paulet had been instructed to provision the fleet to serve at sea until
the end of September. He added: 'I think there will be no failure to do this,
for the Marquess Treasurer carries out everything concerning your majesty's
service more efficiently than do the other ministers.'[490]

On land, attempts were made to improve the militia in case of an invasion. Paulet moved 400 soldiers to the Isle of Wight during January and
a further 300 to Portsmouth to defend the Solent. In March, gentlemen

were ordered to return to their homes to help defend the country and martial law was implemented against deserters, spies, mutineers at musters and against possession of heretical and seditious books. Parliament sat from 20 January to 7 March and passed an act which was to improve attendance at, and organisation of, the musters. A further act for the 'having of horse armour and weapons' detailed what every man was to provide in the way of weapons and armour, based on his wealth. Musters had been called periodically since May 1557 but attendance was poor and morale low and these two acts intended to remedy this. Lords Lieutenant to organise defence and the raising of troops for service overseas were appointed to the coastal counties which would bear the brunt of repelling an enemy force and Lord St John was put in charge of Hampshire and the Isle of Wight. On 12 April 1558 Paulet was given a general commission of lieutenancy to cover all the counties of England and Wales which were not already under such authority (28 counties in central England and Wales) and to use martial law against rebels, traitors and other offenders. These counties included London and the surrounding shires where he would organise the mustering of forces to defend the city.[491] Paulet was also a member of the Council of War which included Paget, Pembroke, Browne, Clinton and Hastings.[492]

Mary's marriage to Philip had ultimately resulted in the loss of Calais and left England with a huge debt brought about particularly by the escalating cost of maintaining the fleet and the large sums spent on the country's defences. If Mary had managed to avoid war during her reign, as her grandfather Henry VII had done, the country might have been in credit when she died. Instead, Elizabeth I inherited a debt of as much as £300,000.[493] As 1558 passed, the Privy Council increasingly needed an end to the war to stop the drain on the country's coffers and they wanted the return of Calais; but France would not relinquish the town. At the end of September, in preparation for negotiations with the French, Philip asked Mary to send him Paulet, Lord Chancellor Heath, Lord Admiral Clinton and Secretary Boxall. However, Paulet, Clinton and Boxall were 'all so sick and weak that they be in no wise able to travel out of their chambers'.[494] Clinton had fallen ill at Portsmouth on 24 August and Lord St John reported that there was much sickness in Hampshire and the Isle of Wight.[495] Paulet may well have been ill for some weeks, perhaps with some other complaint. He had not been at Court since 4 July, although he was corresponding with the Privy Council, and on 8 August he had written to the Queen that he hoped to be well enough to serve her by the following week, since 'God has given

me health of the griff [trouble] on my nose.'[496] When Parliament opened on
5 November the comment that 'even' Paulet and Lord Clinton were attending suggests that they might still not have fully recovered.[497] Although not
fit enough to travel, Paulet was still working and the Queen asked him to
provide copies of all old treaties from the time of Edward III to Henry VII
concerning Calais.[498] The talks with the French made little progress. There
was a stalemate over the future of Calais and, as the Queen's health deteriorated over the following weeks, the talks were delayed until Elizabeth was
on the throne.

Early in 1558 Mary had again thought she was pregnant but, as before,
nothing came of it. By the autumn she was ailing and when Parliament con-
vened most members were aware that she might soon be dead. Parliament
was dissolved after only twelve days on 17 November, the day Mary died.
Shortly before noon Paulet, Norfolk and Shrewsbury rode through London
with heralds and trumpeters as Elizabeth was proclaimed Queen. At Mary's
funeral the painted effigy which had been placed on her coffin on the
chariot was carried into Westminster Abbey ahead of her body. Paulet, on
horseback and bearing the banner of the arms of England, was among the
great procession of mourners who returned to the church the following day,
14 December, for the mass and burial. For the third time Paulet was named
as an executor of a monarch's will, for which service he received £500.[499]
Philip was also named but he never returned to the country. His connection
with England was severed. In a letter to his half-sister, the Princess Dowager
of Portugal, he wrote: 'The Calais question cannot be settled so soon, now
that the Queen, my wife, is dead ... I felt a reasonable regret for her death. I
shall miss her even on this account.'[500]

Those councillors who were ardent Catholics were also going to miss
Mary. Others looked forward to the reign of the new Queen. The three
predominant features of Mary's reign were the Spanish match, the return
of Catholicism and the war against France, none of which had the whole-
hearted support of the Privy Council or the people. The country did enjoy
five years of comparative stability under Mary, experiencing only one relatively localised rising, and the government continued policies proposed
during Edward's reign such as the reorganisation of the Exchequer. Like
Edward's reign, however, Mary's was too short and several of her successful
policies such as reform of the navy and customs duties only came to fruition
under Elizabeth. Sadly for the eldest daughter of Henry VIII, the two achievements she probably considered her triumphs, the return of Catholicism and
the Spanish connection, were both quickly undone by Elizabeth.

14

A New Queen and the Restructuring of the Exchequer

Paulet stayed in London for several days after Mary's death, waiting to learn if he would retain his seat on the Privy Council. Elizabeth's first council of eight men met on 20 November and was selected from her own supporters and from councillors who had served Mary and had ridden out to greet the new Queen at Hatfield. The following day Paulet was called to join other nobles in escorting Elizabeth into London two days later. The Court assembled at Charterhouse and, by the time Paulet made his first appearance at the Privy Council on 27 November, the number of councillors had risen to fifteen; it finally settled at nineteen members in early 1559. Of these, seven were new councillors, eleven had served on Mary's Privy Council and ten on Edward's. Only Paulet had served as Privy Councillor to Henry VIII, Edward and Mary.[501] Elizabeth's decision to appoint so many councillors who had served her sister illustrates her expectation that their first allegiance would be to her as monarch and that they would, therefore, be supportive of her religious intentions even though some of them might lean more towards Catholicism than Protestantism. In describing these men and their acceptance of Elizabeth's faith, Sir Robert Naunton wrote in 1641 'so pliable and obedient they were to change with the times, and their Prince'.[502] Although Elizabeth appointed four nobles who held no official positions, her councillors were primarily officers of state and household officers. She did not appoint a large number of friends and early supporters as Mary had, but even a group of nineteen was a little unwieldy and Elizabeth probably discussed some matters with a smaller, inner council prior to consideration by the full gathering. Like her sister, Elizabeth did not always take their advice. If the Privy Council was not unanimous in its proposals Elizabeth sometimes deferred making a decision.

After attending five Privy Council meetings, Paulet's attendance became sporadic. During the first six months he was present at less than a third of the meetings at Court, even though the Queen and Council were at Westminster for most of the time. A proposal in 1559 that the Lord Chancellor, Lord Treasurer, Lord Privy Seal, Lord Great Chamberlain and Lord Admiral were to be councillors working away from the Court may have been formalising an existing situation and might explain Paulet's long absences from the Council at Court.[503] Perhaps, without the demands of attending meetings, these officers were better placed to execute the orders of the Queen and their peers. The Privy Council was meeting between four and six times a week, sometimes seven, and by the spring attendance had settled at between eight and twelve councillors. With his long experience Paulet was an obvious candidate for this inner council but either work or infirmities restricted his attendance. He had to wait for confirmation that he would retain his position as Lord Treasurer. On 17 December the post had still not been filled although 'The vast political experience of the Marquis of Winchester causes it to be generally supposed that he will remain treasurer.'[504] He was, indeed, confirmed in the post before the end of the month.

With her Privy Council established, Elizabeth was able to turn to the matter of her coronation at Westminster Abbey on Sunday, 15 January 1559. On the previous day all the Court assembled at the Tower to accompany her in procession to Westminster. Along the way the streets were hung with tapestries and costly materials, banners and streamers. The Queen, accompanied by 1,000 people on horseback, was carried in an open litter so the people could see her and the procession stopped along the way to watch the pageants staged in her honour. One depicted Henry VIII and Anne Boleyn while others portrayed her as a great ruler and judge and praised her virtues and knowledge.

One of Elizabeth's first actions after her coronation was to return England to the Protestant faith of Edward VI's reign. When Mary died, the majority of Englishmen were Catholics, especially in areas away from London and the south-east. After Elizabeth's accession, Protestants began to worship openly, trials for heresy ceased and there were demonstrations against Catholicism. One incident occurred in Austin Friars church, next to Paulet's London house. Part of the building, which had been granted to him by Edward VI, was being used by the local Italian community for their Catholic services. Many Protestants were impatient that the Queen had not immediately forbidden Catholic worship and, on Christmas morning 1558, a group of them broke into the church after the Italian consul refused to give them the door key. The Italians complained about the incident to Paulet who responded by shrugging his shoulders and asking them not to refer the matter to him. The Italian consul then complained to the Lord Mayor who also avoided the issue and referred him to the Privy Council, who in turn expressed concern but does not appear to have taken any action.[505] Although the councillors may have been reluctant to proceed against Protestants, Paulet's response was more likely influenced by the fact that his wife, Elizabeth, had died on Christmas Day.

Soon after her coronation, the first of Elizabeth's Parliaments opened on 25 January and, to her annoyance, demonstrated that there was opposition to her plans for religious change. The Parliament passed measures that authorised the collection of the new customs dues and recognised Elizabeth's right to the Crown. It also considered controversial measures concerning the religious changes Elizabeth wanted to make. A bill was introduced to reinstate the supremacy of the Queen, to allow the use of the 1552 prayer book with the sacrament in two kinds and to repeal the Marian heresy laws, thus allowing Protestants to worship in safety. The Commons agreed to the bill but it was changed by the Lords. They were prepared to allow Elizabeth to take the supremacy if she chose but they would not confer it on her, and they were prepared to allow communion in both kinds but they would not repeal the heresy laws. This new package would not fully restore Protestantism and the Queen was not satisfied. Instead of dissolving Parliament before Easter the Houses were recalled on 3 April.

During this second session Paulet clearly displayed his attachment to the Catholic faith and, by holding firmly to his own beliefs, he was forced to vote against the majority of the Lords. Two bills were introduced, the first – the Supremacy Bill – proposed bestowing on the Queen the title of Supreme Governor of the Church rather than Supreme Head, and denied the Pope any right to exercise his jurisdiction in England. The bill also allowed for communion in two kinds and the repeal of heresy laws. The Commons passed the bill but in the Lords it was sent to committee. Paulet was one of the fifteen members of the committee who amended the bill to protect Catholics against being tried for heresy. All the bishops and Lord Montague still voted against it but the bill was passed.[506] Once again England was split from Rome. The country was set to move towards more reformed services and religious toleration even in the event that the second bill, for Uniformity in Religion, should be defeated. The Uniformity Bill detailed changes to the form of worship, proposing to bring back the 1552 prayer book with alterations – or rather compromises – such as amalgamating the Communion sentences used in the prayer books of 1549 and 1552. More divisive was the proposal that denied transubstantiation but allowed for the presence of God in the Eucharist for those who 'fed on him in faith'. The bill was passed on Friday 28 April with a narrow majority of only three. Paulet headed a list of nine temporal lords who joined nine bishops in voting against it.[507] It was not a foregone conclusion that the Uniformity Bill would be passed and perhaps this realisation encouraged the nine lords to oppose it. Not one cleric had voted in favour of these religious changes. Churches began to remove altars, rood lofts and images, and communion cups replaced chalices but in many congregations change was slow as people waited to see if Catholicism might return yet again. A further bill to dissolve those monasteries Mary had established ensured that the laity could retain possession of church lands. However, Paulet actually voted with the bishops against a bill to return land of the Winchester Bishopric to lay owners, a vote which could have prevented him regaining ownership of Bishops Waltham Abbey.[508] The bill was passed.

When Parliament was dissolved on 8 May, after nearly fifteen weeks, Paulet had attended 80 per cent of the sessions. Sir Nicholas Bacon, Lord Keeper of the Great Seal, was Speaker of the House and when he was absent on 4 March Paulet, as the most senior lord, had stood in for him. The Lords' votes for some bills are recorded for this Parliament and because he was not afraid to show his opposition to Elizabeth's plans, Paulet has at last left a clear indication of his religious leanings. He did not object to the Queen being Supreme Head of the Church and so did not want to maintain allegiance to the Pope, but he did believe in transubstantiation and had worked to amend the Supremacy Bill so that Catholics could not be condemned for heresy. His voting record on these issues certainly marks him down as being a Henrician Catholic, following Henry VIII in favouring a Catholic form of worship but in rejecting the Pope as Head of the Church. His contemporaries accepted him as a Catholic and in 1567 Paulet's name headed a list, probably written for the Pope, of supposedly Catholic English nobles.[509]

Only one of the bishops agreed to accept Elizabeth as Governor of the Church and the rest were deprived and replaced by bishops more amenable to her views. Nicholas Heath, Archbishop of York, and Thomas Thirlby, Bishop of Ely, were both at Paulet's house at Austin Friars when they were deprived of their offices on 5 July 1559. The Act of Uniformity ordered regular attendance at church every Sunday and Holy Day with penalties for non-compliance but this was not strictly enforced. Neither was the order that recusants, the Catholics who refused to attend church services, were to be reported to the authorities. For many Catholics, public conformity to Protestantism could be a mask for Catholic worship in private.

While Parliament was sitting the Court was resident at Westminster but Paulet still only attended occasional Privy Council meetings. However, the Privy Council and parliamentary records of attendance for early February may be incorrect since they leave insufficient time for him to travel home for his wife's funeral. Elizabeth was buried at Basing at the beginning of February. He and Elizabeth were married for 49 years, a noteworthy achievement in a time when death could take people early and it was not unusual for those who lived long to have been widowed and to have taken several spouses. To enable her burial to be delayed for several weeks after 25 December when she died, her body must have been placed in a lead-lined coffin. This was taken on a carriage from London to Basing on 4 February in readiness for her funeral three days later. Paulet is recorded as being present at Privy Council meetings on 4 and 6 February and also in the House of Lords on 4 February. This left very little time to travel to Basing and, if he did travel home, he spent little time there, returning to London to attend the Lords again on 9 February.

Elizabeth's funeral procession displayed her attachment to the Catholic faith by including four banners depicting saints, carried at the corners of the coffin, as well as banners of her husband's arms. Along the way, money was distributed to the poor. At Basing the coffin was placed in the church inside a 'herse' or hearse. This was a framework of timber, large enough for people to move inside, which was used to display the family's arms on small pennants and as a stand for candles. The importance of the dead person was indicated by the number of candles, pennants and other heraldic devices that were used. For Elizabeth's herse there were eight dozen pensels (small pennants or tapering flags) and the same number of escutcheons (shield shaped flags) which displayed Paulet's arms, while the whole edifice was further decorated with 'angels and archangels' and more banners. By comparison, at the mass in St Paul's for the Queen of Spain in 1555, the herse had four times as many pensels. As was usual, the funeral was followed by 'great cheer' with a distribution of charitable gifts of money and food and the mourners returned to Basing House for a great dinner of fish, meat and venison. During 1558 Paulet lost not only his wife but also his brother George, who died in August, and his daughter, Eleanor, who died in September and was buried in Westminster Abbey.

Paulet was 74 when Elizabeth died but after he had attended the Privy Council on 29 December, only four days after his wife's death, the Spanish ambassador wrote that Paulet 'looks younger and better than I have ever seen him'.[510] Most of the available images of Paulet were probably painted in the late 1550s or 1560s and portray an elderly gentleman dressed in a high-necked black doublet and a black coat trimmed with fur. His white shirt has a gathered edge around the neck, the precursor of the Elizabethan ruff, and on his head is a wide, flat black bonnet. Presumably made of wool or velvet this has a crown with a flat brim and is set upon the black coif which covered his hair and ears. Hanging around his neck is the Garter collar with a pendant of St George, and in one portrait, on the hand which holds the Lord Treasurer's white staff he wears two rings. The ring on his little finger could be an interlinking or gimmal ring which was sometimes used as a wedding ring to symbolise the joining of two people, although it was not common in the early sixteenth century for men to wear wedding rings. The ring on his index finger shows a design that appears to be a falcon with wings outstretched. His emblem was a golden falcon and this ring was his signet, which he used when sealing letters. His face is old and lined, his moustache and long narrow beard are white. He looks dignified and every inch the elder statesman.

Although the ambassador thought Paulet looked well, at 74 years old he was now the oldest member of the Privy Council by sixteen years and problems with his health became increasingly frequent. Personal details about his life are scant but of those available a surprisingly large proportion concern his illnesses. Beginning with the bloody flux in 1545, references are often not very specific. He appears to have had recurring problems with his nose – 'the griff on my nose' in 1558 seems to have been a long-term problem which still troubled him in 1571, and in August 1559 he was troubled with a 'catharre'.[511] During the 1560s his health problems became more debilitating and, although they sometimes kept him from Court and from work, he maintained his place on the Privy Council and in the Treasury and was still appointed to commissions. In 1563 Bacon, Pembroke and Cecil were commissioned to execute the office of the Lord Treasurer while Paulet was ill.[512] In January 1564, after a long absence from

Court, he was summoned to an important meeting of the Privy Council with the exhortation not to be put off travelling because even though 'the journey may be somewhat painful' he need not stay at Court long and while there need not leave his lodging.[513]

Paulet's age may have brought him ill health but the experience and wisdom he had gained over the years ensured that he commanded the respect of his fellow councillors. However, new men were rising to prominence and foremost amongst these was Sir William Cecil. Cecil was chosen by Elizabeth as Secretary of State and was her closest adviser for most of the reign. Although Paulet and Cecil were initially on good terms, Paulet became disillusioned with Cecil's foreign policy. Even as early as 1559 they held differing views on the best way to handle the political situation in Scotland. England's relationship with Scotland was affected by the relationship between England and France. On 2 April 1559 the two countries ended their war with the treaty of Cateau-Cambresis, which allowed France to keep Calais for eight years after which it would be returned to England. If, however, England did not keep the peace the French were to pay 500,000 crowns and keep the town. The French were also to encourage peace on the Scottish border. The young Queen of Scotland, Mary Stuart, was in France with her husband, Francis, while her mother, Mary of Guise, who had ousted the Earl of Arran, was Regent in Scotland. In September 1559 Paulet was chief mourner at a mass in St Paul's for the King of France, Henry II, who had died from wounds received in a joust. His death left Francis as King of France and had serious repercussions for England and Queen Elizabeth.

With the Guise family in control in France and Scotland, and Mary now Queen in both countries, her claim to the throne of England became a more serious threat to Elizabeth. The Scots were fed up with French troops and French rule in their country and a group of rebel Protestant lords calling themselves the Lords of the Congregation asked Elizabeth to help them oust the French. She hesitated, aware both of the cost of military involvement and that any move on her part could violate the treaty and remove any chance of regaining Calais. Money and weapons were sent secretly in August 1559 but the Privy Council could not agree over open involvement. In December 1559 Paulet, Petre, Sir Nicholas Bacon, Sir John Mason and Dr Wotton were all against war but agreeable to clandestine aid while Arundel resisted any support for Scotland. But the majority of councillors supported Cecil in favouring war. Paulet, Petre, Bacon, Mason and Wotton eventually consented to war but

Elizabeth liked a consensus. Knowing of their original doubts she still hesitated before finally agreeing to send an army to lay siege to Leith and a fleet to prevent the landing of more French troops. The siege was unsuccessful but Paulet was not downhearted and he wrote to Cecil on 12 May 1560 that 'worldly things would sometimes fall out contrary, but if quietly taken could be quietly amended.' He believed it was pointless to lament what could not be changed and that the 'misfortunes should increase the Queen's courage to apply the revenge'.[514] However, all was not lost and, when a storm prevented the French landing more troops and Mary of Guise died, England and Scotland agreed a truce in July 1560. By this, Mary Stuart acknowledged that she had no claim to the throne of England and that Elizabeth was the true Queen. Most of the French troops were to leave Scotland, which was to be ruled by a council of Scottish nobles. The Scottish Parliament acted quickly in August to stop Catholic worship and to remove Papal authority. Religious reformation took place. Only four months later Francis II died and Mary returned to Scotland as Queen where she was forced to accept the Reformation and government by the Protestant party.

After the treaty with Scotland was signed, Elizabeth set out on progress through Surrey and Hampshire spending a few days at Basing House. From there Paulet wrote a letter to Cecil telling him of the 'black counsels' concerning Cecil which were being told to the Queen. Cecil had travelled to Scotland to negotiate the treaty but on his return to England he found himself no longer in such high favour with the monarch. Some in the Court resented the influence he was beginning to exert over Elizabeth and were talking against him. In particular, he found himself being supplanted by Lord Robert Dudley who had aspirations to marry Elizabeth. In his letter to Cecil on 24 August 1560, Paulet wrote that there would never be sound counsel until there was a smaller number of councillors in whose advice the Queen had absolute trust. He believed that they would all work for no reward and that Cecil, who gave the most of himself, would receive the least thanks. Indeed, the benefit of Cecil's good counsel was hindered by the lack of esteem in which the Queen now held him. Paulet continued by advising Cecil to bear with the situation, while he would 'play the part of a good servant' and tell the Queen the truth.[515] Three days after Paulet wrote the letter, Cecil arrived at Basing. When he was at Court and close to the Queen it was more difficult for his enemies to talk against him.

For Paulet, the progress to Basing was a memorable success and the Queen was 'most splendidly entertained, and with all manner of good cheer'. Indeed she was so impressed with his house and hosting that she bewailed the fact that Paulet was so old saying that 'if my lord Treasurer were a young man, I could fynde in my harte to have him to my husbande before any man in Englande.'[516] To the 26-year-old Queen, Paulet, at the age of 76, was truly ancient.

A visit by Elizabeth to Sir William Petre at Ingatestone Hall in 1561 gives a flavour of the preparations Paulet made before the Queen arrived. The giest or itinerary was delivered to Petre six weeks before the event although much of the preparation took place during the twelve days before the Queen's arrival. Workmen built ranges and sheds. The house was cleaned and the royal suite perfumed and hung with the finest hangings. Servants covered great distances buying wine and meat, and great quantities of food were prepared to be served on the best plate. Every host did his best to impress the Queen with his wealth and generosity. The cost of Elizabeth's two or three days with Petre was about £136. This was relatively modest when compared with the £389 Lord Rich paid for a visit by the Queen or the £577 which Sir Nicholas Bacon spent during four days of entertaining her. As the reign continued Elizabeth expected more and more elaborate hosting and the bills rose until courtiers were spending over £1,000 to host her for just a few days.[517] Queen Elizabeth visited Paulet at Basing on two occasions, during August 1560 and August 1569. Paulet records that the first visit lasted for six days and cost him £2,000 while the latter cost £1,000 for five days. These were unusually long visits and could be seen as an indication both of Paulet's status and of his ability to bear the cost of the feasting and entertainments.[518]

Paulet's term as Lord Treasurer for Elizabeth saw several schemes which had been proposed during previous reigns finally put into practice. The deaths of several officers who had opposed his plans provided the opportunity to increase his authority by placing his own men in the Exchequer. His concerns about the loss of money stored in tellers' homes were shared by the Queen and in April 1562 Paulet, with Sir Richard Sackville the Under-Treasurer, and Sir Walter Mildmay, Chancellor of the Upper Exchequer, set about examining the 'ancient' methods of storage and accounting with a view to re-introducing them, a feat he had failed to achieve during Mary's reign. Attempts by Paulet to create a central deposit store for surplus cash were not supported by the tellers who were using the money in their keeping as a temporary source of investment to supplement the income they received from salaries, fees and bribes. Rather than replace the existing system of accounting, he established a version of the ancient methods, overseen by his own clerk, which gave him more control of the Queen's cash. Between 1558 and 1566 a sum approaching £300,000 a year was paid into the receipt. However, the tellers were not the only men who saw these sums as an opportunity to borrow and invest. Paulet, too, may have used Crown money for his own purposes and his debts were still unresolved when he died. The problem of tracing money was compounded by the practice of officers issuing money to themselves to pay for expenses or of using their own money to pay costs and then reclaiming from the Exchequer.[519] In 1562 when part of the ordnance house in the Tower was overloaded and gave way, Paulet purchased an empty nunnery at Minories, by Aldgate, to use as a store for armour and weapons. The Queen was against the purchase because of the cost and it appears that Paulet used his own money. However, the following year, once the store had proved its usefulness, the Queen bought the site from him.[520]

Much attention was given to balancing the budget to cover government spending and inflation. In June 1561 a financial council was established to examine what revenues might be expected from the Exchequer, the Court of Wards and Liveries and from the Duchy of Lancaster, and to list any debts due to the Crown from Mary's reign. Paulet joined Mildmay, Pembroke, Arundel, Cecil, Bacon and Sackville on this committee.[521] Efforts were also made to economise and to raise income by selling land, collecting debts and through taxation. The purity of the coinage had been a concern for many years and re-coinage had been proposed during Edward VI's reign. Much of the good coin – that with a higher silver content – was either overseas or hoarded and, at Elizabeth's accession, there were at least four different standards of coin in circulation. Re-coinage began in September 1560 to restore coins to 'fine moneys … of one sort of fineness, richness and goodness'.[522] In October the justices in each town were commanded to collect together 'four or five hundred pounds of base money and send them sorted' to Paulet and Sackville with a guard of one or two 'substantial' men, and the coins would be replaced by new money.[523] Paulet, Mildmay, Sir Thomas Parry, Cecil and Sackville were to oversee the minting and the issue of the new coinage. The coins were melted and refined and then made up in new proportions with a higher percentage of silver to lead. Within a year the re-coinage was almost completed. New coin to the value of £758,102 was issued for £666,267 of base coin used so, even allowing for expenses, the government made a profit on the exercise.[524]

Trade played a huge role in England's economy and Paulet was closely involved in improving the country's overseas business. Regulations were imposed on merchants, both English and foreign, controlling imports and exports and charging customs. Trading by foreign merchants was more heavily regulated although some enjoyed greater privileges than others. During the summer of 1560, Paulet was dealing with the Hanse, a guild of German merchants who enjoyed special trading rights with England. A meeting on 3 June was postponed because Paulet was ill but four days later he was well enough to continue the negotiations and the following month he was one of the signatories to a commercial treaty with them. In 1563, when the Netherlands temporarily banned trade with England and the exchange rate fell, Paulet and Mildmay looked at ways of counteracting this problem. Their proposals to increase exports and decrease imports in new markets were obvious responses but the idea of establishing an international bank to stabilise exchange rates, although not accepted, was more innovative.[525]

The income from the new customs rates was directly related to the quantity of trade through England's ports but the higher dues were encouraging smuggling. During the Parliament of 1559, an act was passed to prevent the evasion of customs by regulating where and when goods were landed and loaded. Paulet may have been one of the instigators of the act and he, with Sackville and Mildmay, was responsible for drawing up the details of the regulations. Particular goods were to be handled at specific quays so, for instance, fish were only to be loaded and unloaded at Billingsgate. Goods were only to be landed during daylight and at wharfs where 'customers' (customs officers) were on duty to oversee matters. Enforcement of these rules was poor due to a lack of customers and because of corruption where the movement of uncustomed goods was being allowed. One solution to this was to put the collection of customs 'out to farm'. This could be quite lucrative for the customs 'farmer' who paid the government a fixed rate for being allowed to collect custom taxes. The more industrious the farmer was, the more profit he could reap. Paulet was not happy with this proposal, preferring instead to use more customers and an efficient accounting system but he was overruled and Sir Thomas Gresham, the Queen's financial agent in the Netherlands, investigated how the farming system worked in Antwerp. The plans to farm customs went ahead despite Paulet's lack of enthusiasm for the scheme. In 1570 the customs officers and Paulet were ordered not to obstruct the wine farmers in their activities, an order which was repeated after he continued to support the customs officers.[526]

Gresham's support for customs farming may have strained an already tense relationship between himself and Paulet. In 1560 he accused Paulet of trying to ruin him by falsely telling the Queen that he, Gresham, had retained £50,000 of the Queen's money. He believed that Paulet had twice before talked against him, in both Edward VI and Mary's reigns, and that Paulet resented the fact that Gresham worked on secret instructions from the Queen. Gresham asserted that Paulet did not care how things turned out as long as his own 'turn is served'. The animosity between them did not cease and three years later Gresham believed that Paulet had tried to reduce his allowance.[527]

Less controversial than farming out customs was Paulet's rebuilding of the Exchequer and finance offices at Westminster. In 1558 the Exchequer employed about 80 people but a similar number were also employed privately by the officers.[528] The merging of the finance courts into the Exchequer and the increase in customs business placed a greater load on the existing accommodation. A new Exchequer building was constructed at the north end of Westminster Hall at a cost of £8,393 8s 11½d, the most expensive non-defensive building project during Elizabeth's reign. Much of the work was carried out during the twelve months from spring 1565. A new store in which to keep the records was built, alterations were carried out to the Receipt, and the Customs House on Thames Street was rebuilt for the more modest sum of £1,319 0s 5d.[529]

4 June 1561 had been a hot and sultry summer day in London with the threat of thunder all afternoon. The Queen was at Greenwich with many of the Privy Council but Paulet and Sir Nicholas Bacon had remained in the city to manage the affairs of the country. It was just past five o'clock and they were about to leave Westminster Palace to return to their homes when a messenger arrived, much agitated and out of breath. He had ridden as fast as possible through the crowded streets with a message from the Lord Mayor. Between gasps he told the two men that they were needed to save the city. The Cathedral of St Paul was alight and as the fire spread through the church there were fears that it might spread to the surrounding buildings.

Paulet and Bacon called for their horses and as they rode into the city they joined the press of people who were making their way towards the column of smoke curling up ahead of them. They forced their way through the crowd and soon reached the church. The air was full of smoke and noise – the roar and crackle of the fire, the sound of falling timbers and stone – and everywhere there was great activity. Men shouted out instructions and people ran hither and thither although it was difficult to see what was being achieved. The two men handed the reins of their horses to the messenger and strode towards the Lord Mayor who was deep in conversation with the Bishop of London. The Mayor explained that between one and two o'clock in the afternoon there was 'marvellous great fiery lightning' and 'a most terrible hideous crack of thunder'. Many people had seen a 'long and spear pointed flame of fire' run through the top of the spire of St Paul's. By five o'clock smoke was pouring out from the spire while flame broke out around it in a circle like a garland. Paulet jumped as, with a mighty crash and a great spray of sparks, the cross and eagle at the top fell down through the roof of the south transept. The mighty spire, said to be over 500 feet high, looked like a great candle shooting flames up to heaven. The heat forced Paulet to back away.

The Mayor and Bishop were considering whether proposals to shoot down the steeple or for men to scale the church and hew down the roof would contain the fire but these plans were considered too perilous and impractical because of the height of the church and the lack of axes. It was apparent that little could be done to save the building, the fire had too strong a hold, and so Paulet and Bacon took control turning their attention to preventing the flames reaching surrounding houses. Burning embers were falling all about. Slowly the two men managed to create good order out of the confusion. Paulet ordered the onlookers away from the cathedral in case the walls should collapse. He organised men and women to fill buckets at the little conduit on Cheapside and throw the water upon the roofs and wooden walls of the houses. Ladders were brought so that men could reach and pull down any burning embers that fell upon roofs. There was great noise and activity but now people had a purpose. The fire raged through the church and within an hour the steeple was burnt down to the battlements and most of the roof was consumed. As the timbers fell they set light to the north aisle and to the body of the church so that, by 10 o'clock when the fire was beginning to subside, only the vaults were preserved together with the two low aisles of the quire, part of the north aisle and a small part of the south aisle.

Paulet looked around him and raised a prayer to God. Although all the timber was burnt and all the roof lead melted, the fire had been enclosed within the stone walls of the church. Not one of the surrounding buildings had been lost. Paulet's work was done and as he returned home he reflected on the importance of St Paul's to London. It must be rebuilt. Perhaps, if the Queen, the citizens and the clergy gave money speedily for its restoration, it was possible that rebuilding could start before the end of the month.[530]

Paulet was efficient and experienced but it seems that he may have been irritable when the Queen and Privy Council did not take his advice.

On 6 December 1562 there were rumours that he was threatening to resign his Treasurership and his office as councillor after his advice on two issues of 'grave importance' had been ignored and he was not prepared to be ignored a third time.[531] From the timing of these rumours it is probable that one of these issues was England's involvement in fighting in France. In early 1562 there had been a massacre of Huguenots in France and Elizabeth went to their aid, offering to fight in exchange for control of Le Havre until Calais was lawfully returned to England. English soldiers were sent to Le Havre late that year but when the war ended in March 1563 the French Catholics and Huguenots joined together against the English. The garrison was finally defeated by plague, and because Elizabeth had broken the terms of the Treaty of Cateau-Cambresis all hope of recovering Calais was lost. Paulet was against the venture because of the risk to the claim on Calais.[532] Five years later, on 29 February 1568, he wrote to the Queen that his many years of experience had shown how necessary possession of Calais was to the English to ensure the defence of the coast between Portsmouth and Dover. He wished it was again under English control.[533]

The issue over which he was not prepared to be ignored a third time was most probably religion. Paulet was unhappy about proposals to impose new penalties on those who opposed the Queen's claim to supremacy and maintained that the Pope held authority within England. He and his supporters were not strong enough to defeat new laws which were to be introduced after Christmas but they intended to try to reduce their harshness.[534] In the event Paulet's contribution to the Parliament was minimal. He was very ill, attending only five sittings in three months, and on 3 May Pembroke and Cecil were ordered to carry out the Lord Treasurer's duties for the duration of his illness.[535]

Paulet's advice had also been recently ignored on the matter of the succession. The question of who would succeed Elizabeth took on a special urgency in October 1562 when the Queen was taken ill with smallpox while at Hampton Court. For a while it was feared that she might die and the councillors were summoned to Court. There were three main contenders as successor: Lady Catherine Grey, sister to Lady Jane and named in Henry VIII's will; Henry Hastings, Earl of Huntingdon who was descended from the Pole family; and Mary, Queen of Scotland. The councillors were not able to agree. The Protestants were split between Lady Catherine Grey and Huntingdon who, although his claim to the throne was weak, had the perceived advantage of being a man. Paulet wanted to go to the lawyers for legal advice but only a few supported him in this and some believed this was an attempt to move towards Catholicism since the lawyers were likely to be Catholic.[536]

Elizabeth's recovery relieved the pressure to name a successor but forced the issue of her marriage. Many suitors were considered during her lifetime but in 1563 the prominent candidates were James Hamilton, Earl of Arran, the Archduke Charles of Austria and Lord Robert Dudley. Cecil, in particular, was against the prospect of Dudley as king and he supported Charles of Austria because of his position as the son of Emperor Ferdinand. Elizabeth would not commit herself but it was an issue which Parliament was determined to settle.

At 11am on 12 January 1563, a procession set out from the Palace of Westminster to Westminster Abbey. Parliament should have opened on the previous day but the Queen would not go out because of the foul weather. Norfolk with the gilt rod of Earl Marshall, Paulet with the cap of estate and the Earl of Worcester with the sword went ahead of the Queen. In Westminster Abbey the Bishops sat on forms on the north side of the aisle and the peers on the south side while they heard a psalm and a sermon before processing into the Parliament Chamber, the three Lords again going ahead of the Queen. In the Chamber Elizabeth sat under the cloth of estate with Paulet standing before her on her right-hand side and Worcester on her left. The lords sat on forms along the sides of the hall, the bishops to the right of the Queen and the nobles to the left, and the Commons stood at the 'barre' opposite her.

Parliament was called, amongst other things, to provide finance for the French war but the topic uppermost in men's minds was the settlement of the succession. Both the Commons and the Lords presented petitions to the Queen setting out the need for her to name a successor and to marry. Still she would make no decision and, on 10 April, Parliament was prorogued. The question of Elizabeth's marriage continued to be of paramount concern to the Queen and councillors and in autumn 1563 negotiations began for her to marry Archduke Charles. The stumbling block was that he insisted on being allowed to worship in public as a Catholic and the negotiations were still continuing in 1566 when, on 30 September, Elizabeth recalled Parliament to grant a subsidy. Lord Keeper Bacon was absent, suffering from gout, and so for three weeks from 5 October Paulet took his place as Speaker. It was an eventful three weeks. Some members of the Commons decided that their response to the subsidy bill would be tied to the Queen's answer concerning the succession.

On Monday, 21 October the Commons asked the Lords to join them in presenting a petition to Elizabeth. The following day Paulet, as Speaker of the Lords, led a delegation to the Queen and explained that the Commons would not attend to the subsidy or other matters until she had agreed to name a successor. He pointed out that Parliament was wasting time and being made ineffective. The others repeated his arguments but the Queen was unmoved, intending to seek advice from lawyers. The Lords spent two days considering the Commons' request before deciding to join with them in a suit to the Queen. The decision was not unanimous – Paulet was a lone voice against the petition. The Queen was furious at the decision to petition her and verbally attacked the Lords when they were in her presence, almost accusing Norfolk of being a traitor and calling Pembroke a 'swaggering soldier'. She chastised Northampton for managing to marry a second wife while his first was still alive and bewailed the fact that she had always believed Dudley would stand by her, before banishing him and Pembroke from the Presence Chamber. Only Paulet, she complained, was not against her. Here we can see the reason Elizabeth kept the elderly man as one of her advisers.[537] She could rely on him to deal honestly with her and not to blindly follow the tide of opinion.

Elizabeth pre-empted the petition by ordering 30 representatives from each House to appear before her. She explained that she did intend to marry and was reluctant to name a successor because of the pressure it would place on that person. She was not prepared to be dictated to by Parliament and forbade any further discussion of the topic. The Commons were not satisfied and continued to draw up a petition regarding the marriage. Elizabeth, realising that no progress would be made on the subsidy, rescinded her order of no discussion and reduced her subsidy claim by one-third. Parliament was content and Elizabeth had finance but the marriage question was still not resolved. Negotiations with Archduke Charles continued and eventually, in 1567, he proposed that he should be allowed to worship in private as a Catholic while attending public Protestant services. Elizabeth asked the Privy Council for their opinion but there was no consensus and she refused Charles.

Paulet shifted slightly on the Woolsack. It was time for him to make his announcement. Slowly he stood up, steadying himself as he did so. His back felt stiff after sitting so long on the great padded seat and it was a relief to stand. A

hush fell through the Parliament chamber as the Lords and Bishops all turned to him. Nearly 60 of the 80 members were present but Paulet was glad that his son, Lord St John, was not. It was hard for him to make this admission and he would rather that his son did not witness it. He cleared his throat and addressed his audience. On this day, 25 October 1566, he announced, the Queen, 'considering the decay of his memory and hearing, griefs accompanying hoary hairs and old age, and understanding that the Lord Keeper would be slow to recover from his illness', had decided that the role of Speaker for the Lords should be filled by Sir Robert Cattelyn, Chief Justice of the Common Pleas. Paulet waited while his words were recorded in the Lords Journal and the clerk read aloud the commission appointing Cattelyn as Speaker and then he walked to take his place with the other Lords as Cattelyn moved to sit upon the Woolsack. It was done. Paulet was not upset at the loss of his position – he had always known that it was only to be a temporary appointment, brought about because he was the senior noble in the House – but he was dismayed that the Queen no longer considered him capable of carrying out all his duties. This was a public acknowledgement that age had finally caught up with him and he wondered how long he would be fit enough to travel from Basing to London to attend the Court. It was hard, even now, to admit that he was old and that death might not be far away. He knew that his memory was not as clear as it had once been and he did tire more easily. It had taken great effort for him to maintain a near-perfect record of attendance in Parliament recently so perhaps it was time to enjoy his leisure while younger men took over.

That evening Paulet sat upon the chair before the fire in his bedroom. It had been a long and emotional day and he was ready to sleep. His servant had helped him to undress until he wore only his linen shirt and had wrapped a cloak about him. The curtains were closed and the room was lit by several candles. Carpets lay on the floor around the bed and an embroidered tapestry was draped across the top of the cupboard at the side of the chamber. The only other furniture was a chest and a press to contain clothes and the large wooden bed. This was like a shallow box with four carved posts at the corners supporting a wooden canopy overhead and around the sides were hung heavy curtains. Clean sheets and blankets were laid on the mattress. A linen head-sheet was placed over the pillows and the whole bed covered with a linen coverlet. Paulet waited while his servant combed his hair and placed his night-cap upon his head and then rose to visit his room of easement, the small chamber in the corner of the room. The wooden board on which he sat over the privy was covered in green cloth to hide the wood and across the hole in the board lay a cushion to block smells rising from the drain below. When he returned to his chamber his clothes had been folded and placed in the chest and the press, the bedding was turned down, a *chamber-pot was placed ready and a wax night-light had been placed on a table near the bed. Paulet removed his cloak and climbed onto the bed, sinking down into the softness of the feathers while his servant blew out the remaining candles, drew the curtains around his master and, bidding him goodnight, withdrew from the chamber.*

15

An Oak, not a Willow

Paulet achieved a remarkable feat by serving at Court for 47 years and emerging unscathed. When asked how he had survived the dangers of his times he replied:

I am a willow, not an oak;
I chide, but never hurt with stroke.

He believed that he had dealt with people gently, that 'he corrected mildly with a willow twig, not with an oaken cudgel' and so did not alienate those who disagreed with him. By using friendship he had made 'his foes his friends' and, certainly, he does not appear to have had any serious enemies, men who were trying to destroy him.[538]

However, since his death the phrase 'a willow, not an oak' has often been used out of context to describe him as a time-server, suiting his policies to the prevailing climate to ensure his own success and safety. Paulet may well have accepted religious and political changes with which he disagreed but, on issues about which he felt strongly, he was prepared to stand against the consensus of opinion and to take a lead in pursuing what he believed was right. He was one of the first to move against both Somerset and Northumberland. He only reluctantly signed Edward's 'Devise' in favour of Lady Jane Grey, after much pressure, and was one of the first to desert her to support Mary as rightful heir. During Elizabeth's reign he became especially single-minded, attempting yet again to return to a more efficient means of revenue accounting and speaking against farming out the collection of customs. He opposed sending troops into France, voted against the bill for Uniformity in Religion and opposed the proposal to petition the Queen to name her successor. With this unbending resolve to hold to his own beliefs, Paulet would be better described as 'an oak, not a willow'.

In August 1569 Paulet entertained a monarch for the final time when Queen Elizabeth stayed at Basing House during her progress. He had hosted four monarchs on five different occasions at great financial cost but he had gained enormous prestige from the honour. He had attained a position of eminence and in 1567 he compiled a book of his family pedigrees and armorial bearings.[539] He was the second peer of the realm after the Duke of Norfolk but, because he had been so aged before reaching a position of high rank and influence, none of his children made especially socially advantageous marriages. All eight had initially married within gentry families. However, in 1554 John was allied with a powerful family when he married as his second wife, Elizabeth, sister to Jane Seymour and the Duke of Somerset and hence aunt to the late King Edward VI. Paulet was surrounded by a large family and he must have attended myriad family events. Two grand-daughters, the children of his youngest son Giles, were baptised in London in July 1562 and August 1563 and he was godfather to several children himself. On 10 February 1557 he had stood as godfather for Julius Caesar Adelmare, the son of a physician to Queen Mary, and two years later he did the same for John White, the nephew of the Bishop of Winchester. Significantly, both these babies were born into Catholic families who would have chosen godparents with strong Catholic convictions. Funerals also played a prominent part in his life as he outlived so many of his contemporaries. Paulet had a long association with Sir Richard Sackville, a cousin of the Queen, and he was an executor when Sir Richard died in 1566. Within two years Paulet's son John, who had been widowed for a second time, married Sackville's widow, Winifred.[540]

During the latter part of the 1560s Paulet spent less time at Court. He was still receiving commissions for matters ranging from the restoration of decayed fortifications in the north of the country to finance issues and the sale of church property.[541] He continued to be a justice of the peace in Hampshire and other counties but his control was diminishing within his home county. For some years, since Wriothesley had died, Paulet had enjoyed a solitary eminence as the senior noble in Hampshire and his family had become very influential. Two of his sons, John and Chidiock, and his nephew, William, were also justices. However, during the 1560s, the removal from office of many Catholic justices left Paulet and his family relatively isolated with little Catholic support and their control declined as the Protestant families took over.

Paulet's influence at Court also waned as his absences and his objections to Cecil's foreign policy isolated him. His previous attempts to oppose powerful councillors, such as Somerset and Northumberland, had been successful but now he was in a minority on the Privy Council and, more importantly, Cecil had the support of the Queen. The councillors had split along religious lines – the older conservative group of Norfolk, Paulet, Pembroke, Arundel and Lord Howard against the larger group of reformers, which included Cecil and Leicester.[542] When Paulet was called to Court in January 1564 he believed that there was 'bitter rancour' between the councillors because of their failure to agree on foreign policy.[543] Paulet most probably shared the concerns of Norfolk, Pembroke and Arundel about Cecil's control of foreign policy and his support for the Protestants in France and the Low Countries. However, there is no evidence that he was involved in any plot against Cecil, or in Norfolk's schemes regarding Mary Queen of Scots.

Norfolk and his supporters had conceived a plan for him to marry Mary, who would then be recognised as heir to the English throne. If successful, the plan would have enhanced Norfolk's position and might possibly have led to Cecil's downfall. As Norfolk was plotting, Spanish ships landed on the south coast of England to escape bad weather and privateers. The ships were carrying money to pay the Duke of Alva's troops in the Netherlands where he was trying to quash a rebellion against Spanish rule. Tense diplomatic relations between the two countries resulted in Elizabeth confiscating this bullion as Alva ordered the arrest of English men and ships in the Netherlands. Elizabeth responded in kind towards Spaniards and their ships in England with the result that all trade between the two countries ceased. The act of taking the money was viewed by some Privy Councillors as being deliberately provocative towards the Spanish and they held Cecil responsible. The conservatives believed that if Norfolk married Mary she could be returned to Scotland as Queen and named as Elizabeth's successor, the bullion could be returned to Spain and cordial relations resumed with Philip, and Norfolk could replace Cecil as chief minister. The conspiracy widened as Norfolk schemed with the Catholic Earls of Northumberland and Westmorland, both of whom supported the restoration of Catholicism. In October 1569 Elizabeth, knowing of the scheme, eventually arrested

Norfolk and a rising by the two northern Earls collapsed. Norfolk spent about nine months in the Tower and the two Earls fled to Scotland. In December Paulet sent a letter containing intelligence about the rising to the Privy Council and that same autumn he was listed as one of the examiners to question Arundel and Pembroke regarding the proposed marriage of Mary to Norfolk.[544] Cecil survived the plot unscathed.

After Norfolk's release from the Tower he continued to scheme, becoming involved with a Florentine banker, Roberto Ridolfi, who acted as a contact with the Spanish and the Pope. The intention was that Alva should send a force to invade England, Elizabeth should be taken prisoner and England returned to Catholicism. Yet again, Norfolk's plans failed and this time he was found guilty of treason on 16 January 1572. A letter from Norfolk to Ridolfi included Paulet's and St John's names amongst those nobles he thought supported the plot but this seems unlikely.[545] There is nothing to suggest that, having accepted so many religious changes during his long life, Paulet was now prepared to sanction the invasion of England by a foreign force in an attempt to reinstate Catholicism. His loyalty to the Crown was never in question and he would never have supported the overthrow of the rightful monarch.

Paulet had retired to Basing by the time of Norfolk's trial and was therefore excused attendance. His workload had been steadily decreasing. In 1568 he gave instructions that when he was at Basing the Exchequer tellers were to take their orders from the Privy Council, and in June 1570 the Deputy Lieutenants of Kent, Essex and Hampshire were given the 'government' of their counties when Paulet was unable to fulfil those duties.[546] The Privy Council attendance records are sparse for these years and do not give a clear picture. The last relatively complete register is for 1565 when Paulet attended a dozen meetings. After that only one attendance is noted for 19 March 1567 but then the following three years of records are missing.[547] He was certainly not sitting with the Privy Council very frequently although documents were still being sent to him. In 1570 he was receiving and signing warrants and being named on commissions although almost certainly the work was being done by the other commissioners. In the summer of 1571 he continued to sign orders and write to the Privy Council from Basing, and the following January Paulet was named on a Privy Council committee.[548]

Parliament sat in 1571 from 2 April to 29 May but Paulet did not attend. However, one matter raised during the course of the proceedings directly related to him. The Commons were asked to vote for a subsidy but they pointed out that the Queen was short of funds because of misuse of money in the Exchequer. Paulet had been unsuccessful in his attempts to improve accounting and remove cash from the control of the tellers to curb corruption. Investigations had recently shown that several tellers had defaulted on repayments totalling over £44,000 of borrowed money. Unfortunately Paulet also had debts, possibly incurred through spending large sums on his own building projects. At his death he may have owed as much as £34,000 to the Crown and a further £12,000 to various individuals.[549] In 1568 he was given permission to sell land and property to the value of £647 11s 10¾d to satisfy some of his debts to the Queen, but it appears that he died in debt. Shortly before his death, in January 1572, he was borrowing money.[550] Even so, he was a very wealthy man and he left sufficient property for his son John to receive an income of between £2,000 and £3,000 per annum.[551]

The document purportedly written by Paulet, and set down in *A Complete English Peerage*, in which he recorded his personal history, was intended as an explanation to Elizabeth of how much of his own money he had expended on behalf of the Crown. He cited the many expenses of the Boulogne War, the loss of income from land promised but not delivered before the death of Henry VIII, the loss of money spent on restoring Bishops Waltham Abbey and the lost rent from the land, the cost of entertaining Edward VI at Bishops Waltham and Basing, and Mary and Philip and Elizabeth at Basing. Finally, he estimated the allowance he should be due, over and above his basic fee, for attendance and travelling expenses during his tenure as Lord Treasurer. Paulet's calculations of what he believed the Queen should consider as her debt to him adds up to the magnificent sum of over £22,000, an amount which would have drastically reduced his debt to her. There is no record of whether the Queen ever saw this document. He also wrote a draft of another letter to the Queen, in April 1571, regarding the origins of her inherited debt but this letter was never finished. Elizabeth had asked for an explanation of the state of her finances and Paulet explained how Henry VIII had left debts having spent his father's fortune and all the money available to himself, how Edward had suffered from the costs of war and how Mary had continued in debt. Elizabeth's debt had been increased by wars, by spending too freely and by losses in exchange rates. Paulet would have liked to confer with the Queen about the matter but at that time was 'so troubled with the humor upon my nose that I am not able to go abroad'.[552]

During the last few weeks of his life Paulet was the senior peer in England. For some years Thomas Howard, 4th Duke of Norfolk, had been the first peer of the realm but he was in the Tower awaiting his execution

and, attainted of treason, his title and lands were forfeited. Indeed, as he lan-
guished in the Tower he was referred to as the late Duke of Norfolk and he
described himself as being 'but a dead dog in this world' and referred to his
'earthly death' before signing himself just Thomas Howard.[553] The Marquis
of Northampton, junior in rank to Paulet, had died of acute gout on 28
October 1571. He had married Helena Snakenborg at Easter, only months
before his death, and confusion among some historians has connected this
marriage to Paulet. During the spring of 1571 the Earl of Rutland received
two letters referring to the marriage of the 'Lord Marquess' who has been
mistakenly identified as Paulet.[554] Similarly, a letter from Leicester to the
Queen concerning 'my Lord Marquis' and his wife, who were then at
Warwick, is incorrectly considered to refer to Paulet not Northampton,
who in fact died at Warwick only four weeks later.[555] The confusion was
further increased by the fact that Paulet's son John, the future 2nd Marquis
of Winchester, married Winifred Sackville in 1568 and a concatenation of
errors had mistakenly identified this lady as William Paulet's wife. After the
death of his only wife, Elizabeth, in 1558, Paulet remained a widower for the
last fourteen years of his life.

Paulet died at home at Basing House between 10 and 11pm on Monday
10 March 1572. He had lived for more than 87 years and was lauded for his
great age. In 1564, when he was probably 80, none of his living contemporaries in government had reached the age of 70 and only four of the
nine men in their sixties were over 65. He was by far the elder statesman
and continued so for nearly another eight years. At his death only the two
clerics, Richard Cox at 72 and Nicholas Heath at 71, were over 70. At a
time when his contemporaries at court lived to an average age of 62 he was
extraordinarily old.[556]

William Paulet was carried in a long funeral procession and buried in the
chancel he had built for his parents in Basing Church, not far from his great
house. Within the church, his coffin was placed inside a large hearse. With
a floor dimension of about twelve feet by nine feet and a height of over
twenty feet it dominated the small building. The top of the wooden frame,
shaped like a cupola, was covered in black velvet and taffeta and was hung
with a gold and black fringe. Around the bottom, the sides were hung with
black baize to a height of three feet to form a low wall around the hearse
and on two sides were openings with gates to allow the coffin to be placed
inside. The top was decorated with many escutcheons displaying his arms
and along the front in large letters was written his motto, 'Love Loyalty'.[557]
It was a grand setting for a man who had played his part in England's

history for nearly 50 years. After the funeral the mourners returned to Basing House for an equally grand feast, with the guests sitting according to their rank in the hall, the chamber and the great parlour.

By the end of his life Paulet had amassed a wealth of wisdom and experience and gave sound advice to those who would listen. When asked how he had lived to such a great age he replied:

> Late supping I forbear;
> Wine and women I forswear;
> My neck and feet I keep from cold;
> No marvel then though I be old.[558]

The advice which he offered to his children perhaps best summed up the belief which had so often dictated his own actions:

> Be obedient to the Crown,
> For that the King elected is,
> and of the Lord appointed.[559]

William Paulet lived by his motto – Love Loyalty. He was loyal to the four monarchs he served and to England, always following what he believed was the right course. By resolutely maintaining his principles, and by living to such a great age, William Paulet is surely more worthy of comparison with the sturdy oak than with a swaying willow.

Paulet Family *c*.1340–1572

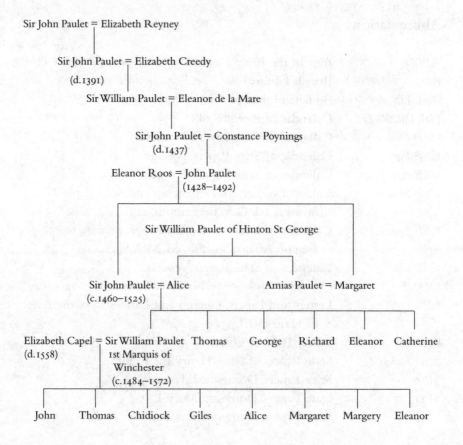

Sir John Paulet = Elizabeth Reyney

Sir John Paulet = Elizabeth Creedy
(d.1391)

Sir William Paulet = Eleanor de la Mare

Sir John Paulet = Constance Poynings
(d.1437)

Eleanor Roos = John Paulet
(1428–1492)

Sir William Paulet of Hinton St George

Sir John Paulet = Alice   Amias Paulet = Margaret
(c.1460–1525)

Elizabeth Capel = Sir William Paulet   Thomas   George   Richard   Eleanor   Catherine
(d.1558)   1st Marquis of
                  Winchester
                  (c.1484–1572)

John   Thomas   Chidiock   Giles   Alice   Margaret   Margery   Eleanor

Notes

Abbreviations

APC	Acts of the Privy Council
BL	British Library
Bod. Lib.	Bodleian Library
Cal. Pat. Rolls	Calendar of Patent Rolls
CSP Dom	Calendar of State Papers, Domestic
CSP For	Calendar of State Papers, Foreign
CSP Rome	Calendar of State Papers, Rome
CSP Spain	Calendar of Letters, Despatches and State Papers, Spanish, ed. G.A. Bergenroth, et al.
CSP Spain, Eliz	Calendar of Letters and State Papers relating to English Affairs, Spanish, ed. M.A.S. Hume
CSP Ven	Calendar of State Papers, Venetian
ODNB	Oxford Dictionary of National Biography
LP	Letters and Papers, Foreign and Domestic, of the reign of Henry VIII, 1509–47
PRO	Public Record Office
State Papers	State Papers of King Henry the Eighth
*SP*10	State Papers, Domestic, Edward VI
*SP*11	State Papers, Domestic, Mary I
*SP*12	State Papers, Domestic, Elizabeth I

1   Bod.Lib. Ashmole MS 836, fs. 211, 214.

2   A. Jacob, *A Complete English Peerage* (London, 1766), pp. 186–8. In his biography of Paulet, Jacob has reproduced part of a document purportedly written by Paulet as a memorial of his services to Queen Elizabeth. Although it is not possible to establish the authenticity of the document there is nothing in the style or content to suggest that it was not written by Paulet. With only a very limited collection of personal papers ascribed to Paulet this document is significant for its autobiographical content. This content does not conflict with the known facts of Paulet's life and some new details concerning, for instance, his role at Boulogne and his sickness in 1544, help to corroborate existing information. *Miscellanea Genealogica et Heraldica,* series V, ed. A. W. Hughes Clarke (London, 1935–37), vol. IX, pp. 142–5.

3   Some sources give the name Elizabeth but it is probable that Alice is correct and Elizabeth (*nee* Denebaud) was her mother.

4   R. Broughton, *A brief discourse of the life and death of the late right and honourable Sir William Paulet* (London, 1572), verse 95; T. Newton, *The Worthye Booke of Old Age* (London, 1569); J.D. Alsop and D.M. Loades, 'William Paulet, First Marquis of Winchester: A Question of Age', *Sixteenth Century Journal,* XVIII (3), (1987), pp. 333–41. There is no reliable corroborating evidence for the cited ages of 96, 97 or 106.

5   PRO C 142/43/56. Inquisitions post mortem were often inaccurate but a date of 1474 would require a large discrepancy of eleven years. Although his birth may have been earlier, without further proof the author has assumed 1484 throughout.

6   C.A.H. Franklyn, *A genealogical history of the families of Paulet, (or Pawlett), Berewe (or Barrow), Lawrence and Parker* (Bedford, 1963), p. 66; Cal. Inq. Hen. VII, I, no. 823; *Miscellanea Genealogica et Heraldica,* series V, vol. IX, p. 144. A birth date of 1474 or earlier would place him in his mid-30s at his wedding, rather old by the standards of the time.

7   Broughton, *A brief discourse of the life and death of the late right and honourable Sir William Paulet,* verses 19, 95.

8   Franklyn, *A genealogical history of the families of Paulet,* p. 66.

9   N. Orme, *Medieval Children* (New Haven, 2001) p. 28.

10 J.D.C. Fisher, *Christian Initiation: Baptism in the Medieval West* (London, 1965), pp. 158–60, 164–5; E. Duffy, *The Stripping of the Altars* (New Haven & London, 1993), p. 281.

11 Fisher, *Christian Initiation*, p.174.

12 J. Guillemeau, *The Nursing of Children* (London, 1612), p.24.

13 Ibid., pp.15, 22.

14 Ibid., p.16.

15 E. Ewing, *History of Children's Costume* (London, 1977), pp.29, 27.

16 N. Bradfield, *900 Years of English Costume: from the eleventh to the twentieth century* (London, 1987), p.67.

17 *Calendar of State Papers, Spanish,* ed. P. de Gayangos et al. 13 vols. (London, 1862–1954), X, pp.18–19; Broughton, *Brief discourse,* verse 41.

18 *Letters and Papers, Foreign and Domestic, of the Reign of Henry VIII, 1509–47,* ed. J.S. Brewer et al. 21 vols and addenda. (London, 1862–1932, reprinted 1965), VI, 465 (p.209).

19 N.Orme, *English Schools in the Middle Ages* (London, 1973), p.124.

20 Ibid., pp.131–2.

21 Ibid., pp.119–20, 123–4.

22 Sir T. Elyot, *Boke named the governour* (London, 1557), folios 23, 15, 52.

23 J. Russell, *The Boke of Nurture,* ed. F.J. Furnivall (Bungay, 1867), pp.18–23.

24 *The Babees Book: medieval manners for the young,* ed. F.J. Furnivall (London, 1908), p.6.

25 Jacob, *Complete English Peerage,* p.188.

26 Broughton, *Brief Discourse,* verses 41–2.

27 Jacob, *Complete English Peerage,* p.188.

28 Sir W. Holdsworth, *A History of English Law,* 17 vols. (London, 1903–72) II, pp.504, 506–7.

29 F.A. Inderwick, *The Inner Temple: its early history, as illustrated by its records,* 5 vols. (London, 1896), I, pp.2, 5, 8.

30 *Three Revels from the Inns of Court,* ed. D.S. Bland (Amersham, 1984), pp.117–118.

31 Inderwick, *The Inner Temple,* I, p.110.

32 *Miscellanea Genealogica et Heraldica,* ed. Hughes Clark, IX, p.144.

33 D. Cosson, 'The Capells of Rayne Hall', *The Archaeological Journal,* vol. XL (1883), pp.67–9.

34 W. Whateley, *A bride bush or A direction for married persons* (London, 1623), p.184.

35 Franklyn, *A genealogical history of the families of Paulet,* p.68.

36 D. Cressy, *Birth, Marriage and Death* (Oxford, 1997), pp.336–7.

37 Whateley, *A bride bush,* p.174.

38 *Miscellanea Genealogica et Heraldica*, ed. Hughes Clark, IX, p.146.

39 J. Stow, *A Summary of the Chronicles of England ... to 1575* (London, 1575), p.545.

40 Jacob, *Complete English Peerage*, p.188; *LP* I i, 257(49); 632(26).

41 PRO C 142/44/94; Alsop and Loades, William Paulet: A Question of Age, p.334.

42 *LP* I i, 969 (23); II ii, 4562; III ii, 2667 (p.1127).

43 *LP* I i, 1221 (6).

44 *LP* I ii, 2574.

45 *LP* I ii, p.1537; *LP* II i, 170, 670.

46 Jacob, *Complete English Peerage*, pp.188–9.

47 Ibid., p.189.

48 *LP* III ii, 3504 (pp.1457–8).

49 *LP* IV i, 214 (p.84).

50 *LP* IV iii, 5407.

51 *Documents relating to the foundation of the Chapter of Winchester, AD 1541–7*, ed. G.W. Kitchin & F.T. Madge (London/ Winchester, 1889), p.51.

52 Jacob, *Complete English Peerage*, p.189. The fees in 1539 amounted to £50 per annum; *LP* XIV ii, 782 (p.326).

53 *LP* IV i, 2000.

54 *LP* V, 1549; VI, 406, 1623; X, 392 (g. 13).

55 *LP* XVI, 947 (55).

56 *Calendar of the Patent Rolls, Edward VI*, ed. R.H. Brodie, 5 vols. (London, 1924–6), I, p.326.

57 *LP* XVI, 136 (2); 242.

58 *Letters of Richard Fox, 1486–1527*, ed. P.S. & H.M. Allen (Oxford, 1929), pp.170–1.

59 S.H. Cassan, *The Lives of the Bishops of Winchester*, 2 vols. (London, 1827), I, p.339.

60 Allen, *Letters of Richard Fox*, pp.101–3, 148,

61 Cosson, 'Capells of Rayne Hall', pp.70–6.

62 *LP* IV iii, Appdx. 67.

63 *LP* I i, 1646.

64 Details of the workings of the Court of Wards are taken from H.E. Bell, *The Court of Wards and Liveries* (Cambridge, 1953).

65 *LP* III ii, 1451 (15).

66 *LP* IV ii, 3471 (18); iii, 5508.

67 *Cal. Pat. Rolls, Ed. VI* , V, p.5.

68 *Calendar of State Papers, Domestic series of the reigns of Edward VI, Mary, Elizabeth, 1547–80*, ed. R. Lemon (London, 1856), p.392.

69 *LP* IV ii, 2673 (3).

70 *LP* V, 80 (11). Idiots and naturals were those whose mental illness was congenital and permanent.

71 Bell, *Court of Wards and Liveries*, p.128.

72 *LP* XV, 942 (112).

73 'Livery' is the legal delivery of property into a person's possession by a writ issued by the Master of Livery.

74 *LP* XVII, 1154 (72).

75 J. Hurstfield, 'Corruption and Reform under Edward VI and Mary: The Example of Wardship', *English Historical Review*, LXVIII (1953), pp.24, 26, 36.

76 Ibid., p.24.

77 *Cal. Pat. Rolls, Ed. VI*, IV, p.195; *Oxford Dictionary of National Biography* (Oxford, 2004), vol. 43, p.163.

78 *LP* IV ii, 4199 (2).

79 *LP* Add.I (Pt.I) 609.

80 *LP* IV iii, 6043 (2) p.2691.

81 S.T. Bindoff, *The House of Commons, 1509–1558*, 3 vols. (London, 1982), I, p.97. There were between 20 and 65 electors for each election in the years from 1542 to 1558.

82 G. Cavendish, *Thomas Wolsey, late Cardinal, his life and death* (London, 1999), p.141.

83 *LP* IV iii, 6436.

84 *LP* IV iii, 6516.

85 *LP* IV iii, 6544.

86 *LP* IV iii, 6748 (15).

87 A. Hawkyard, 'From Painted Chamber to St Stephen's Chapel', *Parliamentary History*, 21 (2002), p.69.

88 D. Starkey, *Six Wives: The Queens of Henry VIII* (London, 2003), pp.440–2; *Calendar of State Papers, Spanish*, IV ii, p.212. Paulet's account of his appointment as Comptroller is recorded in Jacob, *Complete English Peerage*, p.189.

89 A. Woodworth, 'Purveyance for the Royal Household in the reign of Elizabeth I', *Transactions of the American Philosophical Soc.* XXXV (1) 1945, pp.62, 65–6; S. Thurley, *The Royal Palaces of Tudor England* (New Haven & London, 1993), p.158; *CSP Spain* XIII, p.31; 'stirks' are young bullocks or heifers that are 1–2 years old.

90 D.M. Loades, *The Tudor Court* (Bangor, 1992), pp.193–202.

91 Thurley, *Royal Palaces*, p.70.

92 *A Collection of Ordinances and Regulations for the Government of the Royal Household* (London, 1790), pp.220–1.

93 *CSP Spain* XIII, p.31.

94 *Ordinances of the Royal Household*, p.59.

95 Loades, *Tudor Court,* p.64.

96 E. Underhill, 'Examination and Imprisonment of Edward Underhill', *An English Garner*, vol. IV, ed. E. Arber (London, 1882), p.95.

97 See Shakespeare, *King Lear,* II. ii. 13: 'A knave, a rascal, an eater of broken meats'.

98 *Ordinances of the Royal Household,* p.162.

99 Ibid., p.151.

100 Ibid., pp.188–90; P. Brears, *All the King's Cooks* (London, 1999), pp.173–4.

101 *LP* XVI, 380, f. 121b (p.183).

102 *LP* V, 1069.

103 *Ordinances of the Royal Household,* p.148.

104 Ibid., pp.159–60.

105 Cavendish, *Thomas Wolsey*, p.161.

106 *Ordinances of the Royal Household*, p.150.

107 Ibid., p.148.

108 Thurley, *Royal Palaces*, p.174.

109 *Tudor Royal Proclamations*, ed. P.L. Hughes and J.F. Larkin, 3 vols. (New Haven & London, 1964, 1969), I, no. 290 (p. 405).

110 N. Samman, 'The Progresses of Henry VIII, 1509–1529', in *The Reign of Henry VIII: Politics, Policy and Piety*, ed. D. MacCulloch (Basingstoke, 1995), p.62.

111 Bod. Lib. Rawlinson MS. A 195c. f. 300b.

112 Thurley, *Royal Palaces*, p.73.

113 *LP* IV i, 1939 (p. 865).

114 *LP* XIII ii, 1280 (f. 55).

115 *CSP Spain* IV ii, 739 (p.177).

116 *LP* V, 1600.

117 *LP* V, 1705.

118 *LP* V, 1537a.

119 *LP* VI, 830.

120 *LP* VI, 73.

121 *CSP Spain* IV ii, 1072 (p.672).

122 *LP* VI, 1111.

123 *LP* VI, 1186.

124 *LP* VI, 1207.

125 *LP* VI, 1486, 1558.

126 *State Papers of the reign of Henry VIII*, 11 vols. (London, 1830–52) I, ii, XXI (p. 415–17); XXII (p. 418–19).

127 *LP* VI, 1571.

128 *LP* VII, 434.

129 *LP* VII, 529, 980.

130 *LP* VII, 690.

131 *LP* VII, 726.

132 *LP* VII, 1095.

133 *LP* X, 39, 41.

134 *LP* X, 282.

135 *LP* X, 151.

136 *LP* VII, 1114.

137 *LP* VIII, 666 (p. 251).

138 *LP* VIII, 886, 974.

139 *LP* X, 777(5); *Cal. Pat. Rolls, Ed. VI*, I, p.68.

140 *LP* VIII, 149 (33).

141 *LP* VIII, 149 (77).

142 *LP* X, 599.

143 *LP* V, 1754; VIII, 287.

144 *LP* XI, 385 (3).

145 *LP* V, 80 (36).

146 T. Fuller, *The History of the Worthies of England*, 3 vols. (London, 1860), II, p.4.

147 *The Victorian History of the Counties of England: Hampshire and the Isle of Wight*, ed. H.A. Doubleday & W. Page, 5 vols. (London, 1900–14), II, pp.120, 123.

148 *LP* XIV i, 906 (1).

149 *LP* V, 1754; XIV i, 1354 (37); XVI, 503 (11).

150 'Agas' and Copperplate maps in *The A to Z of Elizabethan London*, ed. A. Prockter & R. Taylor (London, 1979).

151 *Cal. Pat. Rolls, Elizabeth*, IV, p.54 (no. 405).

152 T. Allen, *The History and Antiquities of London, Westminster, Southwark and parts adjacent*, 4 vols. (London, 1828), III, p.256.

153 *Cal. Pat. Rolls, Ed. VI*, IV, p.15.

154 J. Stow, *A Survey of London* (Stroud, 2005; first published 1598), p.163.

155   Stow, *Survey of London*, p.93.

156   *Calendar of State Papers and Manuscripts, Venetian*, ed. R. Brown et al 38 vols. (London, 1864–1947), V, p.544.

157   Ibid., p.543. The population of London was estimated at 180,000 in 1554.

158   V.A. LaMar, *Travel and Roads in England* (Washington, U.S.A., 1960), p.5.

159   E. Duffy, *The Voices of Morebath: Reformation and Rebellion in an English Village* (London, 2001), p.169.

160   *Statutes of the Realm* (London, 1810–28), IV (1547–85) 2+3 P+M c.8.

161   F.G. Emmison, *Tudor Secretary, Sir William Petre at Court and Home* (London, 1961), p.206.

162   *LP* VIII, 1018; IX, 192.

163   *LP* IX, 4.

164   *LP* IX, 620.

165   *LP* IX, 639.

166   *LP* X, 848.

167   *LP* X, 782.

168   *LP* X, 797.

169   *LP* X, 848.

170   *LP* X, 908.

171   *LP* XI, 803.

172   *LP* XI, 637, 642.

173   *LP* XI, 580 (p. 232); Franklyn, *History of the families of Paulet etc.*, pp.68–9.

174   *LP* XI, 750.

175   *LP* XI, 755, 776, 799, 803, 800.

176   *LP* XI, 823, 829, 835, 837, 836, 844.

177   *LP* XII i, 734.

178   *LP* XII i, 1013.

179   *State Papers* I ii, LXVIII (p. 508).

180   *Ordinances of the Royal Household*, p.56.

181   Ibid., p.56

182   *LP* VIII, 288; XI, 1291.

183   *LP* XII ii, 911.

184   *LP* XII ii, 1060.

185   Jacob, *A Complete English Peerage*, p.187.

186   Bod. Lib. Rawlinson MS. B.118 f. 14; *LP* XIV i, 477.

187   *LP* XIV i, 398.

188 *LP* XIV i, 573.

189 *LP* XIV i, 662; 'herrode and condytore' – herald and conveyor.

190 *Statutes of the Realm,* III (1509–45), 31 HVIII.c.13.

191 *LP* XV, 139 (p.47).

192 *LP* XV, 14.

193 *LP* XII ii, 379, 380.

194 *LP* XIII i, 471; *State Papers* III, CCLXVII (p. 127).

195 *LP* XIII i, 1021.

196 *LP* XIII i, 999.

197 *LP* XIII ii, 433 – 'he gave honest counsel'.

198 *LP* XV, 316.

199 *LP* XV, 537; *The Lisle Letters,* ed. M. St Clare Byrne, 6 vols. (London & Chicago, 1981), VI, p.116.

200 *Journal of the House of Lords, 1509–77,* pp.146, 149.

201 *LP* XVI, 745 (p.359).

202 *LP* XVI, 931, 932.

203 *LP* XVI, 1395(1).

204 *LP* XVI, 1470.

205 *Journal of the House of Lords, 1509–77,* pp.168, 174, 175.

206 D.E. Hoak, *The King's Council in the Reign of Edward VI* (Cambridge, 1976), p.36.

207 *Acts of the Privy Council of England,* ed. J.R. Dasent (London, 1890–93) vol. I, p.54.

208 *Revolution Reassessed,* ed. C. Coleman & D. Starkey (Oxford, 1986), p.81; *LP* XI, 978, 1028, 1261.

209 *APC* I, p.62.

210 *LP* XVIII ii, p.542. The record of attendance at Privy Council meetings as recorded in the Acts of the Privy Council may not be entirely accurate but does indicate a pattern of attendance.

211 Hoak, *King's Council in the Reign of Edward VI,* pp.125–6.

212 *Ordinances of the Royal Household,* p.155.

213 *LP* XVI, 311.

214 *LP* VI, 465; VII, 690, 726.

215 *State Papers* I ii, XLVI (p.461).

216 J. Buswell, *An Historical Account of the Knights of the most noble Order of the Garter* (London, 1757), p.13.

217 *LP* XVIII i, 451.

218 W.K. Jordan, *The Chronicle and Political Papers of King Edward VI* (London, 1966), p.119.

219 *SP* 12/33/45; *SP* 12/33/47.
220 Bod. Lib. Rawlinson MS. Statutes 40 f. 15894. Contemporary paintings depict the collar with only red roses around white.
221 *APC* I, p.132.
222 Details of the King dining in: Brears, *All the King's Cooks*, pp.164–6.
223 *LP* XVIII i, 675.
224 *LP* XVIII i, 728, 746.
225 *LP* XVIII i, 719; Jacob, *Complete English Peerage*, p.190.
226 *LP* XVIII i, 804.
227 *Tudor Royal Proclamations*, I, no. 219 (p.319).
228 *LP* XVIII ii, 516; XIX i, 1.
229 *The Diary of Henry Machyn*, ed. J.G. Nichols (London, 1848), p.125.
230 *LP* IV, 390 (30).
231 *LP* VII, 9.
232 *The Progresses and Public Processions of Queen Elizabeth*, ed. J.G. Nichols, 3 vols. (London, 1823), I, pp.108, 120. An angell was a gold coin worth 10 shillings.
233 *LP* XIII i, 5; XIV i, 5; XV, 1.
234 *LP* XIX i, 278 (5).
235 *LP* XIX i, 141 (26).
236 *LP* XIX i, 501.
237 *LP* XIX i, 388, 366, 411.
238 *LP* XIX i, 1032 (5).
239 *LP* XIX i, 273 (p.149).
240 *CSP Spain* VI ii, p.270.
241 *LP* XX i, 558.
242 *LP* XIX i, 431.
243 C.S.L. Davies, 'Provisions for Armies, 1509–1550: a study in the effectiveness of early Tudor Government', *Economic History Review*, 2nd Series 17 (1964–5), p.241, n.4.
244 *CSP Ven.* V, pp.350, 544.
245 *LP* XIX i, 675, 694.
246 *LP* XIX i, 704.
247 *LP* XIX ii, 688 (p.406).
248 Jacob, *Complete English Peerage*, p.191.
249 *LP* XIX i, 801, 819.
250 *LP* XIX i, 872.
251 Jacob, *Complete English Peerage*, p.190; *LP* XIX ii, 221.

252 Jacob, *Complete English Peerage*, p.190.

253 *LP* XIX ii,112.

254 Jacob, *Complete English Peerage*, p.190.

255 *LP* XIX i, 970.

256 *LP* XIX ii, 112.

257 *LP* XIX ii, 221.

258 Jacob, *Complete English Peerage*, p.190.

259 *LP* XIX ii, 424 (pp.241–2).

260 *LP* XIX i, 795, 816.

261 *LP* XIX ii, 424.

262 *LP* XIX ii, 334.

263 *LP* XIX ii, 393, 453.

264 *LP* XIX ii, 655, 777.

265 *LP* XX i, 958.

266 *LP* XX i, 671, 846(13) (p.416).

267 *LP* XX i, 821, 922; *State Papers* V, DXXVI.

268 *LP* XX i, 1195.

269 *LP* XX i, 1255.

270 *LP* XX ii, 2.

271 *LP* XX ii, 38; *State Papers* I ii, CCXXII (p. 803); *LP* XX ii, 81; Jacob, *Complete English Peerage*, p.192.

272 *LP* XX ii, 71, 61.

273 *LP* XX ii, 5. Bloody flux was dysentery.

274 *LP* XIX ii, 415; Jacob, *Complete English Peerage*, p.192.

275 *LP* XX ii, 13, 247.

276 *LP* XX ii, 13, 140, 156, 174, 184.

277 *LP* XX ii, 229.

278 *LP* XX ii, 238, 306.

279 *LP* XX ii, 366.

280 *LP* XX ii, 346, 368.

281 *LP* XX ii, 405; Jacob, *Complete English Peerage*, p.192.

282 *LP* XX ii, 706 (8); Jacob, *Complete English Peerage*, p.192.

283 *LP* XX ii, 1068 (34).

284 *LP* XX ii, 814, 849; *Journal of the House of Lords, 1509–77*, p.268.

285 *LP* XX ii, 427.

286 *Ordinances of the Royal Household*, pp.55, 150.

287 Ibid., p.139.

288 *LP* XXI i, 790.

289 *LP* XXI i, 970 (14), (18), (31), (32); 1166 (53), (71).

290   *Original Letters Illustrative of English History*, ed. H. Ellis, 3rd Series, 11 vols. (London, 1969), III, pp.369–72.

291   *LP* XIX i, 278 (4); XX i, 125 (9); XXI ii, 332 (43).

292   *LP* XXI ii, 22, 19.

293   *LP* XXI ii, 44, 58.

294   *State Papers* I ii, CCLII (p. 868); CCLV (p.874).

295   *CSP Ven* V, p.544.

296   *LP* XXI ii, 238.

297   *Journal of the House of Lords, 1509–77*, p.283.

298   *LP* XXI ii, 697.

299   *LP* XXI ii, 696.

300   *LP* XXI ii, 759.

301   *LP* XXI ii, 675, 713.

302   *LP* XXI ii, 770 (85) (p.408).

303   *CSP Spain*, IX, p.6.

304   *SP* 10/1/1; *SP* 10/8/4.

305   *LP* XXI ii, 634 (p.321).

306   *APC* II, p.5.

307   *APC* II, pp.8–9.

308   *LP* XXI ii, 634 (p.321).

309   *APC* II, pp.17–18.

310   *Cal. Pat. Rolls, Ed. VI*, I, pp.42–3.

311   J. Strype, *Ecclesiastical Memorials relating chiefly to religion and the reformation of it*, 3 vols. (Oxford, 1822), II ii, pp.291, 298, 303–4.

312   Ibid., II ii, pp.306–10.

313   *The Literary Remains of King Edward VI*, ed. J.G. Nichols, 2 vols. (London, 1857), I, p.xcv.

314   Ibid., I, p.ccxcii.

315   Ibid., I, p.lxviii.

316   Ibid., I, p.ccxcii–ccxcvii; *APC* II, p.33.

317   *APC* II, p.58.

318   *CSP Spain*, IX, p.52.

319   J. Campbell, *Lives of the Lord Chancellors of England and Keepers of the Great Seal*, 8 vols. (London, 1845–69), II, p.4.

320   *Cal. Pat. Rolls, Ed. VI*, I, p.137.

321   *APC* II, pp.63–4.

322   *CSP Spain*, IX, p.52.

323   Ibid., IX, pp.105, 135.

324   Ibid., IX, pp.199, 244.

325   Ibid., X, pp.165–6.

326   *Cal. Pat. Rolls, Ed. VI,* I, p.177.

327   Ibid., I, pp.66–8.

328   Ibid., I, p.139; *SP* 10/2/9.

329   *SP* 10/8/4.

330   *Tudor Royal Proclamations* I, no. 309; *Statutes of the Realm,* IV (1547–85) 2+3 Ed.VI c.36.

331   *SP* 10/7/5.

332   *CSP Spain,* IX, p.477.

333   Ibid., IX, p.445.

334   A.J.A. Malkiewicz, 'An Eyewitness's Account of the Coup d'Etat of October 1549', *English Historical Review,* LXX (1955) pp.604–5.

335   *SP* 10/9/14.

336   *APC* II, pp.333–5.

337   *APC* II, pp.336–7.

338   *SP* 10/9/24; *SP* 10/9/26; *SP* 10/9/27.

339   *APC* II, pp.337–42.

340   *APC* II, pp.342–3.

341   *APC* II, pp.344–5.

342   *CSP Spain,* IX, p.489.

343   Hoak, *King's Council in the Reign of Edward VI,* p.255.

344   *CSP Spain,* X, p.8.

345   *APC* II, p.398.

346   *Cal. Pat. Rolls, Ed. VI,* III, p.4.

347   Ibid., III, pp.177–8, 189–90.

348   *CSP Ven.* V, p.552.

349   Fuller, *History of the Worthies of England,* I, pp.24–5.

350   *ODNB* vol. 43, William Paulet, p.161.

351   *Cal. Pat. Rolls, Ed. VI,* III. pp.196–7.

352   Ibid., II, p.386.

353   *CSP Spain,* X, p.121; *APC* IV, pp.20, 131.

354   *APC* III, pp.26, 29, 109.

355   *Literary Remains of King Edward VI,* II, p.294.

356   *Tudor Royal Proclamations,* I, nos. 357, 361, 365.

357   Ibid., no. 366.

358   *SP* 10/11/15.

359   Hoak, *King's Council of Edward VI,* pp.273–5.

360   *APC* II, pp.208–10.

361 *APC* XXV, pp.ix-x; A.F. Pollard, 'The Acts of the Privy Council, 1590–97', *The English Historical Review*, 18 (1903), pp.567–9.

362 *APC* III, pp.43, 65, 67.

363 *The Acts and Monuments of John Foxe*, ed. Rev. J. Pratt, 8 vols. (London, 1877), VI, p.160.

364 *CSP Spain*, IX, pp.375, 381–2.

365 Ibid., IX, pp. 444, 447.

366 Ibid., X, p.17.

367 Ibid., X, pp.205–12.

368 *Calendar of State Papers, Foreign Series, of the reign of Edward VI, 1547–1553*, ed. W.B. Turnbull (London, 1861), no. 294 (p.75).

369 *Diary of Henry Machyn*, pp.4–5.

370 *CSP Spain*, X, p.258.

371 *Literary Remains of King Edward VI*, II, pp.308–9; I, p.ccxxvii.

372 *APC* III, pp.329, 349.

373 *Literary Remains of King Edward VI*, II, pp.513–14.

374 *Tudor Royal Proclamations*, I, no. 297.

375 T. Tusser, 'Good Housewives' Lessons', in *Selections from writings of Thomas Tusser* (National Federation of Women's Institutes 1954). Tusser wrote during the mid-sixteenth century on instructions for farming, gardening and household management for wives.

376 *Tudor Royal Proclamations*, I, no. 368; *Cal. Pat. Rolls. Ed. VI*, V, p.173.

377 *Tudor Royal Proclamations*, I, nos. 372, 376, 379, 380.

378 *Diary of Henry Machyn*, p.6; *Literary Remains of King Edward VI*, II, p.328.

379 *Diary of Henry Machyn*, p.7; J. Stow, *The Annales or General Chronicle of England* (London, 1631), p.605.

380 *SP* 10/13/30.

381 *CSP Spain*, X, p.342.

382 *SP* 10/14/38.

383 Stow, *Annales*, p.605.

384 *Literary Remains of King Edward VI*, II, p.343.

385 *APC* III, p.360.

386 *CSP Spain*, X, p.177.

387 Bod. Lib. Rawlinson MS B.118 f. 20; Ashmole MS 840 f. 497. When Paulet was elevated to Earl of Wiltshire his gown was of black satin and cost £5.

388 Bod. Lib. Ashmole MS 837 f. 148.

389 *Cal. Pat. Rolls, Ed. VI*, IV, pp.138–9.

390 *SP* 10/13/64; *Literary Remains of King Edward VI*, II, p.371.

391 Campbell, *Lives of the Lord Chancellors of England*, II, pp.5–6.

392 *England under the Reigns of Edward VI and Mary: A series of original letters*, ed. P.F. Tytler, 2 vols. (London, 1839), I, p.64.

393 *Literary Remains of King Edward VI*, II, p.390.

394 *CSP Spain*, X, p.453.

395 *Original Letters Relative to the English Reformation*, ed. H. Robinson, 2 vols. (Cambridge, 1846–7), I, pp.341–2; p.340. Somerset's four daughters were placed in the care of his sister Elizabeth who, in 1554, married Paulet's eldest son, John, as his second wife.

396 *The Works of John Knox*, ed. D. Laing, 3 vols. (Edinburgh, 1846–64), III, pp.281–3; *Literary Remains of King Edward VI*, I, p.clxix.

397 *CSP For. Ed. VI*, 477 (pp. 190–1); *Literary Remains of King Edward VI*, II, p.359.

398 Ibid., II, pp.360, 362–4.

399 *APC* III, p.399; *Diary of Henry Machyn*, pp.12, 19.

400 *CSP Spain*, X, p.591.

401 *APC* IV, pp.45, 49.

402 *Diary of Henry Machyn*, p.24.

403 *APC* IV, pp.104, 109, 102, 108.

404 *CSP Spain*, XI, p.4; *Cal. Pat. Rolls, Ed. VI*, IV, p.395.

405 *Literary Remains of King Edward VI*, II, pp.498–502; see pp. 552–5 for Edward's set of rules for the Privy Council.

406 Ibid., I, p.81.

407 *Cal. Pat. Rolls, Ed. VI*, IV, p.139; Jacob, *Complete English Peerage*, p.193.

408 Russell, *The Boke of Nurture*, pp.66–7.

409 *CSP Spain*, XI, p.10; W.K. Jordan, *Edward VI: The Threshold of Power*, (London, 1970), p.510.

410 *A Collection of State Papers relating to Affairs in the Reigns of King Henry VIII, King Edward VI, Queen Mary and Queen Elizabeth, from the year 1542 to 1570, left by William Cecil, Lord Burghley*, ed. S. Haynes (London, 1740), pp.145–6.

411 *Diary of Henry Machyn*, pp.30–1.

412 *Cal. Pat. Rolls, Philip & Mary*, 4 vols. (London, 1937–9), II, pp.55–9.

413 *CSP Spain*, XI, p.50.

414 Ibid., XI, p.66.

415 Ibid., XI, pp.69–70.

416 *The Chronicle of Queen Jane and Two Years of Queen Mary*, ed. J.G. Nichols (London, 1850), pp.99–100.

417   *Literary Remains of King Edward VI*, II, pp.572–3.

418   *CSP Spain*, XI, p.66.

419   Jordan, *Threshold of Power*, p.521.

420   J.A. Froude, *History of England from the Fall of Wolsey to the defeat of the Spanish Armada*, 12 vols. (London, 1893), V, p.190.

421   Tytler, *England under the reigns of Edward VI and Mary*, II, pp.201–2.

422   Stow, *Annales*, p.611.

423   Emmison, *Tudor Secretary*, p.111.

424   *CSP Spain*, XI, pp.113–14.

425   *Literary Remains of King Edward VI*, I, p.ccxxvii.

426   *CSP Spain*, XI, pp.150–1.

427   *Chronicle of Queen Jane and Two Years of Queen Mary*, p.15.

428   *APC* IV, p.425.

429   *CSP Spain*, XI, p.151.

430   *APC* IV, pp.322–3.

431   *CSP Spain* XI, pp.343, 428n.

432   *APC* IV, pp.397–9.

433   *CSP Spain* XI, pp.183–6.

434   *The accession, coronation and marriage of Mary Tudor*, trans. C.V. Malfatti (Barcelona, 1956), p.34; *SP* 11/1/15.

435   *APC* IV, pp.313, 323; *Cal. Pat. Rolls, Philip & Mary*, I, p.175; C. Wriothesley, *A Chronicle of England during the reigns of the Tudors*, 2 vols. (London, 1875, 1877), II, p.103.

436   *CSP Spain*, XI, p.332; XIII, p.101.

437   *Cal. Pat. Rolls, Philip & Mary*, II, p.88; *SP* 12/73/59.

438   *CSP Spain* XI, p.332.

439   Coleman & Starkey, *Revolution Reassessed*, pp.166, 169.

440   Ibid., pp.167–77; Jacob, *Complete English Peerage*, pp.193–4.

441   *SP* 11/1/14.

442   *Cal. Pat. Rolls, Philip & Mary*, III, p.81.

443   *APC* V, p.59; *APC* IV, p.369.

444   *APC* IV, pp.397–8.

445   *Cal. Pat. Rolls, Philip & Mary*, I, p.265.

446   D.M. Loades, *The Reign of Mary Tudor*, (Harlow, 1991), p.245 n. 65, p.54.

447   Ibid., p.242.

448   *Cal. Pat. Rolls, Philip & Mary*, III, p.317.

449   F.C. Dietz, *English Government Finance, 1485–1558* (London, 1964), p.208; R. Tittler, *The Reign of Mary I* (Harlow, 1991), p.52.

450 *Tudor Royal Proclamations,* II, no. 390.

451 *Diary of Henry Machyn,* pp.41, 332.

452 Wriothesley, *Chronicle of England,* II, pp.99–100; *Cal. Pat. Rolls, Philip & Mary,* I, pp.74–5.

453 *APC* V, p.68.

454 *CSP Spain,* XI, p.414.

455 *Chronicle of Queen Jane and Queen Mary,* pp.36–7; *SP* 11/2/29.

456 D.M. Loades, *Two Tudor Conspiracies* (Cambridge, 1965), pp.109, 120; *Cal. Pat. Rolls, Philip & Mary,* II, pp.42–3.

457 *Chronicle of Queen Jane and Queen Mary,* pp.59–60.

458 *CSP Spain,* XII, p.167.

459 J. Fox, 'The Imprisonment of the Princess Elizabeth', *An English Garner,* ed. E. Arber, IV, pp.119–23.

460 *The Letters of Queen Elizabeth I,* ed. G.B. Harrison (London, 1968), p.21.

461 *CSP Spain,* XII, p.251.

462 Ibid., XII, p.273; *SP* 11/4/13.

463 *CSP Spain,* XIII, p.1.

464 *Chronicle of Queen Jane & Queen Mary,* pp.167–9.

465 *APC* V, p.54; *CSP Spain,* XIII, p.12.

466 Ibid., XIII, p.443.

467 *Chronicle of Queen Jane and Queen Mary,* pp.144, 82, 77.

468 *CSP Spain,* XIII, p.45.

469 Ibid., XIII, p.23.

470 Ibid., XII, pp.168–9, 220; ibid., XIII, p.101.

471 Ibid., XIII, p.50.

472 Ibid., XII, p.295.

473 Ibid., XII, p.316; XIII, pp.373, 455.

474 Ibid., XIII, p.455.

475 R.H, Fritze, 'The Role of Family and Religion in the Local Politics of Early Elizabethan England: The case of Hampshire in the 1560s', *The Historical Journal,* 25, 2 (1982), pp.272–3; *APC* VI, p.361.

476 *CSP Ven.* VI, i, p.27.

477 *Cal. Pat. Rolls, Philip & Mary,* III, p.546; ibid., V, pp.354–5; *CSP Ven.* VI, ii, p.791.

478 *APC* V, p.169.

479 *Diary of Henry Machyn,* pp.83–4, 70.

480 Ibid., pp.90, 148, 146.

481 *CSP: Domestic Series of the reigns of Edward VI, Mary and Elizabeth, 1547–80,* p.117.

482 J.D. Alsop, 'The Execution of a Peer of the Realm: A note on the 1557 verdict against Charles, Lord Stourton', *Wiltshire Archaeological and Natural History Society Annual Bulletin* (26) (Spring 1980), pp.1–2.

483 *APC* VI, p.427.

484 *APC* V, p.136.

485 *CSP Ven.* VI, i, p.183.

486 *SP* 11/10/61 (1); *SP* 11/10/61 (2); Bindoff, *House of Commons*, III, p.70.

487 *Cal. Pat. Rolls, Philip & Mary*, III p.24.

488 *APC* VI, pp.39–41.

489 Ibid., VI, p.229.

490 Ibid., VI, pp.234–5; *CSP Spain*, XIII, p.394.

491 *Tudor Royal Proclamations*, II, no. 441; *SP* 11/13/10.

492 *CSP Spain*, XIII, p.369.

493 Loades, *Reign of Mary Tudor*, p.357.

494 *CSP Foreign Series of the reign of Mary, 1553–8*, p.395.

495 *SP* 11/13/64; *SP* 11/13/65.

496 *SP* 11/13/53.

497 *CSP Spain*, XIII, p.437.

498 *APC* VI, p.411.

499 Loades, *Reign of Mary Tudor*, p.388.

500 *CSP Spain*, XIII, p.440.

501 Sir Thomas Cheney had also served Henry, Edward and Mary but he died within a month of being appointed to Elizabeth's Council.

502 Sir R. Naunton, *Fragmenta Regalia* (London 1641), p.12.

503 J. Guy, *Tudor England* (Oxford, 1990), p.256.

504 *CSP Ven.* VII, pp.1, 3.

505 *Calendar of Letters and State Papers relating to English Affairs, preserved principally in the Archives of Simancas*, I, pp.16–17.

506 N.L. Jones, *Faith by Statute: Parliament and the Settlement of Religion, 1559* (London, 1982), p.99; E. Jeffries Davis, 'An unpublished manuscript of the Lords Journals for April and May 1559', *The English Historical Review*, XXVIII (1913), p.537.

507 Ibid., p.538.

508 *Journal of the House of Lords, 1509–77*, p.568.

509 *CSP Rome, 1558–71*, pp.265–6.

510 *CSP Spain, Eliz*, I, p.18 (no. 6).

511 *SP* 11/13/53; *Calendar of State Papers, Foreign Series of the Reign of Elizabeth, 1558–9*, no. 1182.

512 *Collection of State Papers … left by William Cecil, 1542–1570*, ed. S. Haynes (London, 1740), pp.383–4.

513 G.D. Ramsay, *The City of London in International Politics at the Accession of Elizabeth Tudor* (Manchester, 1975), p.234.

514 Froude, *History of England*, VI, p.370.

515 *Collection of State Papers … left by William Cecil, 1542–1570*, ed. Haynes p.361.

516 Nichols, *Progresses of Queen Elizabeth*, 1, p.87; E. Lodge, *Illustrations of British History, Biography and Manners in the reigns of Henry VIII, Edward VI, Mary, Elizabeth and James I*, 3 vols. (London, 1838), I, p.423.

517 Emmison, *Tudor Secretary*, pp.237–43, 245.

518 Nichols, *Progresses of Queen Elizabeth*, I, pp.87, 258; Jacob, *Complete English Peerage*, p.193.

519 Coleman & Starkey, *Revolution Reassessed*, pp.184–5, 191–2, 187.

520 *SP* 12/22/15; *SP* 12/30/3.

521 *Cal. Pat. Rolls, Eliz.*, II, pp.92–3.

522 *Tudor Royal Proclamations*, II, no. 471.

523 HMC Report on the Manuscripts of the Duke of Buccleuch and Queensbury, vol. III, pp.8–9.

524 S.E. Lehmberg, *Sir Walter Mildmay* (Austin, Texas, 1964), p.58.

525 Ibid., pp.61–2.

526 Ramsay, *City of London*, pp.153–4, 148.

527 *CSP For. Eliz. 1560–1*, nos. 224 (p.137), 252; J.W. Burgon, *The Life and Times of Sir Thomas Gresham*, 2 vols. (London, 1839), I, pp.326–9, 217.

528 *The Reign of Elizabeth I*, ed. C. Haigh (Basingstoke, 1991), p.102.

529 *The History of the King's Works*, ed. H.M. Colvin, 6 vols. (London, 1963–82), III, i, pp.77–8.

530 W. Seres, 'The True Report of the Burning of the Steeple and Church of St Paul's in London', *An English Garner*, ed. E. Arber, vol. VIII, pp.109–16.

531 *CSP Spain, Eliz*, I, pp.275–6.

532 Ibid., no. 245 (p. 354).

533 *SP* 12/46/38.

534 Jones, *Faith by Statute*, p.175.

535 *Collection of State Papers … left by William Cecil, 1542–1570*, ed. Haynes pp.383–4.

536 *CSP Spain, Eliz*, I, p.263.

537 Ibid., I, pp.590–2.

538 E. Lodge, *Life of Sir Julius Caesar* (London, 1827), p.37; Broughton, *Brief Discourse*, v.118.

539 *SP* 12/42/43

540 *ODNB*, vol. 48, pp.540–1.

541 *Cal. Pat. Rolls, Eliz*, III, c.66/1010/1082; *SP*/12/36/86.

542 *CSP Spain, Eliz*, II, p.204 (no. 151).

543 *CSP Spain, Eliz*, I, p.354 (no. 245).

544 *SP* 12/60/16; HMC Calendar of the Manuscripts of the Marquis of Salisbury, I, no. 1451 (p. 456).

545 *CSP Rome*, I, p.400.

546 M.B. Pulman, *The Elizabethan Privy Council in the 1570s* (Los Angeles, 1971) p.87; *SP* Add/18/80.

547 *APC* VII, p.336.

548 *SP* 12/71/25; *SP* 12/67/4; *SP* 12/83/42; *SP* Add/20/24; *SP* 12/85/31.

549 L. Stone, *The Crisis of the Aristocracy, 1558–1641* (Oxford, 1966), pp.554, 542.

550 *SP* Add/14/16; *Cal. Pat. Rolls, Eliz*, V, c.66/1085/2584; c.66/1090/3144.

551 *ODNB* vol. 43, p.162.

552 Ellis, *Original Letters Illustrative of English History*, III, p.372.

553 *A Collection of State Papers Relating to Affairs in the Reign of Queen Elizabeth from 1571–96, left by William Cecil, Lord Burghley*, ed. S. Haynes, (London, 1759), pp.166–7, 170.

554 HMC The Manuscripts of the Duke of Rutland (1888), I pp.91–2.

555 *SP* Add/19/72.

556 Based on an assessment of 74 contemporary nobles, courtiers and clerics with recorded dates of birth and death.

557 Bod. Lib. Ashmole MS 836, ff. 158;159; 212.

558 Lodge, *Life of Sir Julius Caesar*, p.37.

559 Broughton, *A Brief Discourse*, v. 91–2.

Bibliography

Primary Sources

Manuscripts
Bodleian Library, Oxford
Ashmole MS. 836 folios 158–9, 211–214: funeral and hearse for William Paulet
Ashmole MS. 837 f. 148: creation as Marquis of Winchester
Ashmole MS. 840 f. 497: fees for creation as Earl of Wiltshire
Ashmole MS. 1113 f. 21b: paraphernalia for a Garter Knight
Ashmole MS. 1113 f. 122: installation as a Garter Knight
Rawlinson MS. B. 118 f. 14: creation as Lord St John
Rawlinson MS. B. 118 f. 20: creation as Marquis of Winchester
Rawlinson MS. A. 195c. 300b: expenses for Elizabeth's visit to Basing House
Rawlinson MS. Statutes 40 f. 15894: Statutes of a Garter Knight

British Library
Arundel MS. 151 f. 195: letter from William Paulet to Queen Elizabeth outlining history of royal finances

Public Record Office, Kew
C 142/43/56: John Paulet's will
C 142/44/94: John Paulet's will

Printed

Accession, coronation and marriage of Mary Tudor as related in four manuscripts of the Escorial, trans C.V. Malfatti (Barcelona, 1956)

Acts and Monuments of John Foxe, ed. J. Pratt (8 volumes, London, 1877)

Acts of the Privy Council of England, ed. J.R. Dasent (46 volumes, London, 1890–1964)

Calendar of Letters, Despatches and State Papers, Spanish, ed. G.A. Bergenroth, et al. (13 volumes, London, 1862–1954)

Calendar of Letters and State Papers relating to English Affairs, preserved principally in the Archives of Simancas, ed. M.A.S. Hume (4 volumes, London, 1892–99)

Calendar of Patent Rolls for the reign of Edward VI (5 volumes, London, 1924–26)

Calendar of Patent Rolls for the reign of Mary (4 volumes, London, 1937–39)

Calendar of Patent Rolls for the reign of Elizabeth (9 volumes, London, 1939)

Calendar of State Papers: Domestic Series, of the reign of Edward VI, 1547–53, ed. C.S. Knighton (London, 1992)

Calendar of State Papers: Domestic Series, of the reign of Mary I, 1553–58, ed. C.S. Knighton (London, 1998)

Calendar of State Papers: Domestic Series of the reigns of Edward VI, Mary, Elizabeth, ed. R. Lemon, M.A.R. Green (7 volumes, London, 1856–71)

Calendar of State Papers: Foreign Series, of the reign of Edward VI, 1547–53, ed. W.B. Turnbull (London, 1861)

Calendar of State Papers: Foreign Series of the reign of Mary, 1553–58, ed. W.B. Turnbull (London, 1861)

Calendar of State Papers: Foreign Series of the reign of Elizabeth, ed. J. Stevenson et al. (23 volumes, London, 1863–1950)

Calendar of State Papers, Rome, ed. J.M. Rigg (2 volumes, London, 1916–26)

Calendar of State Papers, Venetian, ed. R. Brown et al. (38 volumes, London, 1864–1947)

Chronicle of Queen Jane and Two Years of Queen Mary, ed. J.G. Nichols (London, 1850)

Collection of Ordinances and Regulations for the Government of the Royal Household (London, 1790)

Collection of State Papers relating to affairs in the reigns of King Henry VIII, King Edward VI, Queen Mary and Queen Elizabeth, from the year 1542 to 1570, from original letters left by William Cecil, Lord Burghley, ed. S. Haynes (London, 1740)

Collection of State Papers relating to affairs in the reign of Queen Elizabeth from 1571–96, left by William Cecil, Lord Burghley, ed. S. Haynes (London, 1759)

Diary of Henry Machyn, Citizen and Merchant-Taylor of London 1550–1563, ed. J.G. Nichols (London, 1848)

Documents relating to the foundation of the Chapter of Winchester, AD 1541–1547
ed. G.W. Kitchin and F.T. Madge (London & Winchester, 1889)

England under the reigns of Edward VI and Mary: A series of original letters, ed. P.F.
Tytler (2 volumes, London, 1839)

HMC Calendar of the Manuscripts of the Marquis of Salisbury, 1883

HMC The Manuscripts of the Duke of Rutland, 1888

HMC Report on the Manuscripts of the Duke of Buccleuch and
Queensbury, 1926

Journals of the House of Lords, 1509–1577 (London, 1771?-)

Letters and Papers, Foreign and Domestic, of the reign of Henry VIII, 1509–1547,
ed. J.S. Brewer, J. Gairdner & R.H. Brodie (21 vols. and addenda, London,
1862–1932, reprint 1965)

Letters of Queen Elizabeth I, ed. G.B. Harrison (London, 1968)

Letters of Richard Fox, 1486–1527, ed. P.S. and H.M. Allen (Oxford, 1929)

Literary Remains of King Edward VI, ed. J.G. Nichols (2 volumes, London,
1857)

Narratives of the Days of the Reformation, ed. J.G. Nichols (London, 1859)

Original Letters Illustrative of English History, series III, ed. H. Ellis (11 volumes, London, 1969)

Original Letters Relative to the English Reformation, ed. H. Robinson (2 volumes, Cambridge, 1846–7)

Privy Purse Expenses of King Henry VIII, from November 1529 to December 1532,
ed. N.H. Nicolas (London, 1828)

Progresses and Public Processions of Queen Elizabeth, ed. J. Nichols (3 volumes,
London, 1823)

English Garner, ed. E. Arber (8 volumes, London, 1877–96)

State Papers of the reign of Henry VIII (11 volumes, London, 1830–52)

Statutes of the Realm (10 volumes, London, 1810–28)

Tudor Royal Proclamations, ed. P.L. Hughes and J.F. Larkin (3 volumes, New
Haven & London, 1964, 1969)

Works of John Knox, ed. D. Laing (3 volumes, Edinburgh, 1846–64)

Secondary Sources

Alexander, P. (ed.) *The Complete Works of William Shakespeare* (London, 1971)

Allen, T. *The History and Antiquities of London, Westminster, Southwark and parts
adjacent* (4 volumes, London, 1828)

Alsop, J.D. 'The execution of a peer of the realm : A note on the 1557 verdict against Charles, Lord Stourton', *Wiltshire Archaeological & Natural History Society Annual Bulletin*, 26 (Spring 1980), pp.1–2.

Alsop, J.D. & Loades, D.M. 'William Paulet, First Marquis of Winchester : A Question of Age', *Sixteenth Century Journal*, XVIII (3), (1987), pp.333–41.

Ascham, R. *The Scholemaster* (London, 1571)

Begent, P.J. & Chesshyre, H. *The Most Noble Order of the Garter, 650 years* (London, 1999)

Bell, H.E. *The Court of Wards and Liveries* (Cambridge, 1953)

Bindoff, S.T. *The House of Commons, 1509–1558* (3 volumes, London, 1982)

Bland, D.S. (ed.) *Three Revels from the Inns of Court* (Amersham, 1984)

Borde, A. *'Sleep, Rising and Dress': Early English Meals and Manners* (ed.) F.J. Furnivall (London, 1868)

Braddock, R.C. 'The Royal Household, 1540–1560: A Study of Office Holding in Tudor England', Northwestern University Ph.D, 1971.

Bradfield, N. *900 Years of English Costume: from the eleventh to the twentieth century* (London, 1987)

Brears, P. *All the King's Cooks: The Tudor Kitchens of Henry VIII at Hampton Court Palace* (London, 1999)

Brigden, S. *London and the Reformation* (Oxford, 1989)

Broughton, R. *A brief discourse of the life and death of the late right high and honourable Sir William Paulet* (London, 1572)

Burgon, J.W. *The Life and Times of Sir Thomas Gresham* (2 volumes, London, 1839)

Buswell, J. *An Historical Account of the Knights of the most noble order of the Garter* (London, 1757)

Byrne, M. St Clare, *The Lisle Letters* (6 volumes, London & Chicago, 1981)

Campbell, Lord John, *Lives of the Lord Chancellors of England and Keepers of the Great Seal* (8 volumes, London, 1845–69)

Cassan, S.H. *The Lives of the Bishops of Winchester* (2 volumes, London, 1827)

Cavendish, G. *Thomas Wolsey, late Cardinal, his life and death* (London, 1999)

Chapman, H.W. *The Last Tudor King* (London, 1961)

Coleman, C. & Starkey, D. (eds.) *Revolution Reassessed: Revisions in the History of Tudor Government and Administration* (Oxford, 1986)

Colvin, H.M. (ed.) *The History of the King's Works* (6 volumes, London, 1963–82)

Cosson, Baron. D, 'The Capells of Rayne Hall, Essex', *The Archaeological Journal*, XL (1883), pp.64–79.

Cressy, D. *Birth, Marriage and Death: ritual, religion and the life-cycle in Tudor and Stuart England* (Oxford, 1997)

Davies, C.S.L. 'Provisions for Armies, 1509–1550: a study in the effectiveness of early Tudor Government', *Economic History Review*, 2nd Series, 17 (1964–5), pp.234–48.

Doubleday, H.A. & Page, W. (eds.) *The Victorian History of the Counties of England: Hampshire and the Isle of Wight* (5 volumes, London, 1900–14, vol. IV, 1973)

Duffy, E. *The Voices of Morebath: Reformation and Rebellion in an English village* (New Haven, USA & London, 2001)

Duffy, E. *The Stripping of the Altars: Traditional Religion in England c. 1400-c. 1580* (New Haven, USA & London, 1993)

Elton, G.R. *England under the Tudors* (London, 1997)

Elton, G.R. *The Parliament of England, 1559–1581* (Cambridge, 1986)

Elton, G.R. *Tudor Revolution in Government* (Cambridge, 1959)

Elyot, Sir T. *The Boke named the governour* (London, 1557)

Emmison, F.G. *Tudor Secretary: Sir William Petre at Court and Home* (London, 1961)

Ewing, E. *History of Children's Costume* (London, 1977)

Fisher, J.D.C. *Christian Initiation: Baptism in the Medieval West* (London, 1965)

Fletcher, A. *Tudor Rebellions* (Harlow, 1995)

Fox, J. 'The Imprisonment of the Princess Elizabeth', in *An English Garner*, (ed.) E. Arber (8 volumes, London, 1877–96)

Franklyn, C.A.H. *A genealogical history of the families of Paulet (or Pawlett), Berewe (or Barrow), Lawrence and Parker* (Bedford, 1963)

Fritze, R.H. 'The Role of Family and Religion in the Local Politics of Early Elizabethan England: The case of Hampshire in the 1560s', *The Historical Journal*, 25 (2), (1982), pp.267–87.

Froude, J.A. *History of England, from the Fall of Wolsey to the Defeat of the Spanish Armada* (12 volumes, London, 1893)

Fuller, T. *The History of the Worthies of England* (3 volumes, London, 1860)

Furnivall, F.J. (ed) *The Babees Book: medieval manners for the young* (London, 1908)

Graves, M.A.R. *The House of Lords in the Parliaments of Edward VI & Mary I* (Cambridge, 1981)

Guillemeau, J. *The Nursing of Children* (London, 1612)

Gunn, S.J. *Charles Brandon, Duke of Suffolk, 1484–1545* (Oxford, 1988)

Guy, J. *Tudor England* (Oxford, 1990)

Haigh, C. *English Reformations: religion, politics and society under the Tudors* (Oxford, 1995)

Haigh, C. (ed.) *The Reign of Elizabeth I* (Basingstoke, 1991)

Hartley, T.E. (ed.) *Proceedings in the Parliaments of Elizabeth I* (3 volumes, Leicester, 1981–95)

Hawkyard, A. 'From Painted Chamber to St Stephen's Chapel : The Meeting Places of the House of Commons at Westminster until 1603', *Parliamentary History*, 21 (2002), pp.62–84.

Haynes, A. 'Supplying the Elizabethan Court', *History Today*, 28 (November 1978) pp.729–37.

Hoak, D.E. *The King's Council in the Reign of Edward VI* (Cambridge, 1976)

Holdsworth, W. *A History of English Law* (17 volumes, London, 1903–72)

Hughes Clarke, A.W. (ed.) *Miscellanea Genealogica et Heraldica*, V series (10 volumes, London, 1935–37)

Hurstfield, J. 'Corruption and Reform under Edward VI and Mary: The Example of Wardship', *English Historical Review*, LXVIII (1953), pp.22–36.

Inderwick, F.A. *The Inner Temple: its early history, as illustrated by its records* (5 volumes, London, 1896)

Jacob, A. *A Complete English Peerage* (London, 1766)

Jeffries Davis, E. 'An unpublished manuscript of the Lords Journals for April and May 1559', *English Historical Review*, XXVIII (1913), pp.531–42.

Jones, N. L. *Faith by Statute: Parliament and the Settlement of Religion, 1559* (London, 1982)

Jordan, W.K. *The Chronicle and Political Papers of King Edward VI* (London, 1966)

Jordan, W.K. *Edward VI – The Young King: The Protectorship of the Duke of Somerset* (London, 1968)

Jordan W.K. *Edward VI – The Threshold of Power: The Dominance of the Duke of Northumberland* (London, 1970)

LaMar, V.A. *Travel and Roads in England* (Washington, USA, 1960)

Lehmberg, S.E. *Sir Walter Mildmay* (Austin, Texas, 1964)

Lloyd, C. & Thurley, S. *Henry VIII: Images of a Tudor King* (Oxford, 1990)

Loades, D.M. *The Life and Career of William Paulet (c.1475–1572): Lord Treasurer and First Marquis of Winchester* (Aldershot, 2008)

Loades, D.M. *The Reign of Mary Tudor* (Harlow, 1991)

Loades, D.M. *The Tudor Court* (London, 1986)

Loades, D.M. *Two Tudor Conspiracies* (Cambridge, 1965)

Lodge, E. *Illustrations of British History, Biography and Manners in the reigns of Henry VIII, Edward VI, Mary, Elizabeth and James I* (3 volumes, London, 1838)

Lodge, E. *The Life of Sir Julius Caesar, Knt.* (London, 1827)

MacCaffrey, W. *The Shaping of the Elizabethan Regime* (London, 1969)

MacCulloch, D. (ed.) *Reign of Henry VIII: Policy, Piety and Politics* (Basingstoke, 1995)

Malkiewicz, A. J. A. 'An Eye-witness's account of the Coup d'Etat of October 1549', *English Historical Review*, LXX (1955), p.600–609.

Millar, G. J. *Tudor Mercenaries and Auxiliaries 1485–1547* (Charlottesville, USA, 1980)

Moens, W. J. C. (ed.) *Register of the Dutch Church, Austin Friars* (London, c.1884)

Naunton, Sir R. *Fragmenta Regalia* (London, 1641)

Neale, J. E. *Queen Elizabeth* (London, 1934)

Neale, J. E. *Elizabeth I and her Parliaments, 1559–1581* (London, 1953)

Newton, T. *The Worthye Booke of Old Age* (London, 1569)

Orme, N. *Medieval Children* (New Haven, 2001)

Orme, N. *English Schools in the Middle Ages* (London, 1973)

Oxford Dictionary of National Biography (60 volumes, Oxford, 2004)

Pollard, A. F. 'The Acts of the Privy Council, 1590–97', *English Historical Review*, 18 (1903) pp.567–9.

Prockter, A. & Taylor, R. (eds.) *The A to Z of Elizabethan London* (London, 1979)

Pulman, M. B. *The Elizabethan Privy Council in the 1570s* (Los Angeles, 1971)

Ramsay, G. D. *The City of London in international politics at the accession of Elizabeth Tudor* (Manchester, 1975)

Read, C. *Mr. Secretary Cecil and Queen Elizabeth* (London, 1955)

Rhodes, H. *Boke of Nurture,* (ed.) F. J. Furnivall (Bungay, 1867, orig. pub. 1577)

Roper, W. *The Lyfe of Sir Thomas Moore, knighte* (London, 1998)

Russell, J. *The Boke of Nurture,* (ed.) F. J. Furnivall (Bungay, 1867, orig pub. 1460)

Scarisbrick, J. J. *Henry VIII* (London, 1990)

Seres, W. 'The True Report of the Burning of the Steeple and Church of St Paul's in London', in *An English Garner*, ed. E. Arber (8 volumes, London, 1877–96)

Starkey, D. *Six Wives: The Queens of Henry VIII* (London, 2003)

Stone, L. *The Crisis of the Aristocracy* (Oxford, 1966)

Stow, J. *A Summary of the Chronicles of England … to 1575* (London, 1575)

Stow, J. *The Annales or General Chronicle of England* (London, 1631)

Stow, J. *A Survey of London* (1st pub. 1603, this edn. Stroud, 2005)

Strype, J. *Ecclesiastical Memorials relating chiefly to religion and the reformation of it* (Oxford, 1822)

Thurley, S. *Hampton Court: A Social and Architectural History* (New Haven & London, 2003)

Thurley, S. *The Royal Palaces of Tudor England* (New Haven & London, 1993)

Tittler, R. *The Reign of Mary I* (Harlow, 1991)

Tusser, T. *Good Housewives' Lessons: Selections from writings of Thomas Tusser* (National Federation of Women's Institutes, 1954)

Underhill, E. 'Examination and Imprisonment of Edward Underhill in August 1553 with anecdotes of the time', in *An English Garner*, ed. E. Arber (8 volumes, London, 1877–96)

Whateley, W. *A bride bush* (London, 1623)

Williams, N. *Henry VIII and his Court* (London, 1971)

Woodworth, A. 'Purveyance for the Royal Household in the reign of Elizabeth I', *Transactions of the American Philosophical Society,* XXXV (1), (1945), pp. 1–89.

Woodward, J. *The Theatre of Death: The Ritual Management of Royal Funerals in Renaissance England, 1570–1625* (Woodbridge, 1997)

Wriothesley, C. *A Chronicle of England during the reigns of the Tudors* (2 volumes, London, 1875, 1877)

Index